ELITE BUSINESS SYSTEMS

INSIDER STRATEGIES OF INDUSTRY LEADING CONSULTANTS

TERRI LEVINE
PETE WINIARSKI

MOtivational®
LEADERS IN GLOBAL PUBLISHING

Published by Motivational Press, Inc.
1777 Aurora Road
Melbourne, Florida, 32935
www.MotivationalPress.com

Manufactured in the United States of America.

ISBN: 978-1-62865-352-6

CONTENTS

———

———

OPENING LETTER

———

Wouldn't it be better to learn from the mistakes of others instead of learning the hard way and paying the price of your own mistakes? You are business owners, business leaders, and independent consultants who are looking to work with the perfect consultant so you can improve your business results. We believe that the best way to improve your business is to hear the real truth direct from elite consultants.

We brought together top consultants for you to get engaged with them and learn from them. As you read their expert advice, open up your minds and interact with their ideas so that you can implement their strategies to grow and expand your business and become more profitable.

We both learned from our own business mistakes and also learned from the mistakes of others. Eventually we got smart and hired mentors who were running further, faster, and exceeding our income and results. We have aggressively implemented strategies to grow our businesses which enabled us to serve more and more clients.

▌ TERRI'S BACKSTORY

Terri founded a coach training school and operated that school for over 20 years. At the same, she was running her own business coaching and consulting firm. While she was extremely successful in her business, she discovered that business coaches were unable to make a good living from just business coaching. She realized that business consultants, however, were able to make a good living and sometimes a great living as business consultants. Here's the other observation though: business consultants often worked way too hard.

In Terri's business she was coaching and consulting about 20-30 hours a week and taking off about 6-8 weeks a year while making a high 7 figure income. This was unlike what other consultants seemed to achieve. She was disturbed about the lack of results in the industry and was frustrated and wanted to do something about it for the other business coaches and consultants she met.

▍ PETE'S BACKSTORY

Pete began in a corporate America setting where he had some really fun and interesting roles that required him to interact with some business consultants that his company had hired. Those early experiences, combined with his direct responsibility in a variety of operations, gave him the perspectives of consulting projects from both sides. From the side of the consultant, Pete was often the person to host and facilitate their projects. From the perspective of the line manager, he knew how to best leverage consulting support to achieve results.

His career moved into formal consulting with the elite firm McKinsey & Company, which provided him the opportunity to work with Fortune 500 companies on their most challenging strategic business problems.

After then playing a role as an executive for a multi-billion-dollar company, Pete went and formed his own consulting company, Win Enterprises, LLC. Win started as just Pete, and then he added some administrative staff, then contractors, and finally consulting staff.

▍ THE LAUNCH OF THE BUSINESS CONSULTANT INSTITUTE

Pete actually hired Terri to help him expand his small consulting company into a formidable seven-figure business. It was during their discussions that they recognized they shared the desire to help other consultants create highly successful businesses for themselves.

We decided to form the Business Consultant Institute as the vehicle to provide business consultants the training and expertise that they require to grow thriving consulting businesses and create more freedom and peace of mind within their companies.

Terri said in a recent interview:

"It felt very important to me at this point in my career to help consultants who wanted to expand their businesses and take them to the next level and share the knowledge tools and information that I had over the past 30 years. Joining together with Pete made perfect sense as we both have different skill sets and the same mission. It also felt very important for me to take coaches and bring them to the next level which is being a consultant using coaching skills. So the blend of working with Pete doing what I love, loving what I do and moving away from training coaches and moving into training consultants is the right thing for me to be doing, and with the right partner."

THE POWER OF THIS BOOK

We are both best selling authors and understand that one of the most important strategies to put in place, as a business consultant, is to grow your exposure and become known as a credible expert. Writing a book or being featured in a movie is a highly impactful way to create that level of exposure. We want to make sure that the consultants we get to know and train (especially those we have the privilege of mentoring) are known by a massive number of people.

It is our desire to bring the best of the best from the consulting industry together so that you, the reader, can get to know who they are and get access to their expertise. Once you find out who they are and read more about what they do and how they think, you can decide to connect with them if your business needs a consulting expert.

What we chose to do was make this opportunity available to high-powered consultants. These consultants who are part of this book have the initiative and persistence to apply business building strategies that are setting them apart from the masses of consultants who frankly do not have everything that it takes to maximize their success. The people in this book are truly special.

They have skills and expertise that are in demand by small and large businesses. The elite consultants in this book include those who can

» help solve strategic problems

» drive revenue up through new marketing strategies

» handle and shift your leadership challenges

» spark innovation

» reduce your costs and make your company more profitable

» help you grow with sustainable, long-term success

» lead full company transformations

The consultants featured in this book are the real deal.

It's really important when you are putting together a collaborative book to choose the best of the best in the industry you're representing. Many, many consultants had an opportunity to be a part of this book. We picked the top experts in the consulting industry based upon their credibility, authenticity, expertise, and ability to get their message across. We are excited to bring their knowledge and wisdom together in one place that represents the collective mind that will help you in the world of business consulting today as well as in your own business or industry today. This is a stellar roster that we've pulled together – all in one resource for you.

With the incredible lineup of talented consultants who have contributed chapters in this book, you have in your hands a enormously insightful guide for you the business leader to accelerate the goals that you have for your organization. As you flip through the table of contents and the chapter headers you will certainly find multiple topics of interest that will give you insights about some of your biggest challenges in your company. By reading the powerful messages here in these chapters you are tapping into some top cutting-edge thinking that can help you shift your results immediately.

Imagine if you were sitting in a room and have the top business consultants in front of you and could get their help and advice. That's what you have when you hold this book in your hands: elite business consultants helping you, guiding you, and advising you and your company.

This is a remarkable resource from a collective mastermind of information. If you want to improve your business, increase your revenues and profits, this book is a must-read and one you will want to have on your bookshelf as a reference for years. We also suggest you share this with others that you know who own a business or who are business consultants themselves.

For those of you who are business consultants, this book provides you with a tremendous number of interesting perspectives that will help you make decisions about how you should move your consulting business forward. It is critical for you to have well-defined areas of expertise that are represented with your unique frameworks and methodologies.

By reviewing the chapters here you will have some insights to those distinctive perspectives from industry leading consultants. This truly is a benchmark for you and a level of expertise that you can now aspire to achieve yourself.

 Read each chapter and see which consultant's advice you resonate with. You may find gems of wisdom from within different chapters. We encourage you to circle or highlight those golden nuggets of advice that seem to jump off the pages for you.

Reach out to the various consultants in the chapters. You may want to speak with them about getting help in your business or to gather more information from them about how they think and solve problems.

If you find that you yourself might want more information about launching or marketing your own consulting business, about transforming from a business coach into a business consultant, or even want to add business consulting to your current business model then get in touch with us at BusinessConsultantInstitute.com. Here we share resources, tools, and tips and also invite you to our events and trainings. Now is a great time for you to get more information about the business consultants in this book and about the Business Consultant Institute.

▌ YOU WILL ALSO LOVE THE MOVIE!

We have produced a DVD, also called *Elite Business Systems*. The authors in this book are featured in live interviews about their consulting businesses and their areas of expertise. You will gain some behind the scenes secrets about these elite business consultants in the movie, so be sure to watch it soon after reading this book.

We are excited to continue featuring world-leading experts and elite consultants, and are committed to helping you rise to new heights of success for your businesses. We know you will enjoy this book, the movie, and the other resources we are creating for you!

Best Luck!

Terri Levine and Pete Winiarski,

Founders of the Business Consultant Institute

HOW TO ACHIEVE PERSONAL SUSTAINABILITY AND IMPROVE LEADERSHIP SKILLS

MARYANNE ROSS

It was a beautiful summer morning, they type you just want to lick off the plate of life. I was on my way to a client site in Buffalo, enjoying a gorgeous July sky and loving life. My cell phone rang and when I saw Deborah's name displayed, I snatched it up, and demanded, "Where have you been? I've been calling you for days!" "Oh, I've been sick in bed," she responded in her typical airy way. The thought of Deborah sick in bed was so foreign to me that I took a wrong turn, and struggled to find my way to a site that I had visited every two weeks for over a year. And no wonder, this was a person who hadn't taken a sick day in all the years that I had known her! She went on to describe her excruciating stomach pains and her trip to the doctor....(the doctor? Deborah?) Suddenly, it was as if an elephant had crawled into my rental car and was now sitting on my chest. Everything within me told me that this was terribly, terribly serious.

She followed the doctor's advice, adhered to a restricted diet, and took the prescribed medication. But over the next few weeks the pains worsened and she was hospitalized. I was back in Buffalo when her husband called me with the dreaded diagnosis. It was cancer, already metastasized to other sites in her body. At this point, she was on what she referred to as "designer drugs," and she was able to speak to me of the coming surgery and aggressive chemo. She reminded me that she had done horrible things to her body and now was paying the price for her choices. We tried to make light of the situation. I vowed to shave my own head if the chemo caused her hair to fall out and we planned to buy and wear red hairpieces. The surgery was scheduled for the Thursday before Labor Day weekend. She pulled through the surgery, but passed away on Labor Day, without ever fully regaining consciousness.

Even as I struggled to cope with the loss of my dearest friend and mentor, I tried to imagine the cost of this loss to her company. Deborah was a mid-level supply chain manager for a tier-one supplier in the automotive industry. She and her staff received raw materials from across the country into a warehouse in Texas, and then re-shipped these materials to five assembly plants in Mexico. She also received finished goods from the assembly plants and shipped them to General Motors and other automakers in North America and Europe. She often worked 12- to 14-hour days, living on coffee, cigarettes, and junk food by day, and relaxing with cocktails and fast food by night. But the risk of losing this outwardly healthy and dynamic 53-year-old woman was so far removed from the minds of her employers, a succession plan had never been considered.

The costs associated with being out of balance - Now, I will fully admit that Deborah's story is an extreme one, but many stories of life-threatening and chronic illness affecting company leaders and workers are becoming more and more common. And the costs to their organizations are staggering. According to research by Integrative Nutrition, Huffington Post and other researchers, corporations are spending over **two trillion** dollars a year on healthcare costs, but only

2% of that is spent on prevention! Some researchers put the number higher and cite "presenteeism" (employees who report to work, but are too sick to perform their duties properly) as being more costly than absenteeism and turnover.

What is the root cause of these rising costs? I blame the poor lifestyle choices of our workforce and its leaders! Almost 67% of US adults are overweight or obese. Over 29 million Americans are diabetic. These two factors alone lead to chronic and often fatal diseases such as heart disease, stroke, and certain cancers. And it is expected to get worse. Researchers predict a 42% increase in chronic disease cases by 2023, adding $4.2 trillion in treatment costs and lost economic output.

Much of this cost is preventable, since many chronic conditions are linked back to unhealthy lifestyles choices. You also have to ask yourself if you really want employees who are not at their best to be interacting with your customers.

And sadly, there is even more for us to consider. Work-related stress continues to increase around the world, and it affects not only the health and well-being of employees, but also the productivity of our corporations. The Huffington Post recently referred to our workplaces as "broken."

An exaggeration, you think? Consider these alarming statistics. Gallup recently reported that only 32% of U.S. employees are actively engaged in their work. And worse yet, 50.8% of employees were found to be "not engaged" and 17.2% are "actively disengaged." Over 83% of us are reporting higher stress levels than a year ago.

And according to the American Psychological Association the millennial generation tops the charts in stress levels, more than their parents or workplace colleagues. The reasons for the alarming increase in stress and lower levels of employee engagement include longer hours, heavier workloads, tighter deadlines, and poor relationships with managers and co-workers.

But the workplace itself isn't the only cause. I'm firmly convinced that we also contribute to the increase in our stress levels simply by leading lifestyles that have become more and more out of balance.

There is good news and there is a way out of the insanity for individuals and for corporations. As decision-makers and leaders, your call to action is to adopt a more balanced lifestyle for yourself, and invest in training for your workforce, beginning with your leadership team. I like to call my Leadership Program *Personal Sustainability Planning (PSP)*. Before I explain a little more about the program itself, let me explain the name.

You've most likely heard of the business best practice of **Corporate Sustainability**, the efforts of companies of all sizes to reduce the negative impact of their business operations on society and the world. According to **APICS, the global leader and premier source of the body of knowledge in supply chain and operations management**, **sustainability** is the ability to meet the needs of the present without compromising the resources of the future. Managing a sustainable organization involves achieving high performance levels over the long term without engaging in detrimental behaviors in the short term.

The **Triple Bottom Line**, a phrase coined by John Elkington in 1994, is a measure of sustainability that includes financial, social, and environmental performance measures.

When applied to the self, we know that:

1. We need to make a living and build a financially stable future for ourselves and our families.

2. The social perspective is to develop and maintain the relationships that are crucial to our happiness.

3. And the environmental perspective must be our physical, mental, and emotional health. If we destroy our health, all the success in the financial and relationship areas of our lives will be for naught.

A few years ago, I lost a nephew to pancreatic cancer. Before his illness, he was at the pinnacle of success. He was an executive, enjoying an extremely high income; he had the beautiful and loving family, the house, the car, and all the material symbols of success. But his stressful lifestyle and poor health habits took their toll on his body, contributing to the onset of a deadly disease.

Four years later, his wife and children do not cry for the loss of the material things his success afforded them. They cry for him, his smile, the little pet names he had for each of them, his big bear hugs. And it would be the same for you. All the career success in the world will count for nothing if you lose your health and loved ones in its pursuit. You can probably think of famous people who had the talent to achieve great things, but lost it all due to bad decisions and resulting actions, can't you?

So now more than ever, I think that we need a similar *triple bottom line* metric to ensure that our very lives are as sustainable as our businesses. I'm firmly convinced that this same framework can (and should) be applied to our own lives and taught to employees at all levels in our companies.

Getting our priorities straight - Far too many individuals spend the bulk of their time and energy in the pursuit of career and financial success, and compromise their health and relationships in the process. We believe that once we have the career success, once we're financially secure, we can go back and mend the broken relationships with our loved ones. We believe that those dreaded illnesses that are a result of stress and poor lifestyles will happen to someone else. Too often, we're wrong on both counts.

This is where my *triple bottom line* approach to developing leadership skills in your company employees through ***Personal Sustainability*** comes into play. As leaders and managers we must recognize that we can't lead others until we learn to manage ourselves.

We can, however, create better life balance and resilience for ourselves. We can model this new and sustainable lifestyle for others, and we can support our teams in the creation of their own plans.

The path is really pretty simple: it involves a commitment to making some lifestyle adjustments. Adjustments that promise to provide you with better health, more career success, more and higher quality free time, and greater satisfaction in your relationships.

How do I know that? Because the habits that I'm going to recommend to you and your staff have been used by the highest achievers throughout history. These habits have been employed by the likes of Andrew Carnegie, Henry Ford, Napoleon Hill, W. Clement Stone, Oprah Winfrey, Jack Canfield, Walt Disney, and thousands of others.

Some of the material that I incorporate into my workshops I first learned from Jack Canfield, co-author of "Chicken Soup for the Soul" and "The Success Principles." I've been a life-long believer in personal development and in 2007, I picked up a copy of "The Success Principles," read it cover to cover, and began applying its wisdom to my own life.

It had such an impact that I wanted to learn more and teach it to others. I attended Jack's Breakthrough to Success program in 2008, and that full-week program helped me to gain greater balance in my own life and increase my own career success, so I decided to enter his first training group and become a Certified Canfield Trainer in the Success Principles.

I love teaching his principles and I have added some business best practices to my programs. Thanks to my 25 years of working and consulting in supply chain and operations management, utilizing the Toyota Lean Production System and other project management tools, I'm able to teach others how to systematically attack the "waste" in our personal lives that keep us from achieving our goals.

This waste that I speak of could be underutilized time, energy, talents, etc. The cornerstone in my workshops is the activities that help people attack the negative and limiting beliefs that hold us back. I believe that the ultimate root cause behind our "out-of-balance lifestyles" is the negative thoughts and beliefs that we think and believe to be true.

This is what drives the stress, the bad choices and the resulting corporate and personal costs. It is the reason that I named my company Mental Apparel. I think we spend a good deal of time choosing clothing that is appropriate to the day's activities or occasion, so that we can put our best foot forward. But we let our minds go unchecked, we let them dress themselves.

So our bodies are well dressed and our thinking is in shambles. This can be as harmful to our careers as showing up for an important meeting in a bathrobe and slippers. And it is just as harmful to our relationships and health.

In my corporate and public workshops, I use a variety of worksheets, case studies, group discussions, and experiential learning tools to convey the best practices of the highest achievers, including methods that convert negative thoughts into their positive and powerful counterparts. For the purpose of this writing, I will share an overview of the steps each decision-maker and leader should employ to gain **personal sustainability** and model the behavior for others.

OUR PERSONAL SUSTAINABILITY PLANNING JOURNEY

As my **PSP** pyramid shape suggests, we begin our journey with attention to our health.

BUILDING OUR HEALTH BASE

Clean up your health act – Start doing the things you know you should be doing. Get the health checks recommended by

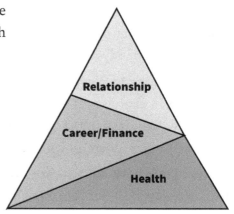

your physician. If you haven't seen one lately, make an appointment and ask detailed questions about what you should be doing to improve and protect your health. Also ask questions about what you should not be doing, and follow the advice.

Start with the standards: Lose weight if you need to, start an exercise program, stop smoking and excessive use of alcohol. And don't think I can't possibly be referring to you. Remember that the statistics indicate that 67% of us are overweight or obese, and 70 million people overindulge in alcohol. Tobacco use is the most important risk factor in about 20% of global cancer deaths, and 70% of global lung cancer deaths.

I don't intend for this to be preachy, I'm on the same journey as you are. I come from a long line of excellent cooks. I love to cook, eat, and entertain, and I use food to soothe my soul. So I have to constantly remind myself that moderation is the key and that there are healthier methods for dealing with stress. Replacing a bad habit with a healthier one is often the key to long-term success in the area of health and fitness.

If you can't do it alone, get help. If you fall off the program (and most of us do), get back on. Don't waste time with guilt and recrimination, just get back on your program and recognize that you are still ahead of those who aren't even trying.

A great way to ensure success in your new habits is to examine the negative thoughts that drive your poor habits. What are the negative messages that you send yourself? Write down a list of the destructive thoughts and then write down their positive turnaround statements. Keep your list handy for those weak moments that we all have.

An example of a negative and limiting belief might be "I'm too busy to keep to an exercise routine." A good turnaround statement might be "There will be days that I can't keep to my desired routine, but even small amounts of exercise will help me in the long run."

Rest your body and mind – Did you know that 40% of Americans are sleep-deprived? Or that 60 million Americans have sleep disorders?

Some of the hidden health hazards of sleep deprivation include higher levels of depression and anxiety. Lack of sleep increases our risk of stroke, heart disease, hypertension, diabetes, and certain cancers. Excessive sleepiness impairs our memory and our ability to think and process information. In other words, burning the midnight oil does not make you more productive, it makes you less so. Talk to your doctor about your sleep difficulties so that you get the rest you need. Try exercise, yoga and meditation instead of drugs and alcohol.

Take small breaks during the day. Even a couple minutes of quiet time can be enough to refuel your body and soul. Get outside every day. Take a walk and breathe in the fresh air. Try to position your desk or workspace so that you get a view of the outdoors even if you can't physically be outside as often as you might like. I've had clients tell me that this one step improved their sense of well-being dramatically.

Practice gratitude – you may be groaning inside and thinking that becoming more grateful couldn't possibly improve your life in any measurable way. If so, I would like to introduce you to Dr. Robert Emmons, professor of psychology at the University of California, Davis. Dr. Emmons' research indicates that gratitude is not merely a positive emotion; it also improves your health if cultivated. As a result, he says, people who practice gratitude will experience significant improvements in several areas of life including relationships, academics, energy level, and even dealing with tragedy and crisis.

I can tell you from my own experience that practicing gratitude for over a decade has improved my outlook on life, helped me to sleep better and achieve more, all with greater peace of mind.

My best advice is to try it for 30 days. Before you go to bed at night, write down five things that happened during the day for which you can be grateful. You can list the big things like health and family and the small things like a good cup of coffee or your desired parking spot.

While you're feeling grateful, make a master list of 100 things that you can refer to when you hit a particularly rough day and you're not especially grateful for anything. Then notice how your outlook starts improving. It is amazing!

I've been using journals and gratitude jars for years. This past Thanksgiving my granddaughters and I created a gratitude tree for the table. We put a large branch into a flower pot and hung all our "gratitudes" on the branches. Soon other family members were adding to our tree. Practicing gratitude will change your life for the better. I promise.

IMPROVING OUR RELATIONSHIPS

Your family comes first – Yes, I said that. Your family comes before your boss, before your big project, before your best client. In the grand scheme of life, all of those work related priorities will pale in comparison to the loss of your loved ones. All of the career success in the world will be hollow if we have no one to share it with. At the end of your life, you will not remember or regret the missed meeting or delayed completion of a project. But you will miss not seeing those first baby steps or that first prom dress; you will miss not making time for that late-night heart to heart talk with your significant other. If you shortchange your family, no matter how good your intentions, you and they will pay an enormous price. Give your boss, your company, your clients a full day's work, but no more. When you leave work for the day, leave physically and mentally. Take this advice to heart. It's the best advice you will ever be given.

Now that you've prioritized your family, leverage the time that you spend with them. Improve your personal relationships through heart-centered conversations.

Why does this matter? Some people are natural-born conversationalist, the rest of us have to work at it. For people in long-term relationships, finding new things to talk about can be especially daunting. But if our intention is to strengthen our relationships with our partners, children, parents, and friends, then playing the role of reporter can open new channels of conversation.

Imagine yourself as a famous talk-show host. Notice when you watch them on TV or radio that they spend much more time asking about the other person and a whole lot less time discussing themselves. Examples of questions that might open new dialog with a family member:

» I really enjoy our time together (or I wish we could spend more time together). What are some new and different things we could do or try that you might enjoy?

» Thinking back over the last year (or two or five), what is your favorite memory of a time we shared? What was your most favorite place that we've been to together? If we could go back and repeat an event, what would it be?

» What was the best vacation you ever took as a child? Where did you go and why did you like it so much?

» Tell me how your parents met.

» What was your favorite family activity while growing up?

» What was the first job you wanted to have when you grew up? What made you change your mind?

» What was your favorite TV show, (or movie or book) when you were younger?

» Whom did you most admire? Whom do you most admire now? Why?

» For older relatives: Where were you/what were you doing when President Kennedy (or Reagan) was shot? When the first man walked on the moon? What did you think about it?

» Of all the holidays we celebrate, which one is your favorite, which one could you do without?

» How did your day go today? What are you looking forward to this week or this weekend? This year?

Here are some more opportunities to open up conversations: Notice what your family member or friends are interested in and ask questions. Examples might be: What do you like best about golfing, weaving, meditating? How did you get interested in that author, sports team, TV series?

Jack Canfield advises us to go deeper. Ask your partner, "On a scale of 1-10, how would you rate our relationship lately? If it isn't a 10, what might it take to make it a 10?" (Warning! Don't ask if you aren't willing to take the answer to heart!)

Whatever conversation starters you choose to use, remember to ask the questions and receive the answers without passing judgement in any way. This includes your tone of voice, inflection, and body language. If you are truly interested in improving relationships, you want to use the information to better understand your loved ones, not pass judgement or sway others to your way of thinking. Ego-centered conversations focus on converting others to our way of thinking. Heart-centered conversations focus on understanding others and their way of thinking.

Don't stop at conversations; take every opportunity to make family time special. Celebrate everything and celebrate every chance you get. Make up your own holidays, like Happy New Month, Autumn Apple-Picking Day, Happy Half-Birthday – you name it and it's yours! And go all out in the celebration! Use the good china, the fancy tablecloth and napkins. Forget about saving those things for a special occasion. Recognize that the occasions aren't special to us; it's the people that we share them with who are special.

We've often been encouraged by our elders to save our best belongings for a rainy day. So we save all sorts of things for decades, things that we and our families could have enjoyed. After we pass on, the things are so outdated that they must be thrown away or carted away for cheap in the estate sale. There was a time when I would lament the slightest chip on the china or stain on the fancy tablecloth. And now I see it as evidence that my family and I are using these things and creating memories. In the same way, the things of my mother's that I most cherish aren't in pristine condition. But the signs of use are evidence of the happiest times that we shared, and bring back the sweetest memories.

There are so many easy little ways that we can show our loved ones how much we care. Leave a sticky note on the fridge; it doesn't have to be more than "I love you." You can even abbreviate, and use the heart symbol. Send an "I love you" or "I'm thinking about you" text message. Include your parents and your siblings in these habits. As someone who has lost my entire birth family, I can tell you that the day will come when you will wish that you had taken a little more time to tell them what they mean to you.

I love Facebook and other social media sites because it allows me to stay in contact with friends and family around the world and it takes very little extra time. I catch up with them by squeezing Facebook into what would normally be underutilized time, like waiting in line at stores, boarding planes, or waiting for the kettle to boil. By all means, keep tight control on social media so that it doesn't become a time drain, but it can be a tremendous asset in allowing you to stay connected to the people you care about.

Think about your "other" family – With a little creativity these same principles can improve your relationships with friends and colleagues as well.

Ponder these questions on the way to work tomorrow. What could you do to let your colleagues know that you respect and appreciate them? How could you practice "How can I help?" on a daily basis? Why would it be important to do so?

I can recall a time, almost twenty years ago, when I was working very hard to help my employers launch a new product line. I was spending long hours getting production processes in place to control inventory. One morning I came to work and found a "Kudos" candy bar taped to my desk. I never did confirm who left it for me, but it meant so much to me that I can still feel the glow that came from the simple recognition.

Also remember that the best approach to a workplace disagreement is to seek to uncover *what* is right, not *who* is right. All too often, we are so determined to convince others that we are right and they are wrong that we fail to recognize that their objections to our ideas may actually be a gift that could prevent a costly mistake. Keep your company's and client's best interest foremost in all conversations. Invite colleagues to shoot holes in your proposals. Listen intently to their feedback, asking as many questions as you can possibly think of. Believe it or not, you will gain more respect and cooperation when you sincerely practice this than you will ever lose.

One of my favorite motivational speakers of all time, Zig Ziglar, had a favorite saying, "You can have everything you want, if you just help enough other people get what they want." This isn't manipulative in any way, not when done with a mindset of truly wanting to help others. When we genuinely look to help other people, they naturally want to help us in return. Be on the look-out for opportunities to make someone else's day, whether or not you think they can help you in return. Model this behavior every day, without fail, and watch your workplace relationships (and your life in general) improve beyond what you might ever imagine.

Believe that the universe is conspiring to do you good, because it is.

The previous paragraphs on doing more for your co-workers than is expected is a perfect segue for some tips on attaining the career success that you dream of. Let's take a look.

ATTAINING CAREER SUCCESS

Be early – Make it a point to get to your desk a few minutes early each day. Have a plan of what you intend to accomplish, but realize that it is only a plan, and that it may have to be adjusted as needed. Put you head down and concentrate on the work at hand. Forget about the internet or your personal business. If there is an urgent matter, take care of it at lunch time or on your break. Vow to give your employer a full day's work for a day's wages.

I don't care if you don't think that your employer is paying you enough. If you agreed to X amount of compensation for X amount of work, then keep your agreement. If you've taken on more work and think you deserve more, make your case in the most professional manner possible. If your boss turns you down, at least you know where you stand. That's far better than being afraid to ask. If you are turned down and you still feel you should be earning more, begin to search for new employment. In the meantime, continue to give one hundred percent effort, and do everything you are asked to do, until the very hour that you clean out your desk to leave.

This has nothing to do with your current employer and everything to do with your own integrity and self-respect. I consult and train for corporations around the world. Whenever I hear someone complaining that they aren't being paid enough to do certain things that they've been asked to do, I cringe and want to shout, "You never will be paid more, because you aren't worth more, not a penny more, than you are being paid now!" We don't climb the ladder of success in reality until we climb that ladder mentally. And there is no shortcut to the top; you have to earn the right to be there.

Be cool – Stay out of company politics; steer clear of gossip and commiserating about the customers, the boss, the weather, or anything else. You may find that some of your co-workers will resent you and believe that you're making them look bad. That's their problem and the best way to handle it is to ignore it.

Be helpful - While we're on that subject, refuse to let anyone's bad behavior cause you to react in kind. Even a bullying boss can be handled by taking time to analyze what is happening and why. Often the bad behavior that we think is directed at us is really an outward symbol of someone else's inward struggle. Be as helpful as you can and refuse to take things so personally.

Be outstanding – If you want to succeed, then you have to be more than willing to separate yourself from the crowd by giving outstanding service to your boss, company, co-workers, and customers. This has nothing to do with what you will get for all this effort and everything to do with what you will become.

Be yourself – Never, ever underestimate yourself or the contribution you can make. Don't try to imitate anyone else either. You will make yourself miserable in the process. It took me years of "suffering by comparison" before I realized that I had my own talents and abilities and that I could either be a poor imitation of someone else or I could strive to be the best version of myself. I want to shorten the learning curve for you, so please take this to heart!

GUIDELINES FOR SUCCESS IN ALL LIFE AREAS

Take 100% responsibility for your life – This is Rule Number 1 in Jack Canfield's Principles of Success and it is the rule that changed my life. Once you realize that blaming anything outside yourself for the circumstances in your life is robbing you of your power, your life begins to change for the better. Once I stopped playing the victim, I was amazed at what I could do. Nowadays, if I don't like the way my life is going in any area, I stop what I'm doing, analyze what isn't working, and take action to change it. If I'm not willing to take the action, then I have to accept the situation. The same will be true for you. I promise.

Have goals in all three primary areas – And put your goals in writing. Dr. Gail Matthews, a psychology professor at Dominican University in California, did a study on goal-setting with 267 participants. She found that we are 42% more likely to achieve our goals just by writing them down. Having written goals helps us clarify what it is that we want. It helps us stay motivated to achieve them. It becomes a marker for celebrating their achievement.

I would highly recommend that you take the time to write down **what** you want and **why** you want it. Think back to when you were in grade school and you wanted to learn to ride a bike: You were willing to fall off, you skinned your knees and elbows, but you got back up and you tried again, because you wanted that fun and freedom. When you were a teenager and wanted to get your driver's license. You knew **what** you wanted (a driver's license), and you knew **why** you wanted it (be independent, be seen as cool by your friends). That clearly stated motivation kept you on track. Even if you slacked on the rest of your homework, you studied that driver's manual. You practiced the driving skills, you learned to accelerate, brake, park and so on. You were willing to do something badly until you could do it well because you clearly understood why you wanted it and what it would mean to achieve it. As adults, we often go from what we want, right to how to achieve it, depriving ourselves of the power of a clearly stated motivation.

Make your goals specific and measurable. This is important because our everyday lives are often hectic and filled with new challenges and priorities. It is easy to forget what it is that we want to be working towards, and why we considered it to be important.

Having a written goal of "making more money" is still vague and unlikely to get results. An example of a clearly stated goal reads like this: "I will earn 150k by 5PM on 12/31/16. This will allow me to pay off my debt and take my family to Disney World on spring break." Now we have a clear concise statement of intention. When our intention is reviewed on a regular basis, and is acted upon, it is a mile marker on the road to achievement. And because the goal is measurable and timed, we can review our progress, make adjustments, and significantly improve our chances for success.

Lastly, take action! – A goal that is not acted upon, no matter how clearly and cleverly stated, is really just a wish. Remember the examples above, of the effort we put into learning to ride a bike or drive a car. Think of other examples from your own life, how you worked through the difficulties of earning a degree, of learning to play a sport or a musical instrument, of learning another language. You kept at it, you practiced, you improved, and eventually you excelled. You most likely created an action plan of some sort, and took action on your plan.

Do that now, with your new goals and dreams. If you're not sure how to start, ask for help, read a book, take a course, search the internet. Start in, adjust as you know more. Trust that as you take the next step, you will see a little bit further and you will know what to do next, and next, until you arrive at your destination.

This will be true of any goal or dream that you have now. You can do it. You can have the things you want, go to the places you dream about, become the person you want to be. It is all possible, as soon as you think it is!

I began with the sad story of a dear friend who was lost because she did not find her own personal sustainability in time. Let me close with a much happier story, of another dear friend who has.

I first got to know Mike as a professional colleague more than 15 years ago. He was smart and funny and we soon became good friends. Mike is a brilliant instructor and trainer with a real talent for helping others realize their importance and worth. But Mike worried me because he had not been paying attention to his health. He was gaining too much weight, and overly indulgent in tobacco and beer.

But Mike has also realized the importance of protecting his good health, and has begun to advocate that we each take stock of our personal habits to ensure alignment with our goals. Mike has lost weight, cut back on tobacco and beer, and increased his exercise. I co-instructed with him just a few weeks ago, and I'm inspired by the physical changes in him.

His secret sauce? Mike is "Happy." Really, that's what he writes on his name tag. And he is happy because he decides to be, each and every day.

I'd sum this up by saying that my friend is well on his way to personal sustainability because he keeps himself focused on all three major life areas: health, relationships, and career/finance – and in that order.

I truly believe that if your action plan begins with Personal Sustainability Planning, you – and your health, your relationships, and your career, will exceed your dreams. So get ready to make some new dreams come true!

MARYANNE ROSS

PO Box 112

East Blue Hill, ME 04629

Maryanneross36@gmail.com

www.mentalapparel.com

703-969-4295

Maryanne Ross, owner of Mental Apparel, is a trainer, speaker, consultant, and coach, with over 25 years of experience in adult education. .She has taught leadership, supply chain, and management courses, and has led team-building and strategic-planning retreats for many Fortune 500 companies, small businesses and non-profit associations. Maryanne is passionate about creating an engaging and interactive environment which ensures that learning is both fun and informative. Maryanne's special passion is the workshop that she calls "Personal Sustainability Planning." It is a totally different type of wellness program, the only process that encourages the workforce to give equal priority to their health and relationships, while attaining career success. Healthy, happy, engaged employees make a major impact on the productivity of their organizations while reducing the 2.3 trillion dollars of poor health and absenteeism costs.

Let Maryanne help your company fully develop its most precious resource, its human capital. Contact her today!

THE TRANSFORMATION CURVE™

DAVID TWEEDT

The Necessary Insight for Selecting the Business Transformation
Approach that Maximizes Your Results

▌ INTRODUCTION

Over my twenty-three-year career I have been blessed with working in, or with, top time-based companies where I either played an active role or personally lead business transformation. When I talk about time-based companies, I am referring to companies focused on quickly and efficiently flowing value to the customers with everything they do which drives short lead-times within each customer interaction point.

My career started at a great company called Wiremold, one of the first United States companies to successfully transform every aspect of how we did business. I was fortunate to play an active role in this evolution and see first hand what worked and how to "do it right."

The culmination of my experiences goes well beyond the awesome foundation I received at Wiremold. In addition to my eleven-year history at Wiremold, I led a transformation in an Irwin Tools plant (A Newell Rubbermaid Company) where we had a lot of fun driving the improvements and increasing our profitability. Adding to this hands-on knowledge is my insatiable drive to research and understand how different companies are winning the business transformation game through high-performance leadership, breakthrough cultures, and well-executed strategies.

All of this fuels my passion at Win Enterprises to work and interact with countless companies to help them realize their potential and achieve breakthrough results. Many of these companies were just starting, in the middle of, or just completing business transformations in one form or another when asking Win to help them take their performance to higher levels.

As I write this chapter, I am looking at two pictures on my desk that inspire me every day. The first is a butterfly leaving a jar that contained a stick and pieces from a cocoon. The caption is, *"Change—Without change there can be no breakthroughs. Without breakthroughs there can be no future."* This picture is accompanied by a second one of a skier on a mogul run. The caption on that one is, *"Goals—Obstacles are those frightful things you see when you take your mind off your goals."*[1] Both quotes sum up how I think about what it takes for a business to evolve.

Business transformation follows a predictable pattern yielding breakthrough results along the way. The key is, first, to identify where your company is today. Next, design the strategy and define the goals to get you to higher results than were previously thought possible. The last piece is to identify which strategies your team will drive and which ones you need help from the outside to drive while simultaneously building the internal capability.

Here, I will take you through where businesses fail and how we, at Win Enterprises, take a holistic view of business transformation using our proprietary framework and approach called the Win Holistic Transformation Model™ (WHTM™). Lastly, I will share how we customize our framework to fit your business and address your immediate needs. We customize our approach based on where your company is on the transformation maturity path that we have defined as the Transformation Curve™.

By the end of this chapter, you should have a general idea where your company stands today with regard to your transformational journey. You will also gain a vision of the high performance environment your company could achieve.

My hope is that you are inspired to take action today to achieve breakthrough improvements within your company. So, without further delay, read on to discover where your company is on the Transformation Curve™.

▌ WHERE BUSINESS TRANSFORMATIONS FAIL

Research has shown 70%—90% of business transformations fail to achieve and sustain the breakthrough results the leadership team desired.[2, 3, 4] This is a dismal statistic, and the source of my motivation to write this chapter. First, I know what it feels and looks like to be part of a team that was very successful in transforming the business, and I want you to have that feeling. Second, the look on associates' faces that are fully engaged and empowered to drive breakthrough change at all levels in the company is priceless. I want to you to see those faces as you walk through your business.

Our first discussion centers on learning from other companies that have "been there and done that." In this age of the Internet where we can "Google" anything, I looked up "Business Transformation Success" and was surprised to see 25.8 million results! This tells me there are many people seeking to find the approach that will yield that success.

What we have found is there is not a "one-size-fits-all" transformational approach. Each company has its own unique culture, history, customers, etc. When comparing transformation tactics, what worked for one company may not exactly work for the next. The constant for the companies that successfully achieved results is the holistic approach where principles remain the same. These successful companies understand their approach evolves as the company matures.

Successful transformations *are aware of* this progression that we refer to as **The Transformation Curve™**. And adapted their strategy along the way versus the weak or failed businesses that held the belief they could copy the exact tactics of another company and just muscle their way through it to get the same results. Yet, before we go much further, I want to make sure we are all aligned when using the term "transformation."

WHAT IS TRANSFORMATION?

I was talking with an entrepreneur the other day when he asked me, "What do you mean by transformation?" This was a very good question because the word is becoming overused, and the definition varies from person to person. Merriam-Webster Dictionary defines transformation, *"as a complete or major change in someone's or something's appearance, form, etc."*[5] This definition is a good start as it reminds me of butterflies and musclebound athletes.

When I think about transformation I remember, as a grade schooler, watching caterpillars transform into butterflies. At Win, we think about transformation as thorough and dramatic sustainable change. Another example is a skinny child that becomes a musclebound athlete. In both examples, the butterfly and musclebound athlete, the change is significant and not reversible.

For our conversation here, I like the definition from BusinessDictionary.com. They define transformation as,

"In an organizational context, a process of profound and radical change that orients an organization in a new direction and takes it to an entirely different level of effectiveness. Unlike 'turnaround' (which implies incremental progress on the same plane) transformation implies a basic change of character and little or no resemblance with the past configuration or structure."[6]

Using this second definition, transformation is not a fresh coat of paint and some new charts on the wall. Transformation is achieving breakthrough results by changing the way the organization thinks and acts. This type of success requires full involvement and teamwork of the entire leadership team. (I could write a whole chapter focused on how to gain this alignment and cooperation across the entire leadership ranks, but I'll save that for another time.)

Assuming we have the involvement and high level of teamwork from the entire leadership team, we are ready to design the transformation that will be successful for your company. This may sound daunting. However, at Win Enterprises, we have figured out what works. There are two major components to this design: the first is assessing where your company currently is in reference to The Transformation Curve™ and the second is co-developing your transformation path referencing the assessment as our starting point, and then using the principles within our Win Holistic Transformation Model™ (WHTM™), which I will describe in the next section.

▍ HOW WE THINK ABOUT TRANSFORMATION

The WHTM™ provides a framework to understand what creates sustainable, transformational results. We created this framework based on over 25 years of experience helping companies and observing best (and worst) practices in action. It comprises three major components that work together to provide comprehensive, holistic, and sustainable results.

These three components of the Win Holistic Transformation Model™ are Organizational Alignment, Supportive Culture, and Excellence in Execution. Based on our experience, all three components must be in place and working together in order for you to achieve and sustain your transformational results. We have found that the "secret sauce" that weaves these three components together includes the customized sequence of implementation activities, commitment and dedication of the entire leadership team, and integration of the Science of Success principles.

▌ THE THREE COMPONENTS OF THE WHTM™

The Win Holistic Transformation Model™ shown below has three main components: Organizational Alignment (outer ring), Supportive Culture (the area surrounding the star), and Excellence in Execution (the five points in the star).

WIN HOLISTIC TRANSFORMATION MODEL™

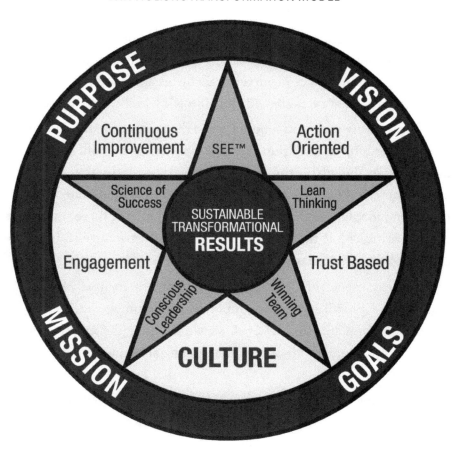

ORGANIZATIONAL ALIGNMENT

Organizational Alignment begins with a well-defined Purpose, Vision, Mission, and Goals for the company. This means these four elements are written in plain English and are understood and referenced in daily decision-making across the organization. Companies typically get tripped up with the belief that defining their Purpose, Vision, Mission, and Goals and posting them on the wall is enough. Defining your Purpose, Vision, Mission, and Goals is just the ticket to enter the game. Integrating them into the daily thinking is one of the keys to a sustainable high-performance environment where breakthrough results are commonplace occurrences. The breakthrough results occur when the organization is aligned and all rowing in the same direction.

I was recently at a client where I asked the group what the company's Purpose, Vision, and Mission message was. No one could answer my question even though the three statements were posted in the conference room where we were having our meeting! This demonstrated what is more commonplace than not. Businesses often have the three statements clearly written—but they fail to design the infrastructure to integrate them into the day-to-day business activities.

The next aspect of Organizational Alignment focuses on the HR systems and practices around employee development and retention. When your organization believes, as we do, that the employees are a company's greatest resource, the organization acts and behaves differently.

This is most evident within the HR systems and practices that are focused on creating a continual learning culture where the future leaders of the company are cultivated from within the ranks of the organization. This type of environment is further supported with an organizational structure, metrics, and "decision rights" aligned to achieve the company's objectives and goals.

The last aspect of Organizational Alignment focuses on the ensuring the reward systems, daily procedures, systems that run the organization, and financial systems that all align and complement each other. The goal of this alignment is to promote the desired behaviors, including the requirement for the different areas of the company to work together to achieve these common goals.

SUPPORTIVE CULTURE

Once we have the strategy identified for Organizational Alignment, we shift our focus to the culture within your company. Greg Brown, CEO of Motorola, has been quoted to say, "Culture trumps strategy every time."[7] It's important to remember that your culture can either accelerate your results or hold you back.

We define culture as your company's collective set of values, beliefs, and actions. Where you cannot necessarily see values and beliefs, you can observe actions. When we assess a company's culture we focus on the patterns of behaviors (actions) that are occurring at each level in the organization and across locations. During these assessments of the company's culture, we typically find both positive and negative aspects. In addition, we sometimes find that actions within the C-Suite team are very different from the front lines. When this occurs, these actions are disconnected and usually not aligned. I witnessed this with a client that has two distinctive cultures between their two locations! As you can see, getting your culture right is critical.

Once we have the results of the assessment, we know where to start with the culture work. The goal is to keep the aspects of your culture that will support your improvements and shift those that are holding you back. I am a strong believer that *if you do not design your culture it will design itself.*

The culture work starts with identifying the core values that will support your company's high performance aspirations. We have identified four core values common within companies with cutting edge high performance. The four core values are:

- » Continuous improvement
- » Action oriented
- » Engagement
- » Trust based

While these four are common in the companies we looked at, they may not be the values best suited for your company. The culture work will identify the core values that best fit your organization. The bottom line is, a company should have no more than 4-5 core values. If there are more then I would question how *core* the values are.

Keep in mind, changing your company's culture will not happen overnight. It requires a well thought through strategy and continual focus over time that includes an objective way to monitor and measure your progress.

Your culture shifting strategy should focus on creating goals for both the associates and leadership at ALL levels. The goal for the associates may look something like, "The associates are inspired, capable, and action oriented and embrace change." An example of a visionary goal for the leadership may sound something like, "Leadership style and team dynamics align with the desired culture and achieve the vision and goals."

The key is designing and implementing the culture shifting strategy that fits within *your company*. Each company is unique and where you start is dependent on where your company is on the Transformation Curve™, which I discuss later in this chapter.

EXCELLENCE IN EXECUTION

The third component of the WHTM™ is the five points in the star within our model, which are:

» Strategy Engagement Execution™ (SEE™)

» Science of Success

» Win's Version of Conscious Leadership

» Winning Team

» Lean Thinking

All five of these areas work together to define the operational standards and leading edge tools and techniques required to drive high performance in your company. The primary driver for these five areas is SEE™ (Strategy Engagement Execution™), which is the approach that aligns the entire organization towards achieving the goals and vision defined by the executive team.

The Time-Phased Strategy Engagement Execution™ (SEE™) approach is a powerful vehicle to help you drive better results through a methodology to increase focus and accountability. The SEE™ methodology provides the leverage within your team to blow out your goals by cascading the company's goals down to the point of impact, defining the metrics and action plans at this point of impact, and assign owners that are driven and accountable to achieve these metrics.

The Strategy portion of the SEE™ model contains four distinct and interconnected inputs which are focused on:

» Institutionalizing your purpose, vision, and mission

» Specific strategic initiatives to shift your culture

» Market and capability building

» Strategic initiatives focused on aligning mindsets to support the first three inputs.

These focus areas play a significant role in supporting the execution as well as building your high performance organization.

I am currently in the process of co-authoring a guide titled, *Rocket Your Strategy Execution Results—The Comprehensive Guide to Strategy Development & Execution For Your Company.* The goal of this guide is to educate the reader on what we have identified as the top characteristics of extremely successful strategy development and execution programs and share with you our SEE™ methodology that contains all these characteristics. Within this guide, we provide a high-level outline for you to understand how using our proven and proprietary strategy and execution approach will guide you to execute that strategy so you can enjoy fast results and reach your full potential for long-term success.

What's exciting about the SEE™ system is that it can be the primary management system you use to achieve your strategic goals and propel your company toward the high-performance environment you are striving for. The natural flow from top-level strategy through the business enables all your organization disciplines to focus on the initiatives that matter. Sales, Marketing, Distribution, Engineering, HR, Customer Service, and Operations all engage their teams to create impressive results.

As you can see, the Win Holistic Transformation Model™ is an extremely powerful framework that not only will drive breakthrough results within your company, it will also create the solid foundation to sustain those improvements and grow the momentum so your team can continually create these breakthrough results for years to come.

Remember, the "secret sauce" that weaves these three components together includes the customized sequence of implementation activities, commitment and dedication of the entire leadership team, and integration of the science of success principles. Customizing the sequence of implementation activities is critical because no one company is exactly like the next.

▌ TRANSFORMATION IS NOT ONE-SIZE-FITS-ALL

As a kid playing outside in the snow, I always wondered if it was possible to find two identical snowflakes. Yes, my engineering-based curiosity was showing itself at that early age. Truth told, I never found two snowflakes that were exactly alike.

We believe the same holds true for companies. We have never found two companies that were exactly the same, which explains why should the transformation strategy be the same? Our position is, it shouldn't! Additionally, we discovered that there are two main variables that need to be considered when developing a company's transformation strategy:

1) The three components of the Win Holistic Transformation Model™ we just discussed and

2) Measurement of these three components in the context of how far the company has matured with respect to the Transformation Curve™.

With respect to the three WHTM™ components: Organizational Alignment (outer ring), Supportive Culture (the area surrounding the star), and Excellence in Execution (the five points in the star), companies are usually further along in one of the three components and in some cases, totally ignore another element. For this reason, we believe in respecting the progress made to date and focus on adjusting the transformation strategy to align the progress of the other components before continuing the journey.

Why is this so important? It comes down to *respect for people*. As leaders we believe that respect is non-negotiable when it comes to creating a truly high-performance environment and breakthrough results. If there has been great progress in one of the three components of the WHTM™ prior to our arrival or if there are pieces of the transformation framework that are in place and working well, then we honor this work and build from it.

It is for this reason that we have found that the optimal solution is a customized transformation strategy. Now, with that said, the elements that need to be in place at each point in the transformation maturity path do not change. For this reason we look at where the company is with respect to the **Transformation Curve™** that focuses on the *maturity attributes* of the three components of the WHTM™.

▌ THE TRANSFORMATION CURVE™

In conjunction with the (WHTM™) framework model we just discussed, we know that businesses follow a predictable pattern as they are driving transformation. We call this pattern the Transformation Curve™. During the initial assessment phase of a business, also referred to as a diagnostic, we reference this Transformation Curve™ to define the sequence of initiatives over 3-5 years that will move the organization towards the targeted sustainable high performance environment. While there are patterns found when assessing a company, we typically find areas further up the maturity path where, at the same time, other areas are in their infancy stage of maturity or non-existent.

In this section, I encourage you to compare attributes and behaviors within each phase of the curve to your company. The following graphic describes the Transformation Curve™ and the phases a business goes through on the way achieve solid, high performance levels of a truly transformed company. It is worth noting that while this graphic describes each of the four phases a business goes through to achieve sustainable transformational results at a high level, without the detailed Transformation Curve™ assessment, it is difficult to truly identify where your business is today.

THE TRANSFORMATION CURVE™

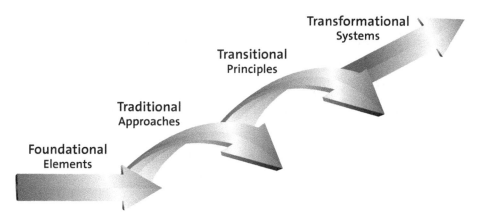

Foundational
Elements

Traditional
Approaches

Transitional
Principles

Transformational
Systems

FOUNDATIONAL PHASE

The Foundational Phase is exemplified by lack of or poorly defined Purpose, Vision, and Mission statement. Before we go further, let's talk about what we mean when we refer to each of your Purpose, Vision, and Mission statements.

Your *Purpose* describes **why you're in business** in the first place and **what inspires your team**. Your purpose statement answers the following three questions: Why are we in business? Who do we serve? Why is this important?

To give you an example, *Win Enterprises, LLC's purpose is to reveal what is possible to business leaders and to help them achieve their full potential.*

The *Vision* statement creates an image to **engage the whole team.** It should be very aspirational, defining the optimal desired future state (the mental picture) of what the organization wants to achieve over time, provide guidance and inspiration as to the organizations' desired achievement in five, ten, or more years, and functions as the "north star." It is intended to align all your employees' daily actions towards accomplishing this long-term result.

At Wiremold our vision statement was to "Be one of the Top 10 time-based companies in the world." Talk about aspirational!

Here are more examples of vision statements are from Win, Norfolk Southern, and Microsoft.

» Win: "Win's vision is a world where companies flourish as cohesive teams having a fun and exciting journey to business and personal achievement."

» Norfolk Southern: "Be the safest, most customer-focused and successful transportation company in the world."

» Microsoft: "Empower people through great software anytime, anyplace, and on any device."

Lastly, your *Mission* defines **how your company will reach your vision and achieve your purpose as an organization** while also defining how you do what you do. It also answers: What is our immediate task at hand? And, how do we differentiate our products and services? Essentially, "What makes us special?" Your mission statement is written succinctly in the form of a sentence or two, but for a shorter timeframe (one to three years) than your Vision statement, and is something that all employees should be able to articulate upon request.

Here are a few mission statements to help get you started:

» Win: "Win's Mission is to help business leaders totally transform their companies so that they can achieve great results and secure a great future for themselves and their employees."

» Nissan: "Nissan provides unique and innovative automotive products and services that deliver superior, measurable values to all stakeholders in alliance with Renault."

» Target: "Our mission is to make Target the preferred shopping destination for our guests by delivering outstanding value, continuous innovation and an exceptional guest experience by consistently fulfilling our Expect More. Pay Less.® brand promise."

WHY CLARITY OF YOUR PURPOSE, VISION, AND MISSION VITAL TO YOUR SUCCESS

If your purpose, vision, mission, and goals are not clear, success will be elusive—if not impossible. Your Purpose, Vision, and Mission statements serve to drive the organization towards consistently serving your customer and aligning your workforce toward improvement activities. Think about this: the absence of, or poorly written Vision and Mission statements, are lost opportunities for:

» Attracting/engaging/retaining talent

» Building organizational culture and

» Increasing productivity while leveraging all resources to success-fully implement a strategic plan

During the foundational phase we look for the company to have a Purpose, Vision, and Mission statements that are written succinctly, in an inspirational manner, and easy for all employees to repeat at any given time. When we get to the Transitional and Transformational Phases, we will expect much more regarding your Purpose, Vision, and Mission statements. In the later phases of maturity, we look at how well these three statements are integrated into daily decision making at every level in the organization. If your company does not yet have well defined Purpose, Vision, and Missions statements then we need to start there.

The way you go about creating these three statements is very critical. This is an opportunity to engage your leadership team and up and coming high performers. We have found that a series of focused activities over a short period yields the foundational drafts for all three statements and the communication strategy for the rollout. From there the internal champion(s) would socialize your Purpose, Vision, and Mission drafts to a select larger group to gain buy-in and expanded engagement.

▌ TRADITIONAL PHASE

The Traditional Phase is where we begin to evaluate the company through the lens of the WHTM™ framework: *Organizational Alignment, Supportive Culture, And Excellence In Execution.* While the Transformation Curve™ assessment goes into much greater detail, I will touch on examples in each of the three components of the WHTM™ framework to give you a flavor to then compare your company with each of the phases of the Transformation Curve™. Within all three components you will notice a pattern of short-term focus, brute force activities, reactive behavior, and silo-focused behavior. The Transformation Curve™ assessment is available by visiting our website, www.CompleteBusinessTransformation.com/TCAssessment.

Let's start with Organizational Alignment. Within the Traditional Phase we would typically find a well-defined Purpose, Vision, Mission. However, many times these statements are not referenced and serve more as great decoration on the walls. When asking associates about these three statements, we find they either do not know they even exist or they know where to point on the wall. The HR systems are also primarily focused on compliance to rules and policies with little regard to employee growth and retention. Finally, the company metrics are almost exclusively lagging metrics in nature. Lagging metrics focus on results at the end of a time period, normally characterizing historical performance. While these metrics are important, they tend to drive reactive behavior versus the more desired proactive behavior observed in the Transformational Phase.

When we look at the Supportive Culture within the Traditional Phase, we tend to see a culture that is a by-product of the company history. While there may be good aspects of this culture, there is little active attention to changing any aspect of it. Within this traditional environment, we typically find: employees are just "told what to do," annual reviews with little to no follow-up, and little time spent growing the next generation of leaders. This view of the workforce generates the perception that the output comes first to the detriment of employee safety and welfare, versus the other way around. This view of the workforce by leadership typically manifests as low employee dedication, high turnover of top contributors, and low employee engagement.

Lastly, Excellence in Execution in the Traditional Phase is characterized by reactive one-off improvement activities that typically address the problem of the day. This is where the Continuous Improvement resource, if one exists in the company, sits on the sidelines and is called to facilitate a kaizen activity to solve today's issue. These activities are not connected from one to the other. These reactive one-off activities are notorious for solving the problem in one area while causing new problems in adjoining functions. We also find problems band-aided without the root cause being identified because everyone is "too busy putting out fires" that they do not make the time to permanently solve these issues. This lack of problem solving manifests as the same issue or problem continually resurfacing over and over.

Companies in the Traditional Phase may have internal continuous improvement (CI) champions (resources who focus is driving process improvement); however, these champions may be new in role or be ill equipped with little practical experience to drive improvements. If the company has CI champions, their focus is on using a small group of improvement tools with little understanding to the principles and desired behaviors the tools are intended to deliver. The CI associates are viewed as the ones to drive the tools, while everyone else continues to do their own jobs. They are viewed as "nice to have" and given little strategic level authority. Essentially, these CI champions in the Traditional Phase are "window dressing" versus critical strategy drivers.

Within the Traditional Phase of the Transformation Curve™, the company strategy, if one exists, is developed and owned by top management with little to no communication to the organization beyond the executive ranks. This strategy is only reviewed quarterly or annually with the board of directors.

As you can see in each of the three components of the WHTM™ framework, in the Traditional Phase, the patterns that emerge center around short-term focus, brute force activities, reactive behavior, and silo-focused behavior. Sometimes these patterns emerge out of necessity. Leadership knows they need to change, but don't yet have new principles to guide new thinking, systems, and approaches.

At this point in the company's transformation maturity, the organization is doing the very best they can with the knowledge they have. While companies in this phase are constrained by their existing knowledge I am in no way inferring that they lack the capability to transform. When we talk with executives whose companies are struggling in the traditional phase, these executives know there must be a better way. They just don't know the path that will get them there.

The way to move your company from traditional to transitional and ultimately into the Transformational Phase requires injecting new knowledge and expertise with external support. These companies require guidance from experts who have personally played an active role or lead transformations. Ideally, these transformation experts have also held leadership roles within industry, which is an advantage when communicating with the executive team because they know what a great transformation looks like from both sides.

▌ TRANSITIONAL PHASE

The Transitional Phase is where we see the initial changes in results and cultural shifts toward your targeted transformational culture. Your targeted transformational culture is the sum of desired values, beliefs, and behaviors your company has defined for the future culture.

In the Transitional Phase examples I share for Organizational Alignment, I will touch on: how the integration of the Purpose, Vision, and Mission into decision-making has evolved, the mind shift of your HR systems, and advancement of metrics driving company behaviors.

For Supportive Culture I describe characteristics of the culture at this phase, increasing employee engagement, and how safety is viewed. Lastly, when talking about the Excellence in Execution component, I describe the development of your continuous improvement program and advancement of your strategy and execution process.

Within all three WHTM™ components in the Transitional Phase, you will notice a shift:

» from short-term focus to longer-term,

» brute force activities give way to defined foundational processes,

» reactive behavior begins to shift to a combination of proactive & reactive behavior,

» silo-focused behavior develops into more cross-functional teams and thinking.

Let's talk about the Organizational Alignment component. In the Transitional Phase, the strategic path is defined for transitioning the organization towards fully integrating the Purpose, Vision, and Mission statements into the daily decision-making is defined, and there has been progress in pilot areas of the company. Due to the communication of this strategy, the company is showing signs of referencing the statements on a semi-regular basis within pockets of the organization.

The HR systems have an employee retention and high-performer de-velopment strategy defined, which is showing good progress, that is well received by the workforce. HR and the executive team have refined the "decision rights" within the organization to shift the decision making to the point of impact and increase employee engagement within the com-pany. The "decision rights" change is also supported by redefined metrics that drive a new level of behaviors and decisions.. The metrics that drive the company are now aligned between departments and have evolved into 50% leading and 50% lagging. All this drives more proactive deci-sion-making and encourages cross-functional teamwork to succeed.

When we look at the Supportive Culture in the Transitional Phase we find the future High Performance Culture defined with specific strategic initiatives included in the annual and three to five year strategies. The company's leadership at every level is focused on engaging the workforce through increased communication and involvement in initiatives designed to shift the culture and improve performance. The leadership message and supportive behaviors demonstrate safety first including defined safety procedure expectations with focus on adherence.

Finally, let's look at Excellence in Execution. In the Transitional Phase, the Continuous Improvement Team operates at the *principle* level versus the *tool* level we saw in the Traditional Phase. The improvement activity is interconnected to achieve business level goals and solve business level problems. Continuous Improvement champions are seen as coaches, mentors, and future leaders in the company. As future leaders of the company, they participate in the strategy development process and own specific initiatives.

The annual and three to five year strategy is developed and owned by middle and top management. The ownership of the majority of the strategic initiatives is now at the middle management level and reviewed monthly by leadership. These monthly reviews are used for two purposes. The first is to celebrate progress and review how challenges will be addressed. The second purpose of the monthly strategy review process is for coaching and mentoring these middle managers to increase their leadership and strategic thinking skills. While this is great news, in the Transitional Phase, the ownership of the strategic initiatives is viewed as "in addition to my regular job" type activity. We will see this view of strategic initiative ownership evolve once when we reach the Transformational Phase.

Comparing the maturity descriptions of the Traditional Phase with the Transitional Phase shows significant step changes in engaging the workforce and yields increased morale and profitability. We have seen a shift from short-term focus to longer-term thinking when solving problems and planning for the future. There is also a significant reduction in brute force activities replaced by well-defined foundational processes and continual process improvement. The general behavior observed in the organization changes from exclusively reactive behavior to more proactive and from silo-focused toward cross-functional teams and thinking.

While you should celebrate when your company achieves the Transitional Phase your work is not done. Long-term sustainability is at risk if you stop at the Transitional Phase. In the following description of the Transformational Phase you'll see what I'm referring to when I talk about sustainability.

TRANSFORMATIONAL PHASE

The Transformational Phase is where we accelerate and anchor the step changes in results. In this phase, we focus on sustainment and full employee engagement. Here, I will go into much more detail than I did with the first three phases, (Foundational, Traditional, and Transitional) because I want to paint the picture for you of what is possible for your company.

For consistency I will continue to touch on: the evolution of integration of the Purpose, Vision, and Mission into decision-making, continued advancement of the HR systems, and continued maturity of the metrics supporting desired behavior when talking about Organizational Alignment.

For Supportive Culture, I will describe characteristics we have achieved within the culture, how this drives high employee engagement, and the role safety plays in the culture. At this point in the company's evolution, we are ready to introduce Win's version of Conscious Leadership.

Lastly, for Excellence in Execution, I will describe the integrated continuous improvement environment, the strategy and execution process, and how the company views comprehensive problem solving.

Organizational Alignment is optimized and obvious to an outside observer. The company's Purpose, Vision, and Mission statements are known and practiced by all associates. They are integrated into daily decision-making processes and each employee understands how their work contributes to achieving the mission and ultimately the vision of where the company is going.

The company attracts high performance talent due in part to the integrated HR systems and practices focused on employee development and retention. Also, remember, top talent knows and attracts other top talent.

The company's high-performance reputation is further reinforced by the focus on driving a learning culture strengthened by the cross functional supported organizational structure and "decision rights" aligned to achieve the objectives. In addition, the reward systems and financial metrics are aligned to promote the desired company behavior.

In the Transformational Phase, the Supportive Culture within leadership is deliberate about driving cultural elements across the total company. This results in an organization that understands and embraces the values, beliefs, and behaviors to achieve the performance results desired. The associates are inspired, capable, action oriented and embrace change.

In addition, the leadership style and team dynamics align with the desired culture. Achieving the vision and goals includes a focus on safety behaviors, awareness, and accountability versus focusing on just the safety results observed in the Traditional Phase.

The leadership understands and embraces the eight elements of Win's version of Conscious Leadership. Four of these eight elements focus on conscious of self and the other four focus on conscious of others. To learn more about our Conscious Leadership model, you can visit our website, www.CompleteBusinessTransformation.com. On the website you can download our assessment to find out if you're a conscious leader.

Our Conscious Leadership requires high emotional intelligence focused on helping you and your team members grow personally and professionally. This leadership style and team dynamics typically yields a 90+% employee engagement. Why is engagement so important? Picture your entire company versus a select few driving improvement and profitability. Intriguingly, a couple years back, Towers Watson published a study where they found the operating margins of high-sustainable engaged companies were 286% higher than low traditional engagement companies.[8] I'll take 286% higher operating margins any day!

Lastly, within the Excellence in Execution component the continuous improvement infrastructure and mindset is ingrained across the entire workforce. The company as a whole understands the principles behind Lean concepts and the behaviors they drive.

Ingraining the Continuous Improvement infrastructure reminds me of a Win client who used the structured problem solving methodology known as *"A3 Thinking"* to create a "problem solving culture" within the company. With this client, we identified internal champions for this initiative who were groomed to be the internal experts. In addition to the problem solving training and coaching that Win provided, these champions were trained in the associated change management and problem solving leadership skills. By co-developing internal champions the client created a sustainable foundation to continue to grow their people with.

Remember, problems come in all shapes and sizes. A company that has matured to the Transformational Phase may adopt a structured methodology to solve these problems which, when ingrained in the organization, would support individual growth while permanently solving these issues.

Like the example above, in a company undergoing change of this magnitude, the CI activities are completely strategic in nature and focus on integrated systems and processes where the business health metrics align and support CI actions. In addition, you may find future leaders in the company are required to rotate through the CI position before assuming their leadership role to ingrain the thinking and better equip them to excel this progressive environment.

Within the Excellence in Execution component, strategically, the entire organization understands how their actions support the Strategy Engagement Execution™ (SEE™) methodology, where the strategic action plans are part of the day-to-day activity. The Strategy Engagement Execution™ methodology is Win Enterprises' proprietary approach that aligns the entire organization towards achieving the goals and vision defined by the executive team. This is accomplished by cascading the company's goals down to the point of impact, defining the metrics and action plans at this point of impact, and assign owners that are driven and accountable to achieve these metric goals.

By comparing your company to the four phases of the Transformation Curve™, you may find your team is further along in one area and just beginning in another. This is a typical discovery when we assess a company to determine where and how to strategically start the transformational journey. Remember, this is a journey. It doesn't matter where you start as long as you and your teams continue to take action to move towards the Transformational Phase of the curve.

▍ CONCLUSION

The good news is you CAN move beyond the hard work and "brute force" mentality associated with *traditional* improvement. With the injection of new knowledge and external support, you can shift to *transitional* improvement and then ultimately sustainable *transformational* improvement.

Dr. W. Edwards Deming said, "New knowledge must come from outside." As you inject new knowledge and principles from outside, you can grow your internal resources and accelerate up the Transformation Curve™.

Ultimately, as your organization matures, you will recognize that the results you achieved in the Transitional Phase are fragile without a fully integrated *transformational* improvement approach. Until then, your results are dependent on the passion and drive of a few critical leaders. Beyond improvement, remember, your culture will hold you back and prevent sustainable improvement unless you also take deliberate actions to evolve your culture towards the characteristics of the transformational phase described in this chapter. This includes culture shifting activity.

Find out if your culture needs to shift. Take this assessment: https://completebusinesstransformation.com/free-culture-shift-assessment.

With guidance to utilize all the components of the Win Holistic Transformation Model™ shown earlier in a sequence of initiatives over three to five years, you will see your results become the natural by-product of your systems and processes. The *culture-focused/values-based leadership initiatives* will also help you reach a tipping point at which time your culture accelerates your progress.

Applying all the components of the Win Holistic Transformation Model™ in an integrated way will ensure your:

- » Workforce is energized and everyone is aligned behind your Purpose, Vision, Mission, and Strategic Goals
- » Improvement activities are aligned and span business wide systems
- » Culture shifts to support and accelerate improvement for long-term impact
- » Efforts constantly deliver results that exceed expectations
- » Systems and processes transcend the reliance on any one individual to hold things together—*you will have experienced true transformation*

The next move is yours. My hope is by reading this chapter you are energized and excited by the possibilities for your company. The good news is the possibilities are endless. The important thing to remember is that this is a journey not a 100-yard sprint. While there will be significant short-term wins, it takes persistence, resilience, and drive to achieve a truly Transformational Level environment. I wish you the best on your journey.

❚ REFERENCES

[1] Successories of Illinois, Lombard, Il.

[2] "70% of Transformation Programs Fail" – McKinsey, September 27, 2013.

[3] Leeman, Ron. "70% of Change Management initiatives fail – REALLY?" LinkedIn, September 14, 2014.

[4] Ward, John and Axel Uhl. "Success and Failure in Transformation - Lessons from 13 Case Studies".

[5] www.merriam-webster.com/dictionary/transformation

[6] www.businessdictionary.com/definition/transformation.html#ix-zz40pzlFm7g

[7] Leadership in the Field: Interviews with Global Leaders. Russell Reynolds Associates with Roger O. Crockett

[8] Towers Watson 2012 Global Workforce Study, "Engagement at Risk: Driving Strong Performance in a Volatile Global Environment."

Take The Transformation Curve™ Assessment to see where your company is on its transformation journey.

Visit www.CompleteBusinessTransformation.com/TCAssessment

David Tweedt

Win Enterprises, LLC

134R West Street

Simsbury, CT 06070

+1.860.651.6859

info@winenterprisesllc.com

http://www.CompleteBusinessTransformation.com

David is President, Win Enterprises, LLC. Lean thinking in an engaged high performance culture is core to David's approach based on his two decades of experience with business transformations. David is a thought-leader on organization wide Lean Operating Models utilizing the Win Enterprises' framework, Win Holistic Transformation Model™. He is co-author of *Win The Game – The Ultimate Guide for Your Successful Business Transformation.*

Win Enterprises, LLC helps visionary business leaders breakthrough their biggest challenges to create superior results. Based on the Win Holistic Transformation Model™, we customize a powerful strategy and execution process so you can enjoy fast results and reach your full potential for long-term success. Win Enterprises, LLC is the only consulting company that has integrated the Science of Success with cutting edge business transformation principles to sustain the breakthrough results we achieve together.

If you are not achieving the results you want, then contact Win Enterprises to learn more about how we can help you maximize your results. Please contact our office at +1.860.651.6859 or e-mail us at info@winenterprisesllc.com.

BUILD YOUR BUSINESS BY GETTING ON TV

MARY JO CRANMORE

One of the best, most powerful and sure-fire ways to differentiate your business and elevate your status as a professional is to be featured on television. It's an amazing truism that being a featured interview on the news – local or national – can put a lot of space and distance between you and your competition. Given today's competitive landscape, this is definitely an effort worth your time.

We – as a species – still look at television (even in the age of the Internet) as a powerful medium and those featured on it as "famous" or gods! You see people on TV and your brain automatically assumes there's something special about that person. I found that out myself one summer when I created a local TV show (in a very small media market, by the way) about local business and I was getting recognized in the grocery store all the time! And I was just the host, the vessel – I was the one asking the questions, not answering them. But still – I was elevated in their eyes as someone special with a lot of valuable information to share. It's true – and this is exactly what I'm suggesting you should seriously consider tapping into. Show your special talents, your expert information, your insights and be amazed at the lift in your business. Guaranteed.

Now, I can hear you thinking, "I can't do that! I don't know what to say or how to do this!" I don't know any producers! I don't know how to come up with – let alone pitch a story. The truth is: yes, you can. If you understand a few things I'm going to share with you in this article: from what the producers and the news management teams are looking for, to how to talk with them and how to cultivate relationships, I promise: you will be able to do this with ease.

NEW DAY, NEW TIME

It's also a truism to understand that the incredible innovation in information and how we consume our TV, news and information has radically changed within our lifetime. What used to be "the only game in town" (ABC, CBS and NBC) has now transformed into a bountiful harvest of opportunity for face time. Never has it been easier to grab your 15-minutes of fame – each and every month!

What's changed? A few things. First, there are a lot more outlets for content – your content. There are local, regional and national shows. There are cable outlets, podcasts, local news feature-based and news-based programming. Remember when it was just the 6pm news? Now, local stations are pumping out 5-6 hours of programming each DAY. That's a lot of time they need to fill.

The biggest thing to change, though, is social media. Understand you now have more access to these folks – but now they have more access to you. Most producers will focus in on your social media immediately. See what kinds of content you're putting out and what kind of following you're getting: that's a good indicator of how you'll play on TV. Keep that in mind and keep growing your following.

YOUR BEST WEAPON

With all of that time to fill, your best weapon in becoming "business famous" is very simple: your mindset. You need to understand – believe

– that producers NEED you. It's hard filling a show every day. Big stories are rare, especially in small towns. They have lots of space to fill and they need to find interesting, compelling content their audience will CRAVE. That's where you come in, my friend. You have that. You ARE that. All you have to do is shift your mindset: they need you.

They also aren't scary. The faster you shift your perspective on who these producers are, the better off you will be. Most of them are, frankly, kids. They are 20-somethings who want what we all want: to do their jobs and go home. They aren't Lorne Michaels or Lee Aronsohn, or Chuck Lorre (if you don't know who these guys are, look 'em up...some of the most successful entertainment producers on the planet). They are news kids.

Your job is to understand them and use that understanding to your advantage.

Shift your mindset to understand who they are and who you are – you are the one with the content that will help them build audience. That's what they want. Get that set – and you're ready to roll!

GETTING THE MEDIA'S ATTENTION:

"Ya gotta get their attention first."

I remember this joke that my father used to tell – a perfectly awful story about a 2x4 and a mule with the punchline "ya gotta get his attention first."

As disturbed as I was about that joke, there's always a kernel of truth in humor. And, as with this example, there is a lot of truth to this statement when it comes to the media.

Think about it: they have to pay attention to the WORLD. Everything is fair game – and everything is vying for their attention. So, as you may understand, that job can get pretty overwhelming, unless you make some boundaries and guidelines for yourself. I did that at every news job I had – from the NBC affiliate in Ft. Myers, Florida to a position as the executive producer in Portland, Maine to the craziness of *Good Morning, America* and **Dateline NBC**.

The guidelines I'm going to share with you in this chapter are exactly how I would look at any story that came across my desk. Of course, each day is different and you may never know why your story is getting coverage – or not – but you'll at least be armed with the methodology by which producers and news managers make decisions. And that's a BIG advantage.

▌ WHAT MAKES A NEWSWORTHY BUSINESS STORY?

Contrary to what most people think, it's not all blood and guts ("if it bleeds, it leads") – nor is it a pure decision of what's news and what's "fluff" that makes the decision for each news manager. The term we're searching for here is "news judgment" – meaning: "in your judgment, is this story worthy of time in the newscast or inches on the page?" Every news manager has to back up their daily decisions and if they can't, well, then they won't have that job for very long. Reporters routinely pitch ideas they like – but in the end, the producers, the executive producers, the editors and the managers are truly in charge.

I used to know a "good story" (meaning it was worthy of my time to ask questions, write the story, send a videographer or photographer and give it space on my newscast. If you take away commercials, sports, weather, teases and graphical opens, I only had a "news hole of about 11 minutes each day – so the competition can be fierce) if I felt a little "thump" in the middle of my chest. That "thump" – call it intuition or solid news judgment. It rarely was wrong.

So you think that after watching the broadcasts, all those managers must care about is blood, guts, sex, money and fluff? (That's a pretty good guess, if that's what you think.....but I digress...)

It's not that the media doesn't want "fluff" (read: feature stories or evergreen feature stories) – heck, there's a ton of fluff out there. But when the media wants fluff, they want a certain kind of fluff.

It's also not that the media ONLY wants the next Watergate or OJ Simpson – because they DEFINITELY do (notice how they keep trying to turn everything into Watergate and OJ?). But they have shows and websites and publications to fill every day – it would be crazy to hold out for one earth shattering story all of the time.

So – you may be asking – what DO they want? What is the magical combination of elements that make the media sit up and take notice? Even for a "fluffy" feature? In my experience, it's not about a flashy media kit, necessarily, or a pitch-perfect pitch. It's all about the <u>audience</u> – if you can align the story with the right media outlet, there you go.

By far, the biggest test of a good news story is "who cares?" Let's take that "who" and run with it. The question my news directors would always ask me when I advocated for a particular story was "who cares?". They meant that literally – who will care about this story? Why are we doing this story? Most businesses need the most help with this item. It's their business, it's their baby – "everyone within the sound of my voice should care!" But....that's quite literally not true. Understanding "who cares" and then where your audience might go to for this information gives you a path to the correct media outlet who might care about this innovation.

Below is the roadmap to media coverage for you and your business. If you can get even four of the five of these elements right (definitely the first three), you're probably going to score some media or TV time. Here goes:

1. **Timeliness** – There's got to be a reason you are telling me about your story on this particular day. Why today? What makes it important for it to be written about on this day or week? Some stories are considered "evergreen" – meaning they could air anytime. But – before you check this off your list, do yourself the favor of at least figuring out why NOW is the perfect time to run your story.

For example, there's a national story about recent deaths caused by high-speed chases and your company just invented a new tool that helps the police stop high speed chases before they start. Your timing is perfect.

2. **Innovation** – Obviously, new stuff is news, by it's very definition. The trick here? Who is it news to? And why? Who is that audience and where can you find them? You won't always have the luxury of perfect timing when a new invention or product or service is launched. If there's no "timing" element, then the key will be – is it the RIGHT press outlet, correct reporter on the right beat or the perfect audience for your story. (see number 3)

3. **Relevance** – Relevance is in large part about the "who" is watching that media outlet or reading that periodical. You must align your story with the choice of media for a story to get coverage. You also need to think about relevance in terms of what's going on in our culture, in our mindset, nationally or internationally. In other words, is your story connected to something that's happening in our society right now? That's called "localizing" and it's very popular with the local news to take something like a national trend or issue and show how it's connected to someone or something right here in your hometown.

4. **Uniqueness** – This is about scarcity. When people talk about how the world is crashing down and all the murders that happen – look, it's right there on TV! Yes, that's true, but the vast majority of us NEVER come in contact with an actual murder. In fact, most murders are not random – they are committed by someone the victim already knows. So – when Chicken Little says "the sky is falling" I say – "it's on the news because it doesn't happen that often. It's a rare occurrence – that's what makes it newsworthy." Can you speak to this with your own news story? Is it a rare occurrence? Is it something that's different or special? If it happens

all the time, you need to beef up the other four elements to make your story newsworthy.

5. **Wow Factor** – Don't underestimate the cool, whiz bang, gotcha to news, either. To truly get a sense of whether you have this one covered, check it out with someone who's in your target audience. If they say "wow – that's cool" then eureka! This wow-factor is by far, the toughest one to get. Something can be unique and relevant and not have a lot of pizazz. But don't worry – if the audience cares, it will still score a hit.

Now that you have a good sense of what they look for from a big picture perspective, let's talk specifics. What is the actual story you will pitch?

First off, there are only two kinds of stories. Really? Yes...only two.

The first is time sensitive – meaning that it's relevant to today only – tomorrow, it might become the proverbial "fish wrapping". The second is evergreen Yup, just like it sounds, it's a story that can be pitched anytime. Simple, right?

Now, I've put together a fairly comprehensive list of ideas to get you started within both of those categories. Can you think of others I haven't included? Here are the best of the best ideas that catch a producer's eye.

TIME SENSITIVE:

1.   Announce something new.

     » Do you have a new product offering? A new feature in your product? Even a new free offer? Did you update a product or service? A BOOK? That's news your customers or prospects may want to hear about sooner rather than later.

2.   Tie-into breaking news as it breaks.

» Is your business or product relevant to breaking news? Monitor the news with an eye to finding items that relate to your business.

3. Events: Tie-into annual events or holidays (or create your own).

» Can you tie into a special event or commemoration? What is the time of year that people are thinking about needing your product, needing your program, needing your book, what time of year are they talking about you?

4. Raise a controversial issue or tie into one.

» This is the very critical concept of your "core story" – and what that means is you keep updated on where your industry is and you have a point of view about it. What do you think? This is a key differentiator AND it provides tremendous value for your clients.

» Who is an expert of getting a lot of publicity that you disagree with? You can go back to that same reporter who wrote about them and say, "Actually this is my opinion...."

» Reporters can do follow-up stories and that's a prime way of just piggy backing onto somebody else's story.

» Do you have innovative ways of doing something? Is there a lot of misinformation in your topics? Are there scams or frauds going on around now that you can comment on?

5. The second part of "core story" concept -- Pitch yourself as part of a trend

» Is there something that's increasing or decreasing in your field right now that you can comment on? Is there a niche popping up and is there some way for yourself to be tied in to that trend?

» You could be noticing an upcoming need, demand or problem which you're already addressing right now. If you pitch yourself as part of a trend, you also want to keep in mind if anyone else can comment or is also part of this trend. Helping a reporter find you as well as other sources makes doing a story – and their job – easier.

NON-TIME SENSITIVE STORIES

1. Promote your personal story

   » This is where you are the main story, it revolves around you. It could be a profile, a review of your product or service or your book.

2. Do something for charity

   » I'm not advocating doing charitable work just to get publicity. What I am saying is, if you are doing something charitable–out of love–then you may as well maximize the situation and get publicity from it.

   » For best results, local initiatives do best. Target your local newspapers, radio and TV, because they're going to be the ones most interested in it.

3. Do a survey – consumer insights are always interesting.

   » In all likelihood, you're doing some kind of market research for programs and services you want to develop. Why not share your results? This could position you further as an expert in your field.

   » I've seen survey results released that have just a couple of hundred respondents. Even a short survey with interesting results can be the basis for a story. However, do make sure you follow best practices in research so nobody can criticize your methodology and question your results.

   » Another way is to watch new studies or survey results that are published, and tie into them. Comment on the results. What bold, outrageous and provocative statement can you make about them?

4. Help people solve a problem – this is like Pete – helped them set their goals and stick to it (good story to launch around the New Year)

» You're in business because you help people solve problems. How you help people solve problems is a story idea!

5. Write an op-ed

» An op-ed is a letter to the editor clearly expressing your opinion about something. It's not a pitch. Instead, you write why you feel the way you do about a particular story they recently published.

» Of course, tie it into your business somehow, but keep in mind it shouldn't be a blatant pitch for your business. When you sign off, for example, make sure to include your branding (see number 14 above) and your official email address and website.

» And bonus number one....and irresistible method (thank you, David Letterman) Issue a Top Ten List that connects with your service or brand: Top Ten Mistakes People Make.....

» ....bonus number 2: this is TV-centric, but every year in November, February, and May (July is also a sweeps month, but it's diminished in it's importance over the years) – TV stations in markets across the country still produce special reports and series for this sort of antiquated system. If you have an idea for a series – for example, a water testing service might volunteer to test water in multiple towns for the "Is your drinking water safe?" series...that's going to cost them money, but it's worth it's weight in TV gold.

» ...bonus number 3: what about a regular series that you could pitch? A garden center sponsors the weathercast on Thursdays and Fridays and they do a little gardening advice piece. The station shoots it and edits – and the garden center is featured and gives advice to the viewers....More promotion than straight PR, but it still counts as great coverage.

▌ YOU DON'T NEED A PRESS RELEASE ANYMORE

Yes, you read that right. Press releases are a bit passé ....old school....an out of date method of communicating as sure as chisel and rock, pen and ink and parchment paper. If you want to get the attention of those news producers, the worst thing you can do is blend in with the hundreds of boring releases they get everyday from folks who don't know any better.

What you're going to do now is something more immediate, more relevant, hipper, more to the point, fresh and updated. It's called a pitch – and it has it all over a press release. Why? Because it connects the dots for the producers and does their work for them. What do we understand about Millennials? They would prefer you did their work for them much more than making them do the work for you. I do not mean this as an insult whatsoever. These folks have a hard job. They're working at a very fast pace and a lot is expected of them. The easier you can make it on them to include you (and the better you do at that on camera) the more they will love you and have you back – get it?

▌ YOUR PITCH

As you can see by the main points in this chapter, the content is really the most important part of this process. If you can get good at understanding what a good story is then you can screw up almost every other part of this (or not do it perfectly) and still be featured all the time!

Story is critical. Not only the story you're pitching but your story.

Let's take a moment to translate what you've come to know as your "elevator pitch" or sales conversation. How will you shift what you've been saying about yourself so it's media friendly? Here's a very easy way to position yourself by using story. Focus on your WHY. That's it. We don't need to know all about you – we just need to know what drives you that relates to why we care about the content you're about to deliver. I help clients all the time shifting their long winded stories down to precision talking points and it's very simple: do you have a short story that encapsulates why you do what you do? Is it compelling? Is it riveting? Does it connect the audience to you immediately? If not – we have some work to do.

Here's how I talk about why I left the TV news business – Good Morning, America, in particular – to work with businesses to help them tell their stories.

Interviewer: So tell us, how did you get to where you are now, teaching large and small companies to use story to create massive success?

Me: Let me tell you a little story I think illustrates that point. I was working as a field producer for GMA in New England when the first Iraq War was launched. We got word that the first kid killed in Iraq was from Skowhegan, Maine – my territory. So, I had to get in my car....and drive to Skowhegan....and knock on his family's door..... and talk to his mother on the very worst day of her life. I am the angel of death....and I want you to tell me all about it. And it was there and then that I realized I didn't want to talk to people on the worst day of their lives any more. I wanted to instead be a tool of inspiration – and I wanted to help others become an inspiration, too. I quit that very week.

(When I tell this story – I get very deliberate....I slow it down....I give those words power and when I tell it – there's silence. They're riveted. I have them – and I know it. Do you have a powerful story that shares your "why"? Start using it. Today.)

This is one of the most important things you will do – share yourself in such a way that shares the value and your vulnerability at the same time. This is the ultimate in authenticity and if you feel the power in your words, so will they.

This is how you connect to your audience, both in social media as well as on TV. Don't be ashamed of your failures, your mistakes, your critical moments – these are the stuff of growth and life and the energy of that is irresistible.

Now – how can you use this example to start telling your story in a short, memorable and riveting way? You want connection. That is the first step to knowing....liking....and then, trusting. By sharing yourself – viewers now know you.....and that's powerful stuff. This is how you convert potential customers into clients.

Back to your pitch. Once you have your story down, can you start to fit these puzzle pieces together? What is it about your work that you can share and connect it to events happening in the world? Here's an example for you.

I have a wonderful client, a financial advisor who is passionate about retirement. Yes, that's right: retirement. What do we know about retirement in the news? We can first put together a Google Alert about retirement and see what others (reporters, TV producers, pundits, experts) are writing about retirement. We weave his personal philosophy into the story-development process and BAM, here's what I came up with (a series idea, no less!).

▌ REGULAR SEGMENT TREATMENT IDEA

(Available for in-studio, weekly series)

You can't pick up a newspaper these days without reading how American's are failing at money, saving, spending and worst of all -- saving money for retirement.

Social Security May Be Bankrupt in 12 Years, 33% Cut In Benefits Looms, screams a **NewsMax.com** finance article.

The Huffington Post says a ***New Study Reveals American's Aren't Saving Nearly Enough for Retirement***

And...from high interest charges to unclaimed tax refunds to wasted food and bad health habits, USA Today shows us we just can't get it together with ***20 Ways Americans are Blowing Their Money***

Charlie Epstein, the best-selling author of two books and a wealth building expert who helps everyday people achieve the life – and retirement – of their dreams (also known as their "Desirement") says these statements <u>don't go nearly far enough</u> to really get at the issue American's have with money.

"We do not do a good job as a culture of teaching our children about money," says Charlie. "We simply hope the kids learn it on the streets or in school. It's a ridiculous strategy and why we find ourselves in the situation we have today."

Charlie points to rampant spending, skyrocketing credit card debt, record bankruptcies and defaults on students loans. "It's simply not sustainable."

Each week, Charlie will bring the viewers information they can put to work immediately, creating for themselves the options and the self-reliance that comes with being in charge of their financial lives. Examples of weekly segments include:

- » **The Myths of Money**: many things we commonly believe about money simply aren't true (and worse, they're hurting our ability to save and build wealth);

- » **Money Mindset**: Removing the emotion from money allows us to have clarity around our financial choices – shifting into the mindset called "Desirement Planning" allows for your life to shift in all manner of ways – what you do is up to you. Charlie helps you identify

- » **Topical Money**: What's happening in the news or the markets that is affecting your ability to save and grow your financial nest egg.

- » **Fiscal Fitness**: Taking stock of where you are now and where you want to be – indicators of trouble ahead or smooth sailing.

- » **The Defender**: You're not the only one making decisions about your money. What to do to protect yourself – and thrive – in the face of a variety of financial threats: market downturns, on-line identity theft,

Charlie is on a mission – a mission to educate and as his second book proclaims, "Save, America, Save". What does he advise? "We all have so many incorrect assumptions, beliefs, it's time to turn all of those incorrect blocks on their heads and start teaching American's what it means to have money, use money as a tool and start building some real wealth for themselves."

MEDIA KIT: http://www.charlieepstein.com/media-kit

YouTube/LinkedIn/Twitter/Facebook

Contact Mary Jo Cranmore 860-709-4216

or mjcranmore@clientcyclemarketing.com to book Charlie today!

Do you see how this blends Charlie's expertise with what's happening in the news and in our cultural mindset about retirement? This is an evergreen topic and I've also given the producers several options for the kinds of stories that Charlie can offer?

Now...how we pitch this kind of story to the media.

❚ THE PITCH

The part of this process that always seems to intimidate even the most accomplished among us is: picking up the phone and actually talking to a producer.

Keep in mind the mindset piece we talked about, the relevance (what's going on in the world in relation to your industry and topics) and how important you are to moving that forward for their audience. You're there to advance the understanding and give information that's relevant and helpful.

Let's do your preliminary work. Assuming you've been doing your social media work – pumping out great content and really working to help your audience and clients, it's time to find your media targets.

You're going to want to start with your local market first. There are 210 TV Markets in the USA – the ranking is purely based on population

– there are no "better" or "worse" depending upon designation – just larger and smaller. Typically, the smaller markets are easier to crack – they have a smaller audience. Do you know which TV market you're in? If not, Google search the Nielsen TV Market Rankings – here's what you'll find:

2015-16 Nielsen Designated Market Areas (DMAs)

» New York (#1)

» Los Angeles (#2)

» Chicago (#3)

» Philadelphia (#4)

» Dallas-Fort Worth (#5)

» San Francisco-Oakland-San Jose (#6)

» Washington, D.C. (Hagerstown) (#7)

» Boston (Manchester) (#8)

» Atlanta (#9)

» Houston (#10)

» Tampa-St. Petersburg (Sarasota) (#11)

» Phoenix (Prescott) (#12)

» Detroit (#13)

» Seattle-Tacoma (#14)

» Minneapolis-St. Paul (#15)

» Miami-Fort Lauderdale (#16)

» Denver (#17)

» Cleveland-Akron (Canton) (#18)

» Orlando-Daytona Beach-Melbourne (#19)

» Sacramento-Stockton-Modesto (#20)

» St. Louis (#21)

» Charlotte (#22)

» Pittsburgh (#23)

» Portland, OR (#24)

» Raleigh-Durham (Fayetteville) (#25)

» Baltimore (#26)

» Indianapolis (#27)

» San Diego (#28)

» Nashville (#29)

» Hartford & New Haven (#30)

» Columbus, OH (#31)

» San Antonio (#32)

» Kansas City (#33)

» Salt Lake City (#34)

» Milwaukee (#35)

» Cincinnati (#36)

» Greenville-Spartanburg-Asheville-Anderson (#37)

» West Palm Beach-Fort Pierce (#38)

» Austin (#39)

» Las Vegas (#40)

» Grand Rapids-Kalamazoo-Battle Creek (#41)

» Norfolk-Portsmouth-Newport News (#42)

» Oklahoma City (#43)

» Harrisburg-Lancaster-Lebanon-York (#44)

» Birmingham (Anniston and Tuscaloosa) (#45)

» Greensboro-High Point-Winston-Salem (#46)

» Jacksonville (#47)

» Albuquerque-Santa Fe (#48)

» Louisville (#49)

- » Memphis (#50)
- » New Orleans (#51)
- » Providence-New Bedford (#52)
- » Buffalo (#53)
- » Fresno-Visalia (#54)
- » Wilkes-Barre-Scranton-Hazleton (#55)
- » Richmond-Petersburg (#56)
- » Little Rock-Pine Bluff (#57)
- » Mobile-Pensacola (Fort Walton Beach) (#58)
- » Albany-Schenectady-Troy (#59)
- » Tulsa (#60)
- » Fort Myers-Naples (#61)
- » Knoxville (#62)
- » Lexington (#63)
- » Dayton (#64)
- » Wichita-Hutchinson Plus (#65)
- » Honolulu (#66)
- » Charleston-Huntington (#67)
- » Green Bay-Appleton (#68)
- » Roanoke-Lynchburg (#69)
- » Tucson (Sierra Vista) (#70)
- » Flint-Saginaw-Bay City (#71)
- » Des Moines-Ames (#72)
- » Spokane (#73)
- » Omaha (#74)
- » Springfield, MO (#75)
- » Rochester, NY (#76)

- » Toledo (#77)
- » Columbia, SC (#78)
- » Huntsville-Decatur (Florence) (#79)
- » Portland-Auburn (#80)
- » Madison (#81)
- » Paducah-Cape Girardeau-Harrisburg (#82)
- » Shreveport (#83)
- » Syracuse (#84)
- » Champaign & Springfield-Decatur (#85)
- » Harlingen-Weslaco-Brownsville-McAllen (#86)
- » Waco-Temple-Bryan (#87)
- » Chattanooga (#88)
- » Colorado-Springs-Pueblo (#89)
- » Cedar Rapids-Waterloo-Iowa City & Dubuque (#90)
- » Savannah (#91)
- » El Paso (Las Cruces) (#92)
- » Baton Rouge (#93)
- » Charleston, SC (#94)
- » Jackson, MS (#95)
- » South Bend-Elkhart (#96)
- » Tri-Cities, TN-VA (#97)
- » Burlington-Plattsburgh (#98)
- » Greenville-New Bern-Washington (#99)
- » Fort Smith-Fayetteville-Springdale-Rogers (#100)
- » Davenport-Rock Island-Moline (#101)
- » Myrtle Beach-Florence (#102)
- » Evansville (#103)

» Johnstown-Altoona-State College (#104)

» Lincoln & Hastings-Kearney (#105)

» Reno (#106)

» Boise (#107)

» Tallahassee-Thomasville (#108)

» Tyler-Longview (Lufkin & Nacogdoches) (#109)

» Sioux Falls (Mitchell) (#110)

» Fort Wayne (#111)

» Augusta-Aiken (#112)

» Lansing (#113)

» Youngstown (#114)

» Fargo-Valley City (#115)

» Springfield-Holyoke (#116)

» Peoria-Bloomington (#117)

» Traverse City-Cadillac (#118)

» Eugene (#119)

» Macon (#120)

» Lafayette (#121)

» Montgomery-Selma (#122)

» Yakima-Pasco-Richland-Kennewick (#123)

» Santa Barbara-Santa Maria Valley-San Luis Obispo (#124)

» Monterey-Salinas (#125)

» Bakersfield (#126)

» Columbus, GA (Opelika, AL) (#127)

» La Crosse-Eau Claire (#128)

» Corpus Christi (#129)

» Wilmington (#130)

- » Amarillo (#131)
- » Chico-Redding (#132)
- » Columbus-Tupelo-West Point-Houston (#133)
- » Wausau-Rhinelander (#134)
- » Topeka (#135)
- » Rockford (#136)
- » Monroe-El Dorado (#137)
- » Columbia-Jefferson City (#138)
- » Minot-Bismarck-Dickinson (#139)
- » Medford-Klamath Falls (#140)
- » Duluth-Superior (#141)
- » Beaumont-Port Arthur (#142)
- » Salisbury (#143)
- » Lubbock (#144)
- » Odessa-Midland (#145)
- » Palm Springs (#146)
- » Wichita Falls & Lawton (#147)
- » Anchorage (#148)
- » Sioux City (#149)
- » Erie (#150)
- » Joplin-Pittsburg (#151)
- » Albany, GA (#152)
- » Rochester-Mason City-Austin (#153)
- » Panama City (#154)
- » Terre Haute (#155)
- » Bangor (#156)
- » Wheeling-Steubenville (#157)

» Biloxi-Gulfport (#158)

» Binghamton (#159)

» Bluefield-Beckley-Oak Hill (#160)

» Sherman-Ada (#161)

» Gainesville (#162)

» Idaho Falls-Pocatello (Jackson) (#163)

» Missoula (#164)

» Abilene-Sweetwater (#165)

» Yuma-El Centro (#166)

» Billings (#167)

» Hattiesburg-Laurel (#168)

» Clarksburg-Weston (#169)

» Quincy-Hannibal-Keokuk (#170)

» Rapid City (#171)

» Utica (#172)

» Dothan (#173)

» Lake Charles (#174)

» Elmira (Corning) (#175)

» Jackson, TN (#176)

» Watertown (#177)

» Harrisonburg (#178)

» Alexandria, LA (#179)

» Marquette (#180)

» Jonesboro (#181)

» Bowling Green (#182)

» Charlottesville (#183)

» Laredo (#184)

- » Grand Junction-Montrose (#185)
- » Butte-Bozeman (#186)
- » Lafayette, IN (#187)
- » Lima (#188)
- » Meridian (#189)
- » Bend, OR (#190)
- » Great Falls (#191)
- » Greenwood-Greenville (#192)
- » Twin Falls (#193)
- » Parkersburg (#194)
- » Eureka (#195)
- » Casper-Riverton (#196)
- » Cheyenne-Scottsbluff (#197)
- » San Angelo (#198)
- » Mankato (#199)
- » Ottumwa-Kirksville (#200)
- » St. Joseph (#201)
- » Fairbanks (#202)
- » Victoria (#203)
- » Zanesville (#204)
- » Helena (#205)
- » Presque Isle (#206)
- » Juneau (#207)
- » Alpena (#208)
- » North Platte (#209)
- » Glendive (#210)

Then, find the stations in your market and look into who's who at those stations. You'll probably be fairly familiar with these stations already, given that you're a member of the community and most likely, their viewing audience. Are there shows you like? Do they do a feature-based show (no news content, more informational and entertainment in nature)? The person you're going to want to talk to is probably the producer, but here's what you ask when you call the station.

You: Hello...I'm looking for the person who books interviews for the 6am morning news. Can you help me find that person?

Or

You: Hello – I wonder if you could help me? I'm looking for the person who books guests on the morning news.

Then – shut up and let them help you! Don't launch in to your pitch until you have that decision-maker on the phone. If the person says "they're not available right now – can I take a message?" Ask for the person's name first and then ask if they know when that person will become available. If you're getting no where, say no and hang up and try later.

The schedule of a news station is pretty much the same in every city. Morning news from 4-7a – that means that producer probably comes in at 11pm and works overnight to produce the show. Then, the day-side producers arrive during the Today Show – or GMA – and prepare for the day. They usually meet after the final "local news cut in" on the Today show – meaning, they're meeting around 8:30 or 9a.

This morning meeting is extremely important. They decide what each reporter will be assigned and where they're going to get the content for their noon and afternoon news at this time. They'll meet again at 2:30 when the 11pm producer arrives to fill him or her in on what's happening with news staff throughout the day.

Your job is to try and avoid high stress times: the half-hour before each newscast is usually frenetic. No one wants to hear a new idea during that timeframe. Stick to 10am or 2pm as good, safe times and go from there. Keep calling until you reach that producer/booker – and don't leave a ton of messages. The only one you'll want to leave is AFTER you speak with that producer as a follow-up. That's it. Until then, call, ask for help, try to talk to the producer.

SHOWTIME!

Now – you have the producer on the phone. It's show time. This is effectively an audition – but don't get freaked out. It's where you get to SHINE!!

Here's what you say:

"I have a segment idea for you. I've been watching and notice you do a lot of health related topics. I can show your audience how to make healthy dinners for kids 7 days a week in under 10 minutes a day....."

OR

"I have a segment about making healthy meals for kids 7 days a week in under 10 minutes a day....I think it would make a great segment for your audience. I notice you focus quite a bit on healthy living and this would be a perfect addition."

OR

"I have a segment idea for next week during school vacation (super relevant to her audience) – 10 super entertaining things you can do with your kids that won't kill your budget."

OR

well...you get the idea.

Now – you've got her attention.

Share with her how you could make this visual – it's an interview for sure, but in what way can you make it a TV interview (don't forget – it's video!) The cooking – super easy – they've been doing cooking segments for decades. The school vacation idea might be a great one for a reporter to come out to your place and do what's called a "package" or "series" – this is not live in the studio. Rather, it's interviews and video and they put it all together back in the editing room of the station.

If you get to this part in the conversation, you've got her. Go with it! Ask her what her preference would be, what day or day for the interview or production. Don't hesitate to nail it down. If she puts you off, schedule a second conversation and send her follow up email information. BUT – your goal is to set a date – then and there.

Do you see how this is starting to work?

A common question I get is, "can I email my pitch?" The answer is yes – that method is both less effective and more effective at the same time. First, you haven't interrupted them with a phone call (positive) but it's a lot easier to push you off. I typically use email as a follow-up method.

▌ THE STORY, THE PREP AND THE PITCH

These three elements outlined for you here in this chapter gives you a great head start on your media career. There is a lot to each of these elements and you now have in your possession the roadmap to becoming a regular on local – or even national media. Your job now is to turn your attention to connecting these dots with your own expertise, your own material and your own media market or favorite shows. I'd love to hear more about your success!

Mary Jo Cranmore

Brand Storyteller, Video Marketer & Expert Media Placement

www.maryjocranmore.com

www.firstcalltalent.com

email: mj@maryjocranmore.com

Mary Jo Cranmore is a journalist and storyteller who helps companies powerfully connect with their customers through video. Starting out as a TV news producer, writing and crafting interesting and viewer-attractive stories, she learned to build an audience. During her time in the media, Mary Jo worked at NBC & ABC network affiliates and then as a field producer for *Dateline NBC* and *Good Morning, America*.

Since working in news, Mary Jo has built strategic marketing and video content programs for small and large companies, including Discovery Channel, Ann Taylor, Kraft Foods, Gillette and Verizon. She currently runs a strategic messaging and branded content marketing service as www.maryjocranmore.com and serves as Creative Director at First Call Talent, placing guests and experts on national network and cable news organizations such as CNBC, CNN, FOX Business.

STRIKING ASSESSMENT GOLD: HOW TO PROFIT FROM OPPORTUNITIES FOUND IN ONE DAY

DAVID W. GARRISON

█ RUNNIN' WITH THE DEVIL

Just imagine, you're running a business, division, department, or team, and things aren't going so well. The people in charge want to know what you're going to do about it and fast. Fast as in the next 30 days! What do you do? How do you come up with improvement ideas? Where do you get the information on what to improve? What is working and what isn't? Is it a financial problem? Customer Service? Quality? Or perhaps accidents or injuries are starting to mount? What would you do and where would you turn?

All of these are legitimate and important questions to answer, but how and in such a short time frame? Plus, you'll need enough data to support your analysis, after all the devil's in the details! This is where a proven assessment tool comes into play. By following the guidelines I'll show you here, you'll be able to understand what is working and what is not, and how it's impacting your business. As I say, "I can tell you what the workplace looks like by understanding your books, and can tell you what your books look like by understanding the workplace."

WHO'S ON FIRST?

When first assessing a business, whether transactional, such as insurance or financial companies, healthcare, or manufacturing, you need to have a feel for what you'll see and how it will impact future activities. There are many things to look for and questions that can be asked. By focusing on operational metrics, one can understand how the business is being run and if it is running well. In addition to operational metrics, understanding cultural aspects can tell a lot about whether the associates are engaged in helping the company succeed, how leadership manages their associates, and if problem solving is a strategic advantage used to improve the business's processes.

Assessing this and combining both financial clues as well as operational clues allows you to make a much more thorough review of the business and determine where the opportunities lie. Whether you are looking to benchmark the business, do business with them, or even purchase them outright, this assessment will show you what to focus on first.

THROUGH THE LOOKING GLASS

First let's look at the windows into the processes for all companies who have embarked on a lean improvement process or have done the necessary self-reflection to have set up a few key metrics by which they can tell the health of the process and the business. (Note, if they have not done this then that will be one of the first areas to look to improve upon). The classic metric categories you will see in most companies revolve, to some degree, around: Safety, Quality, Delivery, Continuous Improvement and Productivity, both Costs and Inventory. These are listed in the order of importance based on my experience and being able to study some of the greatest companies in the world. Typically, you should see metrics prominently displayed throughout the organization you are assessing, and not hidden away where only the senior managers can use them as methods to shame people into improvements...or even "beat" them into submission as I've also seen. The end goal is to make sure everyone is on the same page no matter what level of the company they are at. This means we should have these metrics at all levels such as: Corporate, Division, Plant or Office, Line or Group and even at the smallest working team level.

By having these metrics for all to see it is akin to being at a football game where the scoreboard puts everyone on the same page simply with a quick look. You can tell who is winning, the time left in the game, who has the ball, where the ball is and how many timeouts each team has. You can also look at the field and see the "standard work" everyone is using to play the game...what is inbounds and out, where the first down marker is, what down it is, and where the goal line is to score points. All of that gleaned by simply looking at the field and the scoreboard. Imagine if you were touring a facility and everything was that easy to discover. In minutes you would know all you would need to and then could "dig" into more details than what your eyes can discover.

❚ TEN FINGERS & TEN TOES

All of the major metrics mentioned above have some key clues or details that can help lead you to learning how well run the company is and where the opportunities for improvement are. For example, SAFETY, the most important metric any company has whether manufacturing or otherwise, can be assessed by looking at or asking about the number of lost time accidents in a period often called recordables.

Recordables are the most severe injuries that take place; companies must report these to the government. If a company has a high number of recordables, or an increasing trend, then a flag needs to go up as to what could be causing this and further how much it is costing the company. It is also a clue as to possible discipline issues which may show up in other areas within the company. (Discipline is meant here as the ability to consistently perform a task or think at a high level based on training, not the punishment for having an issue or problem.) If the company cannot keep its workers safe or thinking about safety all the time, there is a definite question as to what is going on. In the financials, you would see this in a higher than normal cost of Workers Compensation, or an increasing trend in that cost area.

As an illustration of the importance leaders should put on SAFETY, as VP of Operations, I would always end our daily meeting with my associates by saying, "Make sure you come in and leave with ten fingers and ten toes. I don't want anyone doing anything that jeopardizes your safety. It's more important to hit our safety goals than our productivity goals. So keep it safe and steady today." I would sacrifice any number to make sure I had a safe environment and everyone worked in a safe manner. However I rarely had to sacrifice anything as every associate practiced safety in everything they did every day, because they bought into my vision of "everything starts and ends with safety".

"THE PURSUIT OF PERFECTION"

The second most important metric to look at while reviewing a business is QUALITY. It is defined as the measurement of how well your processes do at producing a 100% perfect part, outcome, letter, surgery, or whatever your "product" is every single time. This can be measured both internally as the "product" is produced and externally based on customer returns or complaints. Commonly these are measured in parts per million (ppm) or as a percent. For example, if your "product" was to produce 100% accurate medical bills for every patient billing opportunity, and your process is measured externally by customer complaints or call backs where they have financial issues, 15%, may sound pretty good. However, if you are the customer and you get one of the fifteen out of every hundred that are incorrect, you would not be impressed. Even more to the point, think of the administration cost that would be needed to keep up with all those phone calls, questions, rebilling, and worst case scenario refunds in addition to all the negative feelings customers would have about using your service. Negative quality can quickly become a demotivator for a consumer of a good or service. From this we will get world class processes run by world class associates and leadership who deliver exceptional results for our customers, shareholders and stakeholders.

From the internal perspective of the business, good quality can keep a business from having to perform rework to fix something that was done incorrectly or to scrap out something if it cannot be salvaged. Again, this applies to any type of business, you just have to figure out how it manifests itself within the given business. In a transactional world, you will not have a pile of parts waiting to be run through a repair process nor will you see the multiple times someone has to send a letter regarding the same topic because they were not given correct or complete information the first time. In this case, you would need to look into the computers and especially the email queues to see the "piles" of work that are a result of poor quality.

Once again, I must emphasize this does not mean the person doing the job cannot do it well but, as studies have shown, 95% of the time a problem caused in a process is due to a bad process and not a "bad" associate. (E. Deming, 1992) It is our job as managers to make sure we help create perfect processes and well trained people who know how to run these processes in order to take care of our customers or clients.

▌ "WHEN IT ABSOLUTELY, POSITIVELY HAS TO GET THERE"

DELIVERY, the third key metric, is again a customer facing metric. It is the measurement of how well we deliver our "product" on time to the request of the consumer, customer, or client. As you are assessing a facility or company, delivery metrics should be posted in each department, line, unit, or at a minimum the last place the company "touches" the product before it goes to the customer.

Delivery metrics can take multiple forms: 1. On Time Delivery to Request Date (the purest delivery metric based on the date the customer wants the good or service) 2. On Time Delivery to Promise Date (the date the company promises to deliver, not necessarily when the customer wants it), and 3. a Level Loading chart which shows the imbalance in a process depending on how much variation there is in the scheduling of the delivery of goods or services. The costs of poor delivery can be seen in expedited freight costs to ship something out over a premium route or method vs. standard ground and paid for by the company to try to make up for a late process or issues that have caused delay in the delivery of the good or service.

Another question to ask in the delivery area is, "What is the lead time?". Lead time is the elapsed time from order to delivery. If the lead time is within reason, and competitors in your industry are similar, then a customer will not see "average" as a positive or a negative. However, if the company you are analyzing or a competitor can figure out how to make a shorter lead time feasible and cost efficient then it could be a huge differentiator for the market. You would see this show as a spike in sales when the new campaign or promotion is launched.

Probably one of the best examples of this lead time concept is Domino's Pizza. Back in the 1980's, Domino's was a pizza start up that actually filled its pizza orders out of a mechanic's garage. However, their typical delivery process was improved upon when they guaranteed "hot, fresh pizza in thirty minutes or it's free". This new campaign promise caught on with the college campus near where they started their first store and the rest is history. They had found a way to beat the competition without incurring a significant cost, and lived up to that promise of a 30-minute delivery or its free. If they had not been able to stand behind the promise, the financials would have backed up the problem in showing inflated employee costs for driving or making the pizzas, or in refunds given due to greater than thirty minute deliveries. Either way the success or failure of the idea would be evident on an operational or financial evaluation with a pretty quick look.

THE SECRET SAUCE

The rate at which a company can take ideas from their associates and turn them into operating improvements is a huge factor in a lean assessment. Associates who are empowered to not only come up with suggestions, but also the method of implementation for solving a problem are truly the improvement engine of the company. CONTINUOUS IMPROVEMENT can be measured in Ideas Implemented per Associate, on an average basis, not literally how many each person turns in and are accepted, and how much the total savings are on an annual basis from all the ideas that are accepted. Many companies who have figured this out will brag about their process and associates during a tour of the facilities. Many in fact will have the associates lead this portion of the tour or discussion, as it again shows the engagement and buy in. If you do not see or hear about continuous improvement, a red flag or warning, should go up as this would be a huge opportunity for savings, or improvements in many areas of a business. There is nothing like harnessing the power of tens, hundreds, or even thousands of great people to help improve the company versus having only a select few managers do it from their offices or conference rooms.

"I WANT IT ALL AND I WANT IT NOW"

Last but definitely not least is PRODUCTIVITY. Productivity is the measurement of improvement of a process or function from one year to the next. It is therefore highly tied to the costs of a company and can be most often viewed in the material or labor content of a product or service. Year over year, when a company can make improvements to become cheaper, faster, or better than their competitors without sacrificing SAFETY or QUALITY, they will be able to see their margins expand and thus make more profit out of each dollar of sales. Frequently, companies will have a chart that shows sales increasing while headcount stays constant. This is a great indicator of productivity being driven in the workplace. As a mentor of mine once told me, "Productivity is all about doing more with the same or doing the same with less."

A quick tip as to how to evaluate how much labor is going into producing the product or service being delivered is to do a blink test. For a blink test, simply close your eyes, when you open them count how many people are actually touching or adding value to the product. Also count how many are standing around or not doing anything that adds value to what the customer is purchasing. This percentage of value added, those working on the product vs. those who are not, is typically around 50% or lower. If a company can pass the blink test at around 80% that is outstanding and it implies that most of the people at any given time are working on something the customer is willing to pay for.

Obviously this is only a snapshot and rough evaluation, but that is all you get as you are walking around and doing a quick assessment. As with CONTINUOUS IMPROVEMENT, PRODUCTIVITY is not a metric you will have to look hard for as most companies brag about it. As stated above, if you don't hear or see anything regarding PRODUCTIVITY, or you see many associates standing around and not adding value, you should note this as a huge area for improvement and opportunity to add profits to the bottom line of the business' financials.

HOW MUCH IS TOO MUCH?

Another area of PRODUCTIVITY that many do not consider is INVENOTRY. INVENTORY is the material on hand to make a product, or finished product stored on the shelves in case of significant variation in the customer order rate. Often it is stored in a warehouse and also by where the processes are being performed. I have seen companies with so much inventory it literally goes from floor to ceiling and they will brag that they rarely run out of parts. Now that sounds like a great thing, but when you consider the cost of that entire inventory just sitting there waiting to be put into use, you get the idea of the millions of dollars most companies have "sleeping" or dormant on their shelves.

If you were to reduce a million-dollar inventory to $500,000, then you would be able to take that working capital and use it for something else, say an investment that yields a higher return than 0% which is what the inventory yields. Or you may be able to use the freed up cash for needed purchases. In either case, reducing inventory without impacting service or delivery is very possible, and an area of your assessment to take great care in looking for the clues, as they will very often lead to 50-75% reductions that then become cash available to invest in other areas.

Determining how much INVENTORY is too much is a learned art when doing a quick assessment.   You will gradually get a feel for it. When you're first starting out you will want to evaluate and determine how many people are touching the inventory. In other words, how much labor is required to move parts from one area to another? How many forklifts are needed in a manufacturing or fulfillment environment? How many patients are there in the waiting room or diagnostic offices, or diners waiting to be seated at a table or how many are seated and eating?

Just as manufacturing firms have inventory, other types of businesses do too. You just have to look harder to see what it may be and figure out what they are "producing".   In healthcare, they are producing healthy, happy, pain-free patients, thus the raw material inventory are the patients waiting to be seen and the work-in-process inventory are those who have been taken into a room but not yet been discharged. At a restaurant, the raw material are the diners waiting to be seated, and the work-in-process are those who are eating but have not finished and paid the check. Restaurants also have physical inventory such as the raw materials needed to make the food. They also have finished goods consisting of whatever was made but not sold.

No matter what the business type, inventory exists and in most all cases needs to be lowered as the velocity of product through the business is increased via continuous improvement. If inventory builds, a drain on the financials will occur either through higher working capital with no return or lower revenue from people waiting for an appointment or reservation and not eating or using the services.

▍A CULTURAL REVOLUTION

Metrics can't tell you the whole story, but they get you a good way there. They also help considerably in being able to validate what is happening and how it is helping or hurting the operation income. Another very important aspect of analyzing operations and financials is to ask some questions in key cultural areas to see what answers you get. Now we're not talking about anything proprietary or top secret, but things companies can tell you without much trouble, but which mean an awful lot. For example, I mentioned employee engagement in the CONTINUOUS IMPROVEMENT section, and how the more engaged associates there are the more problem solvers a company will have. This should also turn into less firefighting. By having many people all trying to solve small day-to-day problems, they hopefully will not turn into larger ones that keep repeating. Simply ask any front line supervisor or manager if they would characterize their day as value added, trying to think of how to improve the product and processes, of the company, or firefighting? Most of the time these days everyone is stretched so thin that they do nothing but firefight. They just do not have, nor make, the time to improve the operation or business.

▌ THAT'S GENIUS!

A great lean company knows how to turn having problems from a bad thing to a good one. They are able to teach everyone simple problem-solving techniques for issues they encounter during their workday, and then build a culture to support CONTINUOUS IMPROVEMENT around it. The key is to allow time for people to solve problems even if it means stopping work to do it. I have seen multiple companies, large and small, stop their normal operations and let every associate work on a countermeasure to a problem they or their team is trying to solve for the betterment of the company. This might not be hours on end, but just imagine if your company allowed even 10 minutes once per week for every associate to improve what they do with the help of their supervisors and managers acting as problem-solving coaches. How much could be accomplished, and how much firefighting could be stopped because the problems will no longer exist?

The culture that surrounds a successful problem-solving system, is comprised of supervisors and managers who have changed or evolved from what they used to do or what leadership has typically done in the past. When you look around do you see associates being told what to do for everyday tasks, or are they being coached and mentored so they know what to do when a problem arises? While you are on your tour make sure to notice this, because at first you may not see it or believe it.

Just how lean a company is can, and usually does, depend on how engaged the associates are and how hands off they are managed. This is not to say they are just left managing themselves if they have a problem, but are coached on how to quickly handle those problems when they arise. Simply put, the best companies are the ones who know how to quickly deal with adversity and get back to "standard work" thus minimizing the disruptive impact.

▌SUSTAINING WHAT YOU'VE IMPROVED

While viewing the operations of a company, ask about meetings and walks that occur on a frequent, repetitive basis. Companies who are building the lean culture should hold stand up or reflection meetings to understand where the problems are they've encountered recently and what can be done to eliminate them from happening again, especially if they have an impact on the final customer. Reflection Meetings along with Operation Walks (sometimes called Gemba Walks after the Japanese term Gemba meaning where the work is done and where the truth lies) where leaders tour their own facility or office to review any chart, graph, or visual designed to help see normal vs. abnormal, are important parts of what the leaders must do for the lean culture to prosper. Operational Walks focus on:

Do we have standard work?

Is it visible?

Are we following it?

Is it sufficient to yield a perfect "product"?

Reflection Meetings and Operational Walks are the cultural enablers known as LEADER STANDARD WORK that allows improvements to be sustainable. Sustainability of improvements is what every company who has gone through, or is contemplating going through, a process transformation is looking for. Companies will be able to show you these visuals and describe how teaching is done from management level to management level. This ensures everyone understands what is important to the leadership, and how everyone acts quickly when there is an abnormality to solve it and put it to bed forever, ensuring very little firefighting has to occur now or in the future.

▌THE GUIDING LIGHT

The next key to look for when assessing a company is its Vision, Mission, and Values. Now I don't mean the signs in the lobby or cafeteria that people hear about once a year if they are lucky, but the actual tenet or foundational beliefs that turn into action on a daily basis. In lean this is called TRUE NORTH, and are the guiding principles of what a company strives to be. You will not be able to read or see to understand this, but must ask questions. Everyone at every level should know and be able to say what the TRUE NORTH is, what it means to them, and how it impacts their actions on a daily basis.

For example, at Toyota the True North is, "To contribute to society, by building the highest quality vehicles, at the lowest possible cost, in the shortest amount of lead time; while respecting the humanity of those who do the work" (K. Hanley, 2016). If you were to ask a Toyota associate about how this impacts their work, they would say that no matter what even the smallest issue such as a screw going in crooked needs to be elevated and the problem solved due to the tenet of "making the highest quality vehicles". There does not need to be a supervisor or manager around to help the associate with this thought of stopping the line to find out why the screw stripped, as a matter of fact they are empowered and expected to stop it. Without such beliefs issues would not get elevated, quality would suffer, and the "delivery of the highest quality vehicles" would be in jeopardy.

▌ A REVOLVING DOOR OF DOLLARS

Finally, one last figure to look for and again something you won't see but will have to ask for, is TURNOVER. Why is this important and how can it help when assessing a company? TURNOVER is a very important financial key. It is a tremendous cost driver that if managed properly can save the company significant sums of money, or cost them even more. Companies who have learned to create a win-win value proposition with their associates are able to offer good paying, stable jobs with growth opportunities and a commitment to value their input. This in turn gets the company committed associates who come to work every day, follow their standard work, and look to improve their jobs to make things more efficient.

Job improvement gets back to the CONTINUOUS IMPROVEMENT and problem-solving mentioned earlier, and is the company's competitive edge for keeping them ahead of the competition. If a company has high TURNOVER, they will always be in a training mode and have many people who cannot perform all the tasks needed. Even when someone who is intelligent and very skilled comes on board they must still be trained in the company specific knowledge and behaviors. This training can last weeks, months or even years depending on what level of position we are talking about and the complexity of the product, service, or business.

▌ MINING FOR ASSESSMENT GOLD

While on the assessment you might be inclined to take pages of notes and try to catch everything you see and hear and get it down on paper. If you do this, you will likely miss some of the observations you need to make your quick assessment. Remember this is all done on the fly. To help with this, I have developed a simple tool to quickly aid your assessment and is available for free on my website at www.GarrisonProductivity. com. Simply click the link for the GPS Quick Assessment Tool.

The quick assessment tool that you can download enables you to pay attention during the assessment while allowing you to score key categories of findings on a 1-5 scale: from Must Improve at a 1 to World Class at a 5. The categories to score are:

» People: Employee Engagement & Turnover

» Operations: Safety, Quality, Delivery, Continuous Improvement, Productivity, & Inventory

» Culture: Problem Solving vs. Fire-Fighting, Leadership, & Visual Management

More importantly, the GPS Quick Assessment Tool gives you a guide for your reflection and discussion when the assessment is complete. I always encourage immediate discussion amongst the group taking the tour to review all that each person has seen, heard, and experienced. In this way, little will be forgotten and a great deal of knowledge can be coalesced into one cohesive business and financial overview. Mind you this is not the full assessment tool, but a quick representation of the business to help with the initial assessment. Also the more you work with it and understand it, the faster your ratings will be determined, and you'll be able to get back to observations and questions more quickly.

To show how the tool would work, imagine you are doing an assessment of a luxury resort, including the hotel, restaurant, bars and spa. (This would be about as far from a manufacturing example as you can get.) While you are there, you want to make sure to enjoy yourself and get the full experience. This also allows you to see how they run all sides of the business and fulfill the main objective of satisfying customers.

When preparing for the tour, have a few questions ready to dive into the areas or details you don't see. With all the information that is available online, preparation has become much easier. You can get reviews from customers, a look into the resort including amenities, the company culture and pricing from their website, a review of the financials by reading their latest financials or Security and Exchange Commission filings if it's a publicly traded company, and any current or past articles on the resort from various rating and news agencies. All of this helps you zero in on areas of concern you either want to dig deeper on or look into for verification.

As you're walking around on the assessment, first continuously look for Safety hazards. Typically, this is meant in terms of associates, but in this example it also pertains to the guests. Is everyone following the safety guidelines? Does the staff ensure people have a good time while being safe? Are there signs and placards posted to let everyone know the safety rules? Are the lifeguards on duty at the pool or on the beach as scheduled? If so, use the check-sheet and quickly give them the rating you think describes their Safety practices and Visual Management. Five would be world class and if you can see that safety is a priority in all they do, then rate them accordingly. In a resort you would assume that is always the case, but the closer you look you may find some issues.

Next, as you are touring around and you pass the tiki bar or restaurant, take a look at how efficient the bartenders and servers are at getting drinks or food out quickly. Is there a long line? Is the inventory of unfulfilled orders piling up? The quicker the orders are taken and filled the more guests are served, profit earned, and customers satisfied.

If you do not see short waits, quick service, and lots of happy customers, then you would want to check off a lower rating of 1 or 2 noting that they need to improve Delivery, Productivity, and potentially Employee Engagement. This last criteria, Employee Engagement, is important as it will be the reason someone goes above and beyond for the customer. If they truly believe the True North of the company and can relate it to you as you ask them some questions, then you will find an associate who loves to make people happy and understands that's the most important aspect of their job.

While at the bar, in addition to the inventory of drink orders, take a look at how the bar is set up. Is there a flow to the process? Do bartenders run into each other trying to get something that is only on one side of the bar? Is the setup of the wells identical so that anything can be made at any location? Are there enough bartenders for the crowd size and are they able to move quickly through the orders knowing how all drinks are made?

All of this can be viewed quickly and checked off on the form under Inventory, Productivity, and Delivery. You can even review quality without having a drink or meal yourself, by listening to the guests and what they are saying about the Service and Quality of the food or drinks. No one is ever shy about telling a bad experience or story. If you don't hear anything just look for someone who was just served and ask. Then you'll be able to rate a few more categories.

Along with the quality of the food and drinks, you'll be able to see or ask questions about other areas that pertain to quality. Are the grounds meticulously kept? Are all the facilities advertised available to the guests? There is nothing worse than enticing the guests with a fancy pool, spa, or special type of massage and then not being able to deliver on that commitment. If something is offered and not available, that would signal you to ask some questions as to the reasons and also give them a lower rating on the assessment sheet, maybe a 2 or 3 in Delivery depending on how everything else is going. This will at least give you a point to review when you are going over your findings and their responses to your questions.

The final areas we haven't touched on in the tool are: Turnover, Continuous Improvement, Problem Solving, and Leadership. All of these are more question based than observations. However, if your tour gets you behind the scenes you may see office areas where metrics are posted, the True North is visible, Associate Ideas are being worked on and Leadership is either dictating to or coaching their associates.

If not visible, do not hesitate to ask people in various areas you are touring through. Again, people, even associates, are not shy about telling you what they think if it's an open and honest environment where they look for problems as a way to continually improve. Then fill out the form rating accordingly for what you have seen or the information you have gained from the interviews.

One caveat to always remember, is that no matter what you are told or see on charts, nothing beats what you see with your own eyes. One time on a plant tour, I was shown outstanding safety metrics and chart that showed no accidents over multiple years. This was outstanding, given the very manual labor and heavy nature of the product.

However, when I went out onto the production floor, a very different scenario could be seen. Actually it could not be seen, because of how much dust was in the air. You could not see clearly 100' in front of you.

Not only that but forklifts were running at high speed right through where all the people worked. At one point 8 forklifts all headed into the same intersection from multiple directions and came to a screeching halt just before a spectacular crash. They actually sat there trying to figure out what to do long enough for me to take a picture. There was no way I was rating this site a 5 as the metrics lead me to believe, and as a matter of fact without the company insisting they would improve the safety and air quality we wouldn't have done business with them.

▌ "YOU CAN'T ALWAYS GET WHAT YOU WANT"

Once the tour and questions are complete, you and/or your team must review the findings as quickly as possible so that nothing that has been seen or heard is forgotten. Discuss everything no matter how small it may seem. Not everyone will have picked up on the same things and all the findings are important. Jot down notes quickly and then come back to fill in more details after the discussions have begun.

Use your GPS Quick Assessment Tool to help aid the discussion and point out where there were:

1. Great processes that delivered world class results with excellent people,

2. Average processes that delivered good results as a result of the excellent people working there,

3. Poor processes that delivered fair results with associates trying really hard but not delivering great results, or finally,

4. Poor processes run by people unable to deliver results and not really trying to change or improve.

Note the checkmarks you made on the tool every time you saw an example of that attribute being performed or modeled and the ratings you gave the business. Sum up all the columns and get a total for the assessment. A minimum score would be an 11 if everything you saw and heard was in the Must Improve category. This would be a business that has tremendous opportunities to improve from a metric point of view, but may not have the cultural capability without considerable time and effort, let alone existing capability of personnel at all levels.

A median score of 33 would indicate a business that has hit an Intermediate level of operational excellence. Not all categories may be a 3, some may be higher or lower, but on average they total around the 33 score. This would indicate a business that has processes and personnel that are capable, but that need and for the most part, are looking for improvement.

Finally, a score above 45 or higher would indicate a world class operation operated by highly functioning associates and led by a team of coaches and mentors teaching everyday how to get better. Their processes would yield excellent results and no one would be satisfied no matter how good the metrics look. They would believe there is always room for improvement.

"START ME UP"

Whenever you have the opportunity to run an assessment of a company, whether it is a business you are responsible for, one you are benchmarking, one you are looking to do business with, or maybe even purchase, there are key operational and financial clues that can help make a surprisingly well educated conclusion at the end of a quick tour. Remember to always keep in mind that seeing or finding problems is a good thing. These are opportunities for improvement, and all businesses have them. Some may be better at making them visible so they can address the issues which leads to greater improvements and a competitive advantage, while others prefer to hide them or not expose them as it will cause issues they have to deal with, embarrassment, or even an opportunity for some unwanted "coaching" from above.

Utilizing the ideas I've laid out here can help you understand how the operational aspects of a business can lead to the financial results. These financial results can then give you a window into what the workplace may look like. Understanding what you're seeing and what it means in terms of dollars of opportunity are keys to improving any business. Without seeing both sides of the system, you can lead yourself down the wrong path and cost you or your company vast amounts of wasted time and money.

Good luck with your journey, no matter what phase you are currently in, and if you have any questions on assessing any type of business, please let me know.

David W. Garrison

860.218.5238

Dave@GarrisonProductivity.com

http://www.GarrisonProductivity.com

At Garrison Productivity Solutions (GPS), Dave Garrison has a history of going above and beyond for his clients. From a 25+ year career of increasing responsibility and success, in addition to some of the best lean training from around the world, he has been able to create a truly value-adding business for his clients. Dave leads his company as he teaches, by delighting the customer in everything they do and creating sustainable improvements not only in process but in company culture.

Prior to his current role as President of Garrison Productivity Solutions (GPS), Dave had a long career of holding management positions in a wide variety of industries including paper/chemical production, aerospace bearings and rolling elements, electrical protection and distribution, security devices and sensors, and engine retarding systems. Positions included: VP of Operations, Danaher – Jacobs Vehicle Systems; GM Global Lean Six Sigma, GE Industrial & Lighting ; VP of Manufacturing, GE Zenith

Controls; Master Black Belt – Global MFG & Quality, GE Industrial Systems; Manufacturing Black Belt for 4 GE Industrial Systems' plants in CT, ME, MN and Mexico; Operations Manager, SKF/MRC Aerospace Bearings; Controller, SKF/MRC Aerospace Bearings.

Dave holds a BS in Accounting from Bentley University and an MBA with dual concentrations in Operations and Corporate Finance, from the University of Hartford.

BE THE SOLUTION: EMPOWERING EMPLOYEES, TRANSFORMING ORGANIZATIONS

TERESA D. HUGGINS

Big Vision, Company Goals, and Focused Outcomes: Many employees don't see what the leadership team envisions, nor are they automatically on board with new ideas. Many times this lack of employee enthusiasm and alignment confuses leadership, particularly when despite a tradition of providing quality service, customer-focused solutions, and a commitment to excellence, team members don't seem aligned with the mission or are even happy at times. Additionally, more time is spent analyzing reports while the company culture isn't flourishing. If this sounds familiar, consider looking at the situation from a new perspective of employee engagement and solution-focused conversations resulting in a thriving company culture.

As a consultant for companies, non-profits, and educational institutions, I began to see patterns with how people think, interact, and operate as a unit. I realized that the flaw wasn't in the systems designed for the best outcomes, rather it was about how people were valued and whether or not they felt included in the process. Employees want their ideas to be heard and respected. They want to be appreciated. They want to be recognized from their direct vantage point. They might have a solution that others haven't considered instead of being told "this is how it will be." By creating opportunities for individuals to contribute to the unification of an organization, productivity increases as employees are then vested member of the organization. It no longer is a job to go to for eight hours each day; rather, there is an aspiration to be an engaged contributor to the desired outcomes. Through interactive trainings, group facilitated discussions, and a sense of renewed value, people can connect to one another and begin to see perspectives of different departments, resulting in a common purpose and vision.

One activity at a training yielded a shift in awareness, an expansion in an idea, a release of the limiting beliefs that prevented the company from achieving their desired outcomes, and authentic conversations resulting in an additional contract for this small business worth $42 million dollars! The employees put their doubts—"it won't work" attitudes and frustrations—into open conversation and with guided discussions and activities, they were able to see with a clearer vision by focusing on what can be instead of what was happening.

When we consider looking at the future with innovative ways of expanding our influence, strengthening our interactions, and embracing the opportunities that are yet created, we open to new possibilities and solutions that were once unseen. Others may speak of the uncertainty in the future; however our organizations will be combining intellectual strength, creative solution-based focus, and a unified commitment to create a foundation that will insure the growth of all. Companies that hold a proactive vision, empower its employees to share their ideas, and recognize individual talents will thrive in the future. Creating an organization with strong systems, genuine interactions, and solution-focused communication strategies that strengthen each another will result in your desired outcomes.

So how is this accomplished?

Leadership needs to take time each day to celebrate what is achieved, to recognize the solutions that are generated, and if something doesn't go as planned, make the course correction that is necessary to *begin again* the next day. As you strive for excellence, pause, notice, and stay true to your authenticity.

This chapter offers ideas to consider and language to use that increases success and strategies that can be integrated into your current culture. You may want to consider one idea a day and bring it into your awareness as you work. Review the ideas periodically or meet as a group and consider which ones you may want to adopt as a company focus. Possibly, consider a monthly theme to focus on or design a leadership training program to strengthen the skills of individuals and departments. When the strategies become part of a daily practice, individual strength becomes the strength of the organization.

▌ THE ESSENCE OF A SOLUTION-FOCUSED COMPANY

Interactions with employees is key to a flow that results in efficient contributions. When individual values are aligned with company values and are discussed, trust is developed and potential business increases. Beyond the "on time and under budget" scenario that many clients seek, clients or customers are also looking for dependable, trustworthy people to work with. They seek individuals who are able to understand their perspective, readily listen to their concerns, and are interested in collaborative decision making.

It's management's responsibility to establish the environment that makes this possible. Leaders create sincere commitment to the goals of the company by encouraging camaraderie among employees, a desire to succeed, and a willingness to go beyond an expectation to create a result that is exceptional. As we live from the foundation of the values that make us unique, goals can be reached more effortlessly. We are able to know if it is a "yes" or a "no" to become involved in conversations, decisions, or a project because it is based on values important to individuals and the organization. What are the values of your company? How can you measure them?

The successful qualities that create an engaged employee culture include: trustworthy relationships, individual commitment to excellence, a concern for all involved with a sense of community/family within the organization, a desire to learn more and a willingness to grow as individuals and as departments or teams. Intelligence and creativity are valued, along with excellence in products and services. There is a personal responsibility for outcomes and people see the *big* picture and plan ahead accordingly. Respect for one another's ideas is important to create a culture of unity. People are willing to consider the greater good when resolving challenges and engaging one another in solution-focused conversations, and it's helpful to allow a sense of humor into our conversations. Focused commitment with a sense of integrity for doing what is right when no one is looking yields greater success for all involved.

The concerns of customers and clients must also be taken into consideration. Speak a language they can identify with. For example, if they are in the medical field, patient care and health regulations are important to the decisions they make. If the job is funded through donations, they want to make sure the donors are pleased to encourage future donations. If the contact person is new to the company, they must insure the job is done correctly to insure *their* position is secure. As you help them, you help your own company.

Consider the person you are meeting with as you plan a meeting or a phone call. What are potential questions that may be asked? Prepare some answers in your mind or even write them down. If you receive a question you aren't ready for, be honest and tell them you will get back to them. You might respond like this: "That is a great question and I appreciate you asking me. It is my desire to have a relationship built on trust, so I am going to research that and share an answer with you that will meet your needs." Individuals may not fully understand your perspective if they are not in your field of work, so phrase requests or explanations in the context of *their* work. *The more you can bridge to "what they already know," the greater they will understand what you are saying.*

No one likes to appear ignorant or uncertain, so the more you can speak in a way they can understand, the greater the chance they will want to work with you. Before meeting with a new client, examine their website to see what is important to them, ask someone who knows them what matters to them, and weave it into the conversation naturally. Increase trust by being prepared, flexible, and honest. Hold the outcome you desire in your mind while allowing your heart to feel their concerns so you can be the one that generates solutions for them. Be fully present for others. When you are with someone, be intentional with your focus and desire to be of service to them. Be in the moment, not thinking ahead of your next task or meeting. People will feel the difference in your energy. Simple gestures matter! People want to work with others who genuinely care about their situation.

Responsibility is one's ability to respond. People are going to make mistakes and choices that may be frustrating. The way you respond reflects the essence of the company. Keep focused on what you want to create and more solutions will come forth. Repeat business saves time and money. By establishing relationships, you have a foundation created that you can build upon.

▌ COMMUNICATING FOR A YES!

When presenting to a group of people, find out what their interests are and speak to their interests/needs. The way they hear you is enhanced if they feel you are connected to their mission. Before a meeting, take time to gain clarity on the outcome that you want to create. The greater clarity you have in your mind, the more likely you will be able to answer the questions others pose. Think about possible challenges, obstructions, and frustrations that the client may present and think through possible solutions. Consider the perspective of the listener. How will they hear you? What filters do they use to experience the world? For instance, if the person sees the "gloom" of a situation, then *you* are the one to bring them security and resolution. How you speak to a CEO may vary compared to someone else in an organization, yet treating everyone with respect is vital to employee engagement!

People draw conclusions about a company based on the way we communicate, the words we use, and the way we present ourselves in a professional setting, especially when there is a challenge. If a question comes up that is unexpected, *pause*, know that you have the answer and respond, *or* be honest and let them know you will get back to them and when. Whatever you commit to,be sure to follow through with your commitment. Sometimes we want to respond quickly and may over commit, so know that it is fine to let others know you will follow up with them in a timely manner. Write down this commitment in front of the individual and group. When you get back to the office, take action, even if it is a small step. Ask for help when needed.

One technique I teach is the "Sandwich Approach." When approaching a challenge or a conversation that needs resolution, I follow the following formula: First statement is something positive or affirming, the filling is the area for change, and the last statement is ends with a future expectation. Here is a sample "sandwich": When we were at the meeting, I appreciated hearing that we would receive the materials by _____ date. It is now four days later and the promise isn't fulfilled. This is delaying the completion of the project. What will it take to get the materials here by tomorrow? (They answer). I appreciate your willingness to create a resolution. I am sure we can work through this. Contrast this with: "You said it would be here and it isn't. It isn't working for us and it is very frustrating."

Individuals respond quicker when they feel they are valued and appreciated. It doesn't have to be fake; a genuine approach will create a longer standing relationship.

When you communicate with someone for potential business, create an "image" of the completed project. Connect to their heart by describing the project in a way that will help them reach a goal that is important to them. People will respond more favorably when they can *feel* the experience more than hear the experience. With descriptive words, you create a photo in their mind of the completed project and how it will be the solution to a challenge or something that brings them joy.

Personal internal messages influence our interactions ,and often we are unaware of the power they have in our conversations—and on the outcomes we desire. We think over 50,000 unconscious thoughts a day. Are you aware of the conversations in your head, the judgments that flow through your mind or the fear that enters as you build your dreams? Consider some affirmations that you can remind yourself of your greatness, especially during stressful moments. For instance, instead of feeling overwhelmed, you silently affirm "solutions come easily to me." Rather than feeling no one appreciates me, say, "I am making a significant difference today." It isn't about becoming boastful; it is fueling your brain to discover solutions easily. Your brain will follow the leadership of your thoughts, so be aware of what you are thinking silently and outwardly. It impacts your emotions and your interactions with others.

In situations where you are collaborating with others, be cognizant of conversation stoppers and starters. Are you all focused on the same outcome? Are you listening openly? Humor is great as long as it isn't used at the expense of another. If you are feeling someone isn't contributing to the project, a one-on-one conversation may be better than confronting someone in front of others at a meeting. It is important to create a comfort level with every conversation and build upon the trust that is created to start a conversation from the viewpoint of the client's needs. Listen and learn before selling something. What matters to our client or employee? What holds them back from reaching their goals? What constructs do they need to work within? And then share from that perspective of how you can be the solution to their challenges, their "pain".

Formulas for Success that I created to keep my focus on the desired outcomes are:

Preparation + Performance + Possibility = Productive Results

Intelligence + Imagination = Inspiration

Efficiency + Empathy = Excellent Relationships

SOLUTION-GENERATING CONVERSATIONS

While we often focus on the systems in an organization, success begins with the simple conversations that people have within the organization and with others outside the organization. Having an expanded vision without effective communication strategies diffuses the power of the vision and increases time to create the desired result. By applying solution-generating communication techniques, efficiency and productivity increases for all involved. Clarity in your message and your presence influence outcomes.

"I Statements" remove blame, shame, and judgment from our conversations. An example is: "When I heard we were going to have extra laborers on site to complete the job on time, I expected that would be done. When I see it isn't done, I become frustrated because of an unfulfilled request. What can we do with this situation?" This is a much more positive approach than: "You didn't get the guys on the site like you said and now we are behind."

WHICH STATEMENT WILL YIELD GREATER RESULTS?

Speak with an *anticipated outcome* and people will listen more to your request. For instance, "We expected the payment by _____ and by not having it, we are _____ (challenge). Instead of "you didn't send us your payment." "You" statements create defensiveness and the person shifts from wanting to resolve the situation to wanting to protect their self worth. Be non-judgmental with your conversations. Judgement separates individuals and blocks solutions. "Have you ever considered this?" is a way to shift a person into "solution." Think of the outcome you want and offer it as an idea, supporting a person who may not know what the best way is to resolve a situation. They may feel empowered to make the choice that you desire.

When conversations become confrontational, allow the emotions (energy in motion) to be expressed, yet remember to *detach* from the feeling of the frustration and anger and take deep breaths if you find your body tightening. If you are on the phone, move from the location where you received the challenging news, and disconnect from the frustration for a moment. Stand up, drink a glass of water, and take a moment to calm yourself. You will be able to generate more solutions quickly. And, if you lose your patience, apologize to the person during the conversation, later in the day, or next day. If it was a verbal conversation, resolve it verbally, not by email. Be honest and let the person know what the trigger was for you. This may require spending a few minutes by yourself for you to ponder what created that response.

Structural tension occurs when there is an expectation and it is not being met. When reality is not aligned with expectation, people become angry, frustrated, and confused. The greater the gap between expected outcome and reality, the greater space that is created for conflict and there is less efficiency in resolution of the challenge.

Perhaps the greatest challenge is expressing the appropriate emotions is Email. This mode of communication has become a common conversational instrument, yet we've received little instruction on how to efficiently interact with one another on this platform. I worked for a company once to facilitate one-on-one personal leadership meetings and a mediation. There was a challenge between two departments that impacted the company's ability to make production goals. After time spent with individuals, the realization was that two directors has mis-interpreted emails, felt judged by one another, and created a story line that lasted over a year. With mediation, the issues were resolved and new ways of doing business and relating to others were established and followed through to create efficient practices again.

When you have emails to resolve a conflict, write a response before sending an email. Speak it aloud so you can *hear the tone* that might be perceived by another. Emails become documentation in legal cases. Be cautious of how you respond. Refrain from threats or blaming another (even when another is "at fault"). Phrase the language in ways that reach resolution for both parties. When copying others in emails, be sure to assess how it is perceived and consider the protocol. Be consistent so it doesn't look like you are "reporting to a supervisor."

Emails can be shared with other companies and within an organi-zation. If you read an email, ask yourself, "Am I reading between the lines? Am I adding emotion when there are just words explaining a sit-uation? Am I making conclusions that might not be validated?" If there is something uncomfortable for you in an email, call the person and ask! So many people are avoiding direct contact and *interpreting* what they think is being shared in an email. Never respond to another's frustration in an email. Instead, read it, pay attention to what emotions are surfacing within you and walk away for a moment. Come back to it when you can respond in a neutral way. At times, written communication like emails may be misinterpreted because voice tone is removed. When sending emails, end your message with a phrase that lets the reader understand your intention, such as "in the spirit of open and clear communication, in the spirit of clarifying roles, or in the spirit of..."

Language that Empowers Others

Words have energy and the statements and questions you share will impact the results you desire. Statements that I have found helpful are:

» Have you considered this solution?

» Would you be open to this suggestion?

» Is it possible for us to consider a few options?

» I invite you to consider the idea (or ponder the possibility) _____ (state your idea).

» Let me know me how we can create a mutually agreed upon decision that works for both companies.

» Using proactive language yields positive results. Use:

» "Remember to…" as a replacement for "Don't forget to"

» "I choose to…" as a replacement for "I have to, I should do"

» "I create solutions for…" as a replacement for "Our problem is"

» "What works for me…" as a replacement for "I didn't like this"

» "Let us consider…" as a replacement for "We need to do this"

» "I invite you to…" as a replacement for "I need you to"

When checking for understanding of one's message, say "What I heard was…." and rephrase the other person's comments. That individual will let you know if it is accurate. By doing this, you are letting them know you are listening.

It is important to provide feedback in a way that increases participation. In giving feedback and in evaluating the success of a project, use the following phrases: "What worked for me was…." and "What would work for me better is…" This allows the listener to understand your perspective without feeling attacked or questioned.

When people are feeling uncertain, instead of having them share the "it won't work, it hasn't worked before, it can't be done," use the phrase "up until now" to help them see possibilities that lie ahead. For example, instead of: "We haven't been able to receive the materials on time," use "Up until now, we haven't found a resolution to this challenge. Let's begin thinking of other strategies that we haven't used."

Using non-judgmental language, even when there is a conflicting situation, is important. The more non-judgmental you can be, the greater the probability of resolving the difficult situation. By placing blame on someone or with an organization, you are breaking the trust that is established in a working relationship. By sharing the challenge with another person without judging them, your mind will activate solutions more freely. When we are angry, frustrated, tired, and disappointed, we are unable to see solutions as clearly as when we are in a positive working relationship. For example, "We have this situation here _____ (describe the challenge). We both want to see resolution to this as we have vested interest in the completion of this job. What can we consider as a solution that will work for both of us?" This example creates a partnership instead of an adversarial relationship.

Reformat the power of words. Be aware of how a word changes how you feel about someone or an event.

» Dis-Appointment = Expectation wasn't met and I am feeling something that isn't the way I want to feel.

» Mis-Take = Something happened that wasn't aligned with our goal and we are going to make a change now and look ahead.

» Re-Action = You have a choice what action you will take to a response of another.

» FEAR = Fantasized Experiencing Appearing Real. Ask yourself what is a "real fear" (ex. Safety) and what is something you are imagining that can have a resolution. Live with Trust. Use the same energy to imagine a solution.

» FAIL = Find Answers in Life. While you want to focus on 100% solutions, if there is a failure, what it the relationship with the outcome? How can you use what happened to strengthen your organization?

When you aren't clear what someone is saying or is needing, say, *"Help me understand what you meant by* _____?*"* This will help them know you value them and are listening openly to their comments. If someone is frustrated, let them vent. Do *not* take it personally and ask, *"How can we support you?"* Sometimes individuals just need to share their feelings with someone and may not be asking for anything, yet knowing you heard them is very important. After someone has expressed a concern, you can say, *"We will look into your concern and find a solution that meets both needs."* When you want a solution that the other person may not support you with, use a statement that triggers a solution focus from them, such as: *"What would it take to.... (The outcome you desire)?"* This puts the other person in a solution mode. Instead of thinking of reasons they aren't going to agree, the mind shifts into a different mindset.

I Hear What You Are Not Saying: Research says 80% of communication is non-verbal. Our actions relay how we are feeling without ever sharing words with another. Consider how you sit in a meeting: What you are doing with your hands and your body? Are you focused on the speaker? Does your face share what you are thinking? While there are many different interpretations for body language, often people draw conclusions based on how you present yourself. For example, Are you sitting behind your desk or next to the person in a meeting? Are you facing the person or is your shoulder turned away? Are you looking at your phone while the meeting is going on? If you are with a client or a prospective client (or even a colleague) and you check email or send a text during a meeting, you are saying to the person, your value isn't as great as what is on my phone. If there is an emergency and you need to be notified, ask the person if it is okay to leave your phone on in case you receive a call. They will understand that request usually.

When the best planned conversations turn to conflict, it is important to diffuse anger. When we have an expectation that isn't met and we care, sometimes we become angry at a person. Find a strategy that you can quickly use to release the anger so you can shift in the present moment. If you are in a conflict, use an "I message" that lets the person know what is triggered in you. Take a quick walk, do some stretches in your office, move your body in some way to release the inner tension so it isn't carried throughout the day. When you experience resistance to an idea, when we feel one way and someone is sharing a contrast with us, we will often negate the advice or feedback. Be aware when you feel yourself wanting to "defend your position" and imagine yourself looking through the other person's eyes. Pause and consider how they might be viewing the situation and allow that perspective to be pondered. You don't have to agree; yet, you can let go of the resistance you may be feeling. Holding onto resentment about something that happened that felt "wrong" by an action or inaction by another hurts you more than the other person. When you can talk about it with that individual, stay in the present moment and the interactions will be more productive.

Breathe: When the brain feels "stress" it is unable to see solutions quickly. The body then responds with constriction and distracted thoughts start to form. Tasks take longer and more mistakes are made. When feeling stress and challenge, take deep breaths. By changing one's physiology, the body is able to relax. Even one minute of deep breathing an hour allows the body to rekindle its power. If you are working on a project and tension is increasing, change your position. Stand, if you are sitting, and sit, if you are standing. Move your body and you'll move the energy that is blocking you from the outcome you desire. Be aware of your internal pressure—your own self-talk and the story that you are telling yourself. External pressure must also be factored in. What perceptions do you hold to be true? If you think someone has an opinion of you that is not aligned with who you know you are and you operate accordingly, you are limiting your potential. Remember each person is doing the best they can with their awareness, knowledge and skills that they have. When we interact from this perspective, we can reach a solution with ease.

In discovering what techniques enrich your life, remember to stay open to the possibility of change, and become receptive to the idea that you have the ability within you to transform obstacles into opportunities. I invite you to consider that life can be a joy-filled, wonderful experience and *you* are a player in the game of *LIFE*: Living Fully, Inspiring Thoughts, Finding Solutions, and Empowering Others.

THE FUTURE IS BUILT TODAY: EVERY CONVERSATION IS A FUTURE SUCCESS

As you design the future, think "we" in your focus. The collective talent of the organization is what yields greater results and you have people who care and people who can bring the company into the next generation. Embrace an entrepreneurial spirit by entertaining the idea that each person may have an idea that will expand the influence of the company. You may not be sure if it is viable, yet by sharing with others, you can activate more ideas. As you look ahead to the future, notice the conversations you are experiencing in the community and imagine how your company can become one of the solutions.

How you "show up" in life is how you create your success. Whether you are at work or in the community, people notice how you live and respond to life. Individuals want to do business with trustworthy people, so consider your behaviors and comments wherever you go. Simple genuine actions may yield new business in the future. People notice what you say, how you behave, and if you are aligned with the values promoted by your company.

Remember, *"Be the Solution"* lives within your alignment of self to others. While we often think it is in our actions that we create our results, when we can connect with "being" who we are, we activate a truth within us that allows us to live authentically and to connect genuinely. As you begin to integrate the suggestions in your daily life and model for

others an integrity-based leadership system, you will find more engagement by individuals. By providing leadership development training to
all people, especially for those individuals in your first point of contact
of your company, such as the person who answers your phone, you will
create a culture that clients and customers can identify with and trust.
It is in the establishment of trusting relationships that companies grow
and flourish for generations. It is in recognizing that we can all grow as
individuals, units, departments and teams that we strengthen the viabil-
ity of our expanded vision.

When we believe, we create. When we create, we put into action an
abundant energy that allows us to thrive even during uncertain times.
By honoring the strengths of one, we connect the strengths of many and
create a ripple of possibility that expands beyond our work and into our
daily lives.

Teresa D. Huggins
www.teresadhuggins.com
teresa@teresadhuggins.com
315-525-3296.

Teresa D. Huggins is a Solution-Focused Consultant who engages people
in highly interactive seminars, leadership renewal programs and one on
one coaching. Clients consider new possibilities and expand the vision of
the future for themselves and their organization. As a transformational
thought leader, she collaborates with people to identify change and create results through inspired action. Teresa's dynamic presentations help
employees discover their fullest potential. By promoting communication
strategies that result in a thriving environment, individuals find more

joy and increased motivation to be of service. Her enthusiastic person-ality, wealth of experiences, and commitment to tapping into whatever is holding individuals from reaching their goals leaves the audience with a "can do" attitude and better understanding of how to reach their highest potential. Lives are transformed and companies thrive with an inspired commitment to live their vision. Her website is: www.teresadhuggins.com. She can be reached at: or by calling (315) 525-3296.

YOUR MAGIC BRAND™ HOW TO CONJURE MORE CUSTOMERS AND HOLD THEM SELLBOUND™

ROBERT M. DAVIS

Dr. David Rice, founder of IgniteDDS, co-owns a prestigious dental practice whose work is of the highest quality and integrity. The doctors and staff continually go beyond the call of duty in the service of their patients. The entire philosophy and work ethic of East Amherst Dental Center is summed up in their Magic Brand: *Go the Extra Smile™*.

Tom Peter used to call himself The Tree Guy, which conjures up images of a friendly arborist. But Tom is more than that. When you're about to lose the treasured tree from whose limbs you swung as a child, Tom crafts a sacred vessel from the wood. A one-in-the-world keepsake. Tom transforms trees into works of eternal art. And in creating his Magic Brand, the Tree Guy was himself transformed into the world's first *Master Tree Shaman™*.

The University of Buffalo Surgeons' mission transcends medicine. They go beyond operating on patients to nurturing a healthy community— and beyond diagnosing "where does it hurt" to seeking "where does it *help*?" Their Magic Brand? *UBMD: Wherever it helps.*

UB Neurosurgeons are *Teaching, Healing, Leading the Way*. Owl is *The Wise Choice*, with the most choices for family-friendly orthodontics. Your family receives *brotherly care, brotherly love* at Brothers of Mercy. Nichols School boasts *Exceptional Students, Extraordinary Stories*. DeLacy is *First for Ford*, while Chevrolet buyers are *Happy with Heinrich*. Attorney Arthur Pressman is *Your Ticket to Justice*. Cathy Droz unites women auto buyers with dealerships that are *HER Certified*. Jon Ward supercharges creativity with *Zoom Thinking*.

Izabela Lundberg empowers people from torture and genocide victims to C-suite executives and pro athletes as *The World Messenger*. Kellan *the Cagebreaker* Fluckiger transforms personal and professional lives. Dr. Natasha Deonorain empowers patients and heals an ailing system as the CEO and co-founder of *Conscious Health Solutions* and the *HealthCentric* model of healthcare delivery.

Melinda Xavier helps women and children suffering from hair loss rediscover their inner and outer beauty through *Melinda's Mission*. Ashker's looks like a restaurant, but beyond nourishment they actually *nurture people, culture, creativity and community*.

Home team sports fans eschew big box stores to *Go local—go Laux*. And everyone who wants the tastiest, meatiest, sauciest, genuine, original, bestest, firstest chicken wings in the world knows "The wings that started all the rest, the very first are still the best. *The only way to wing it is to wing it at the Anchor Bar*."

Though focused into a few words, "Your Magic Brand" speaks volumes. Properly crafted, it defines your entire business, drives all your marketing, and creates the most compelling connection with your ideal customers. It's complete, congruent, consistent.

Most brands, however, are mere masks and far from magical. Let's change that. Presto.

INTERNAL. EXTERNAL. ETERNAL.

The real magic happens when you leverage and live Your Magic Brand by continually asking three vital questions:

"Are we living up to our Magic Brand?" (*"How did we go the extra smile for every one of our East Amherst Dental Center patients today? What can do even better tomorrow?"*)

"How else can we live up to our Magic Brand?" (*"What policies and practices should we put in place to help families make their wise choice for our Owl orthodontic services? What if we host seminars and develop new marketing outreach that teaches people how to evaluate their choices, and how to avoid making poor decisions?"*)

"Who must we recruit, nurture, partner with, collaborate with to live up to our Magic Brand?" (*"Let's get the parent company of our primary manufacturer to gift new hairpieces every month to children suffering hair loss whose parents can't afford them in support of Melinda's Mission."*)

Ask this of yourself, your stakeholders, your clients, customers and patients. And act on your answers.

That's how your internal brand becomes congruent with your external brand. That's how you create an engaged, innovative culture that serves all of your stakeholders. That's how your brand *experience* lives up to your brand *expression*.

Your Magic Brand also drives all of your messaging: "Here's how Hamburg Door Company *over-delivers all over Western New York.*" "Do more, be more, live more fully when you *Hear More with Aurora Audiology.*" "Let me be *Your Ticket to Justice.*"

"IT'S ALIVE, I TELL YOU. ALIVE!"

Your business—whether you're a one-person act showcasing your gifts, or a global enterprise selling your goods—is a living entity with its own identity.

Your brand—whether your deliverable is a product, service, inspiration or experience—must also pulsate if it is to truly resonate with real buyers.

Too many brands, alas, are all surface and no substance. They are imposed from the outside, not inspired from the inside. Though they may appear brilliant, beautiful, exciting, compelling, dramatic, and enticing they are, as Shakespeare wrote, "full of sound and fury, signifying nothing."

Others are stitched together into "Frankenbrands". Alive, perhaps, but mixed up monstrosities nonetheless. In fact, Dr. Frankenstein's process—the same process followed by misguided marketers—is exactly the opposite of how a great brand should be created. The doctor tried to put life into his creation as the final stage in his work. But the real secret is to *start* with your real life force, your true creative spark, your own "magic"—and bring *that* to market.

A birthed brand is bred from the bone—with heart, muscle and spirit. It has its mother's eyes and its father's smile. It's congruent. Custom. It captures your magic...casts it into the marketplace...creates compelling corporate-to-consumer, core-to-core connections...conjures more customers...and holds them SellBound.

That's Your Magic Brand.

And this is how to craft it.

DOES THIS BRAND MAKE MY BUTT LOOK BIG?

You may never have brought your brand to market because it doesn't look right, feel right, or resonate with who you really are and what your customers really want.

Perhaps you tried to do it yourself. And that's what you have: a dood-it-yourself brand.

Or you may already have invested thousands of dollars in looks and logos that still aren't right. They just sit there when they should sing and dance and attract and seduce customers from across the room at first sight. And, yet, have the depth required to sustain a lasting, meaningful, mutually rewarding relationship.

Unless your brand is infused with your unique spirit and substance, unless it's authentic and aligned, unless it's genuinely you, you're wearing somebody else's brand. It doesn't fit. It rings false. It's out of place, like polka dot flip flops at a white tail celebrity wedding.

Which could be cool—IF that's truly you.

Otherwise? Well, would you wear a suit or dress that—no matter how fashionable, no matter how fine the fabric, no matter how talented the tailoring—just didn't fit YOU?

Of course not.

So why wear a one-size-fits-all brand that's incomplete, inauthentic, incongruous?

Why settle for mediocre, misaligned, me-too marketing when you can flaunt made-to-measure marketing?

Your Magic Brand fits you because it's *from* you. Totally aligned from the inside out. It begins at your core ... expands into your character ... and is expressed through your costume.

Your Magic Brand begins with you. In fact, it IS you. Manifest and multiplied.

A personal example is in order as a model for your consideration. All of this "magic" metaphor could easily sound silly if it was adopted by most consultants. In this case, however, it's fully congruent. The serious study of the art and craft of magical entertainment has been a major part of my life since boyhood, and the practical application of its persuasion and performance principles informs my work as a master copywriter and creative director. I founded *Magical Life, Meaningful Legacy™*, *Merlinship™*, *The Merlin Marketing Method™* and *Your Magic Brand™*, wrote *Entertaining with Magic*, and created custom conjuring for such companies as Corning, Zippo, Fisher-Price Brands and Mattel. It's partly why Stephanie Frank, bestselling author of The Accidental Millionaire, says, "Robert Merlin Davis is the Magician of Positioning"—and why my branding is baked right into my professional name. *You, too, can live and breathe Your Magic Brand. That's what this manuscript is all about.*

> *"We can't help our customers discover THEIR missing mag-ic until we claim our own."*
>
> ### **Robert Merlin Davis**

▌ YOUR MAGIC BRAND IS THE FOUNDATION OF YOUR MAGIC BUSINESS.

Creating Your Magic Brand follows a deep process called the Merlin Marketing Method™. When you wield its power, you share the best of your authentic, actualized, aligned self with your world—and the world at large.

It is a key factor of your ability to *Live a Magical Life and Leave a Meaningful Legacy.*

When you share your core-built brand with the marketplace, you are empowered to manifest both money and meaning, go beyond commerce to connection, grow customers as well as community, and make not only a living but also a legacy.

▌ YOUR MAGIC MEANS MORE THAN YOUR BRAND.

Before getting to work on the Your Magic Brand, we're going to dig into the underlying concepts that distinguish it from ordinary marketing and branding strategy.

For now, let's set aside color combinations and "creativity." Let's forgo clever wordplay. Let's leave logos till later. That's all the "costume" part of Your Magic Brand.

(In fact, since it's important to decide *what* to say before determining *how* to say it, "Merlin's M.A.G.I.C. Message" intentionally leaves creativity for last. You'll read about it below.)

First, let's look word-by-word at *"Your" "Magic"* and *"Brand."*

"YOUR" Magic Brand is uniquely, unmistakably you and you alone.

Your **"MAGIC"** Brand expresses your core calling and talents.

Your Magic **"BRAND"** drives your marketing by encompassing the total experience of and expression of conducting business with you.

Now let's go deeper.

▌ "YOUR" MAGIC BRAND

The glass slipper fit Cinderella and no one else. The fabled sword Excalibur was wielded by none other than King Arthur of England.

There is to be discovered for you, too, a Magic Brand that is yours and yours alone.

As distinctive as you are, it's developed from your core. Authentic. Genuine. Congruent. It fits you perfectly because it's spawned from within you—not layered upon, adopted by or adapted to you. It represents who you really are so you can live and breathe it naturally, easily, simply. With integrity and authority.

You don't have to fake anything. You don't have to work at it. You don't feel phony. There is absolute alignment with who you profess to be and who you prove to be.

Your ideal customers are drawn to you because they resonate with you. When they meet you and work with you they are not disenchanted and disappointed; they are delighted.

YOUR magic brand is naturally empowering. And it's proprietary. Not mistaken for anyone else and not copyable by anyone else.

YOUR magic brand is 100% YOU.

Because it is, after all, YOUR magic.

YOUR "MAGIC" BRAND

Discovering your magic is such a vital element in this work (you may even call it "the real work") that we will talk about it in greater depth further on. For now, be assured that just as Arthur was mentored by his Merlin in the process, so, too, are you.

YOUR MAGIC "BRAND"

"Brand" is bandied about by everybody, but properly understood by practically nobody. So let's look closely at what a brand really is, what it is not, and how it synergizes with the other elements of sales and marketing that allow you to prosperously translate your brand into your business.

Branding is everything you do and everything you are. It's the total expression of – and experience of – you and your business.

Your logo is not your brand. Logos and jingles and the like are creative brand *elements* that help express your brand through your marketing messaging. But they are not your Brand.

Marketers who say "don't bother with branding" create an "anti-brand brand." They miss the fact that you cannot help but brand yourself and your business. It's automatic. If you don't even try, you present a "don't even try" image by accident. If you go cheap on your wardrobe, photography, production, storefront, staff, media presence or any other element of your messaging, you project a "cheap" brand. So it's best to brand by design rather than default.

> *"The problem with do-it-yourself marketing is that it looks like you dood it yourself."*
> **Robert Merlin Davis**

Of course you do not want to brand at the expense of your business.

You do need to create sales and cash flow, and you can certainly utilize fiscally prudent Guerrilla Marketing tactics. The trick is to build both your brand and your business intentionally.

But before you can even begin to brand your business, you must position it.

YOUR MAGIC BRAND IS BUILT ON THE FOUNDATION OF A POWERFUL POSITION.

The only thing more important than your brand is your positioning. (Another misunderstood marketing concept that we're about to demystify.) Although branding and positioning ideally harmonize and synergize in a symbiotic relationship, it's actually preferable to promote the *right position* simply stated, than the wrong position brilliantly branded.

Positioning makes you The One Specific instead of just another generic. Like The Master Tree Shaman or the founder of Melinda's Mission, or world's first and only Guerrilla Marketing Copywriter.

Positioning is how one brand is chosen among other brands. Branding gets you shopped; positioning gets you purchased.

Both branding and positioning help customers make a choice about what to buy and from whom to buy it. That choice is a matter of *context* and of *contrast*:

Based on the current *context* of their needs and desires, buyers *contrast* you with their other options, and then *choose* where their cash goes.

Looking closer, consumers make considered choices from competitive options, based on their current criteria. Your prospect's present and proximate predilections and preferences inform their purchase.

For example, let's say they want to purchase a pen. If they're on a budget they'll buy The Cheapest Pen. If they want to show off, they'll shell out for The Priciest or Most Prestigious Pen. In a hurry? Grab The

Closest Pen. Drawing Rudolph? Get the Red Pen. Underwater? On a rocket? The Space Pen. Gifting a Bar Mitzvah boy? A fountain pen. (I still own the Parker my aunt sent me from London when I was thirteen.)

Positioning affects pricing, too. When your *waiter* suggests a salad, you tip $5. Your *nutritionist* says "Salad" and you pay $50. Your *doctor* runs tests, examines you, says "Salad" and charges $150. $500 goes to the medical *specialist*. And the Tuscany Trip with the *Celebrity Salad Specialist* where you tour the farm and make your own gourmet signature salad? Pony up $5000. Plus airfare.

"You can't build a strong brand on a weak position."
Robert Merlin Davis

Take a moment to consider these questions to begin positioning your business:

- » How are your ideal customers and clients choosing you?
- » What is their context?
- » What are their criteria?
- » What are their preferences?
- » What are they choosing you in contrast to?
- » How can you be the most favorable choice?

To connect with customers, compel their purchasing and conquer competition, you need Preferential Positioning.

A "preferred position" makes you the best, easiest, most obvious choice for your most desirable clients, customers, patients, audience. Some of the most important pillars of positioning include:

- » **Proprietary** – more than popular.
- » **Purposeful** – aligned with your vision and mission.

» **Passion-Based** – well beyond interesting.

» **Promotable** – not just packaged.

» **Purchasable** – easily bought.

» **Profitable** – sustainably sellable.

» **Prosperous** – not just profitable.

» **Pressworthy** – deserving of media attention.

» **Perpetual** – worthy of posterity.

» **Persuasive** – your perceived position influences your persuasiveness.

» **Personality Positive** – connecting with your core customers at their core.

» **Pervasive** – Internal and external congruency and consistency.

» **Promising** – solving a problem or fulfilling a desire. (And your performance fulfills your promise.)

» **Polarizing** – attracts most desirable clientele; us against them

» **Provocative** – compels people to pay attention

» **Professional** – perceived competence

Hit as many of these as you can. If you have to pick just one, pick Proprietary.

▎ POSITIONING THOUGHT-STARTERS.

Here are a few additional thought-starters to trigger your thinking while pondering your position:

Compared to your competition, you can be:

» The first, best, only, nearest, latest, oldest, cheapest, friendliest, harshest, creepiest, largest, smallest, wisest, whateverest _____.

» The most expensive, most valuable, most practical, most _____.

» Official, doctor-recommended, By appointment to ___, the expert's ____, insider, secret weapon, former, ex-____.

» Today's ___. Tomorrow's ___. Your region's You're your country's ___. The People's ___. Your personal ___.

Are you a visionary or revolutionary? A performer, puppeteer, practitioner, prophet, pied piper, pariah, messiah?

Are you a pitchperson or a spokesperson?

Are you an agent, advisor, advocate, activist, agitator, or authority?

(If you are an authority, be an Authentic Authority.)

Are you a thought leader? (If so, think original thoughts and demonstrate leadership.)

Do you confer, consider, consult, collaborate, compel, coerce or command?

Do you educate, elucidate, entertain, entice or engage?

Now that we've agreed on a few essential concepts of what a brand really is, we can begin to build Your Magic Brand by following the Merlin Marketing Method.

The Merlin Marketing Method is holistic and synergistic. Let's start with an overview.

The process follows eight essential steps. The first steps enable you to *Live a Magical Life*; the latter steps expand your outreach and enable you to *Leave a Meaningful Legacy*.

1. **Define your mission:** Why are you called to step up and what meaningful legacy do you desire to leave?

2. **Deepen your mindset:** Which attitudes and insights must mature within you so you can achieve your mission and enjoy the path?

3. **Discover your magic:** Who are YOU—to yourself and your market? What are your proprietary powers?

4. **Distinguish your message:** What are you compelled to say—that your audience needs and wants to hear? What are your magic words?

5. **Develop your music:** What is your "true voice"—and how are you gifted to best express your legacy message?

6. **Deploy your marketing:** How do you get your word out—efficiently, effectively, and profitably?

7. **Dominate your media:** Where will you be the featured celebrity and voice of trusted authority?

8. **Demand your monetization:** How will you ethically prosper from your lifework, so you can sustain and expand it?

Ready to go deeper? Due to space constraints of this particular work, we can only zoom in on a few of the core components. Future and additional works expand on, and guide you through, the entire process. You'll find more resources at RobertMerlinDavis.com.

Discover your MAGIC: *Who are YOU—to yourself and your market? What are your proprietary powers?*

In a way, there is a sense of "Right livelihood meets personal branding" to discovering your magic and casting it to the marketplace. But it's much more than that.

Discovering your magic means finding out who you are at your core. Because the best position, the best branding, the best business really stems from who you really truly are inside. Some of us have no idea and some of us have too many ideas. Some have achieved a certain "surface success" that is less than who they really are, only part of their totality, misaligned with their mission, and out of synch with the next stage in their career or legacy.

They may have a brand, but it's not Magic.

This work is too deep for a designer, and is most easily accomplished with the guidance of a sort of sherpa or shepherd. (Or, yes, a Merlin.) Here are some considerations and questions to get you started:

» What are you gifted and given to do?

» What are you compelled to do instead of supposed to do?

» What do you do when you're supposed to be doing something else?

» What you want to sustain, live with, and share?

» What moves and inspired you?

» What are you best at?

» What comes easily, naturally, where you're frequently in the zone?

» What are you obsessed about? Can't stop thinking and talking about?

» What did you dream about when you were a kid? What did you play?

» What have you discovered?

» What arcane knowledge have you acquired?

Distinguish your MESSAGE: *What are you compelled to say—that your audience needs and wants to hear? What are your magic words?*

Once you've discovered your magic, your message is defined in a way that can be packaged so people can receive, consume, digest, understand, enjoy and share it.

Ultimately, you seek simplicity. The simplicity you seek encompasses all the complexity, subtlety, psychology and nuance of your messaging in just a few branding elements.

Your magic words hold your customers SellBound. Those words can be spoken, sung, and illustrated.

Your magic words are expressed through three elements:

1. Your name.
2. Your slogan.
3. Your "copy."

Your name is the most important element. The more impactful, the more meaningful, the more uniquely magical your name is, the less work is required by the other elements. (This is why my branding is baked right into my professional name.)

Your slogan—in harmony with your name—creatively expresses your position and brand. It should not be merely a "tag line" that's tagged on your marketing communication. Instead, your slogan sums up and drives the rest of your marketing. ("Go the Extra Smile." "The Wise Choice." "Wherever it Helps.")

Your copy is everything else—in harmony with your name and slogan. The highest level of copywriting incorporates proprietary, multisensory language.

Magic Messaging combines salesmanship and showmanship. You want to craft messaging that's psychologically compelling, competitive, cohesive and consistent across all communication, and that leverages uses all the educational and entertainment aspects of your chosen media.

▌ HERE ARE A FEW RESOURCES TO HELP YOU CRAFT YOUR MAGIC WORDS.

An effective slogan is:

» Easily grasped.

» Easily transmitted. (Speakable, singable.)

» More emotional than intellectual.

» External, internal, eternal, universal.

» Has "legs" (versatile, flexible).

» Can be a "rallying cry."

» Simple and obvious.

» Exclusive, proprietary.

» CUSTOMER driven.

Tactics to craft a viral, memorable slogan include:

» Rhyme.

- » Rhythm.
- » Parallel construction.
- » Rule of Three.
- » Alliteration.
- » Common expression.
- » Twist on common expression.
- » Coin a phrase.
- » NAME as solution.
- » Contrast: Us versus You.

MERLIN'S M.A.G.I.C. MESSAGE

Contemplate these five elements when creating and evaluating Your Magic Message:

Media – Be where your prospects seek information, entertainment, community.

Actionable – Don't just go for the gut; go for the gold. Make your message easy to act on, especially by skeptical people resistant to change. Put all the ingredients, instruction and implementation in place for purchase and consumption.

Grounded – Make an honest promise, rooted in reality, with credibility and managed expectations.

Integrated – Be consistent and cohesive across all media and all messaging from lead generation to lifetime customer value.

Creative – Express Your Magic Brand by leveraging all the informational, educational and entertainment tools and techniques of the relevant media.

MERLIN'S 5 LEVELS OF COPYWRITING

The higher the level, the more compelling your copy. Start at level one and don't stop until your magic words are as magical as possible:

1. **Informative**. Simply state the facts.
2. **Interesting**. Back up the facts with emotional content.
3. **Entertaining**. Sugarcoat the facts with intriguing content.
4. **Persuasive**. Boost the facts with psychological content.
5. **SellBinding!** Lightening-bolt the facts with all of the above, plus compelling, connecting content and passionate presentation.

SellBinding messages are sales scripts on steroids. It's not enough to show and tell; you must show and sell.

Sellbinding messages go deeper than features and benefits. They connect core-to-core with your customers, addressing their hidden pains, pleasures and passions.

Sellbinding messages are bulletproof. They predict questions and build in the answers. They preclude objections by disarming them. They assume the sale, the upsell, and the cross-sell.

They are fun to read, watch and listen to. In fact, they're the kinds of messages that people would pay for, stay up all night consuming, and give to their friends and family.

They leverage the irresistible, dramatic, storytelling techniques of classic movies, love letters, first dates, midnight whispers, giggles, gossip and ghost stories, eavesdropped arguments, scandal rags, naught jokes and grandpa's stories.

In other words, they're Your Magic Words,

▌ EDITING YOUR MAGIC WORDS

It's true that good writing its re-writing. Follow these steps to hone your work for maximum effectiveness:

1. **Edit for corrections.** Clean up errors, check consistency, accuracy.
2. **Edit for content.** Include intellectual, emotional, motivational

content.

3. **Edit for clarity.** Be clear, concise, and don't confuse your customers.

4. **Edit for concept.** Is the content interesting and entertaining?

5. **Edit for character.** Does the copy express Your Magic Brand personality?

6. **Edit for cash.** Does the copy present a compelling, persuasive sales message...ask for the order...and make it easy to take action?

▍ MOUNT A CAMPAIGN.

Magical messaging is more than a one-off commercial. Instead, create a campaign that tells an ongoing story over time, throughout your customers' buying cycle from consideration through compliance.

Remember that one of the first tenets expressed in Guerrilla Marketing is that consistency breeds familiarity, comfort, and trust.

Consistent brand messaging elements include your name and slogan, logo, languaging, music, format, and spokesvoice.

Develop your MUSIC: *express your true voice and talents.*

You express and share your message through your preferred personal medium—speaking, writing, teaching, coaching, healing, leading, parenting, painting, selling, performing,

After the creation of your message comes the craft of your message. The more you master the methods, tools and techniques of your means of expression, the more your music will connect with, move and motivate your customers and community.

More than technical proficiency, developing your music allows you to express your true "voice," and technical mastery allows you to express it fully.

Deploy your MARKETING: *Be heard, valued, well paid and prosperous.*

Marketing encompasses everything from branding to networking to advertising. It is deployed via various media to communicate with your prospects and customers.

Your marketing plan supports your business plan. Strategy precedes tactics. Some considerations for its development include:

» Who is your most desirable clientele—in detail and depth?

» Where do they congregate, commune, seek education and entertainment?

» Who influences them?

» What do you want? Connection, control, celebrity, credibility, community, commerce?

» What resources do you have? Need?

Dominate your MEDIA: *deliver and amplify your voice and message.*

Media channels are continually changing. Platforms come and go, free and paid, public and private. All have their place. You can't do it all, though; here are some guidelines:

» Broaden your definition of media to include "Where your prospects go for entertainment, education, community."

» Focus on selected media that you can "own" through continual, consistent content and communication.

» Work with a synergistic multimedia mix, both traditional and new.

» Master the tools of the medium you choose.

» Create your own media.

» Remember that YOU—your voice, your gestures, your words, your image—Are your media, too.

» Commercial messages become cultural messages, so create them with intention, integrity, longevity and legacy in mind.

» Do something newsworthy; Intrigue, poke and provoke.

Demand your monetization: *How will you ethically prosper from your lifework, so you can sustain and expand it?*

For those who are not yet entirely comfortable "selling" or receiving money as remuneration, take comfort in knowing that Your Magic Brand lessens the need to "sell" because it creates a compelling core-to-core connection that attracts the customers, clients, community and patients who most resonate with you. And when you follow the Merlin Marketing Method you are in alignment and integrity so there is absolutely no seedy selling.

Keep in mind, too, that pricing is part of your positioning.

In addition, money is not necessarily the only form of remuneration available to you. For those who prefer other types of exchange, I have coined the term "energetic commerce." If this resonates with you, you are welcome to act accordingly within your own entity and enterprise.

▎THE MOST IMPORTANT REASON TO CREATE YOUR MAGIC BRAND.

My first marketing lesson came, when I was four, in a treasure chest. It looked to the uninitiated like a shoebox.

It was a gift from Dad, who once worked for Jack and Jill Joke Shop in Boston. Inside the box were some props from the shop. One of them was a classic effect called the Ball and Vase from which a little red ball disappears. I don't know how, but mine vanished completely. Gone for good.

That day, in a Long Island basement, began the search to reclaim my missing magic. It led me through the years to study the inner workings of marketing, magic, and the human mind. My mission evolved into inspiring and empowering others to Live a Magical Life and Lead a Meaningful legacy.

To the uninitiated it looks like marketing.

With My Magic Brand built right into my middle name.

Now it's your turn.

I believe all of us, including our customers, are looking for their own little piece of lost magic. When we deliver our products, services and experiences, we can help them find some of that missing magic.

That's marketing at its deepest, most powerful, most persuasive level.

That's why it's so important to create Your Magic Brand through the Merlin Marketing Method. Because we can't help our customers discover THEIR missing magic until we claim our own.

Robert Merlin Davis

http://RobertMerlinDavis.com

Robert@RobertMerlinDavis.com

(716) 903-2727

PHOTO CREDIT: Tess Moran Photography

Robert Merlin Davis is the founder of *Magical Life, Meaningful Legacy™: The secrets of aligned, authentic achievement*, *Merlinship™: Timeless Wisdom for Legacy Leaders*, *Your Magic Brand™: How to conjure more customers and hold them SellBound™*, and *The Merlin Marketing Method™: The Science and Sorcery of congruent, creative commerce*. As an award-winning branding and positioning strategist and creative director, broadcast executive, and the world's first and only Guerrilla Marketing Master Copywriter, Robert has helped clients from local to global manifest millions by leveraging the secret methodologies of master marketers and magicians. He is also an accomplished jazz pianist and journalist, and the most proud dad in the universe.

For more resources and updates on forthcoming multimedia courses, consulting and creative development, please visit RobertMerlinDavis.com.

RISING TO THE TOP: PROVEN STEPS TO BUILDING A PROFITABLE SERVICE BUSINESS

MEGGIE JONES HALE

"What you *get* by achieving your goals is not as important as what you *become* by achieving your goals."

Henry David Thoreau

If you knew the details of the earlier part of my life, you would bet that I was destined for failure. Born into an extremely dysfunctional family, I was kidnapped by my abusive father when I was five. By the age of fifteen, I had successfully petitioned the school court to commission for the right to be my own guardian. With determination and ingenuity, including attending my own parent-teacher conferences, I was able to graduate high school. Yet, the difficulties of life weighed heavily upon me, and when I was twenty-one, I was almost successful in committing suicide.

At the time, I was living in a basement apartment, and I had a plan. My landlords were going camping, and I had the opportunity to end the deep emotionless void in which I was living. As luck would have it, my landlords returned, I was resuscitated, and I woke up two days later in the intensive care unit extremely angry. It was the first emotion that I'd felt in more than three weeks. When I was released, the next emotion to rise to the surface was embarrassment, and that was the impetus for leaving town. A year later, I had fallen in love and married. Deep inside, however, I didn't really believe that my husband loved me. I had been so physically and emotionally abused by my father that I felt like a walking mistake.

Nevertheless, something inside of me kept me going—along with my two daughters. I entered college and began my studies in the medical field. However, I was convinced that I possessed only borderline intelligence and expected to slide through with barely passing grades. At the end of one semester, I was sick with strep throat, and I was convinced that I flunked my psychology final. Upon confessing my concern, my professor informed me that I'd received the highest score in the class. This was the turning point in my life. I realized my father had lied to me and that I could do anything. I was a superwoman. After years of self-deprecation, I acknowledged my value and the gifts, talents, and skills that I could contribute to humanity. Just a few short years later, by the time I was twenty-nine, I had gone into business and started an assisted-care facility that catered to hospice patients. By thirty-six, I had opened a day spa, with an investment of $1,000, a sub-lease, and a month's free rent. I made it happen. The spa grew from 1,000 to 7,000 square feet in three years. I later expanded the business to occupy 10,000 square feet. Now, I share my success formula with other spa owners and service-base providers—and I am building a business that will support many of my philanthropic desires to help young women.

▋ THE KEYS TO MY SUCCESS

There is no one fell-swoop method to rise to the top of one's field. Throughout the developments of my business, I found there were, however, several keys that must be put into play for anyone to achieve success.

One is passion to serve and make people's lives better—that's your "why." Instead of staying stuck in the belief system that my earlier experiences had instilled in me, I placed stock in the value that I bring to the world. When you own your own business, there has to be something more to get you out of bed in the morning than money. Your mission has to be the driver. The second is the ability to focus on what needs to be done rather than what's hard and difficult. All too often, many of us get stuck in the quagmire of "victimhood," and put our attention on what's going wrong in our lives—rather than what we can do about our difficulties. Granted, sometimes life throws us too many hurdles at once and it's easy to get discouraged. That's when shifting our attention to what's right in our lives can set us back on the path to finding solutions to the problems we face. Thirdly, I'm always continuing to develop. It's a sad thing in life when people think they have all the answers and cease growing. Self and professional development are a must for any business owner.

However, perhaps the biggest asset I possess is my ability to be an outside-the-box strategist. This is the skill I've been able to teach clients when analyzing their businesses to find the weak areas where resources are being drained—and those areas that can be enhanced to increase their Return on Investment (ROI). Thinking outside the box is required at all levels—whether we're focusing on customers service or implementing new marketing techniques. Additionally, this can only occur when we give ourselves the time and space to be creative and to look objectively at what's working in our businesses and what's not.

OUT-OF-THE-BOX STRATEGIES

Provide Incredible Customer Service

The simplest way to build your business is for your customers to talk up the town about you. It's about being "you" and sharing your genuine concern for their well-being by creating experiences that leave your clients feeling better about themselves and about their lives.

Yet, how do we get them to walk into our establishment in the first place? We begin by building that relationship.

Building relationships is most important component of starting or growing a business. And we do this by adding value. Spas can offer a service—such as a complimentary make-up session with a hair cut, or a color analysis to help customers pick the colors that are going to make their skin glow. Glamour photos or a dozen roses can be offered for anyone who purchases a day of beauty services. Weight loss clinics and chiropractic offices might offer a body fat weight analysis or a complimentary consultation with the doctor. Additionally, educational articles are great giveaways for weight-loss clinics and chiropractic offices. Some suggestions might be, "10 Recipes for Optimal Health" or larger content ebooks such as "100 Recipes on How to Eat Comfort Food and Stay Low Glycemic."

Amp Up your PR

Any press is good press is an adage in the marketing world; however, it's much better to create your own good press to achieve great results.

Start with print or online publications. There are different sections of newspapers and magazines where many of your ideas can land. "Letters to Editor" is just one where you can share your opinions about a number of topics. Writing a good press release can often serve as an article to fill space in a pinch—as long as you're providing some value— meaning fresh information that isn't designed to sell.

When writing press releases, understand that the people who will give you space in publications have busy schedules, demanding bosses, and tight deadlines. This means submitting releases that are timely and relevant to current events, complete with all the information they need, including your contact information. One of the best ways to get press is to send the press release to the executive producer or editor directly and offer them the first scoop.

Tony Barker, of Tony Barker Music says, "The bottom line here is to demonstrate how helping you helps them with their job. Get good enough at it, and you'll be the one they call when they need space to fill on a deadline."

Additionally, position yourself as an expert and write an article about the key issues in your field. It's a cost effective way to market and get PR. If you are willing to write about five articles per week on subjects in your area of expertise, there is a very good chance that these articles can go viral. For instance, if you are an esthetician, you can do a feature on cleansers and toners, one on wrinkle fillers, another on the best masques for different age groups, and so on.

Remember, too, many articles have readers comment boxes at the end of online articles. Get in the habit of reading the works of other experts in your field. Leaving a comment, adding your perspective, or supporting the author's may garner you some notice. Make sure your contact information is in the resource box for online newsletters. Chances are you'll be called on in the future as a resource for a journalist's assignment—or potential customers might just search your Facebook page or website and pay you a visit.

If you're writing muscles are a little weak, begin with a blog on your website or post tips of the day on Facebook. Or hire a ghostwriter to assist you in spreading your message across the world.

Radio interviews are also a super strong way to garner the attention of potential customers. They're easy and effective. You get to share your wisdom with the potential of tens of thousands of listeners from the comfort of your office or your home—and possibly even in your pajamas.

Once you get on one good radio station then other reporters might want to interview you, too. Radio personalities might opt to do their show from your place of business—which might lead to a co-marketing opportunity by teaming up with a local coffee shop or restaurant to bring in food.

The key is to know who your customers are, what they read, what stations they listen to, and where they socialize.

NETWORK–VIRTUALLY AND IN PERSON

Developing a strong social media presence is mandatory for success. Many times if you provide great value, your connections will grow. Keith said that if you have 100,000 active followers that your business could be worth over $15 million.

Show up at local events. There are a number of different groups that meet every week, where you can distribute product samples and some value-added gift certificates. Your business can also be the place where people gather. Establish your own meet-up group around topics that promote your business and that are near and dear to your heart.

Holding educational seminars and charging $10 or so for the event will bring the curious through your doors. Hairdressers can do a style night or a blow-out event. Estheticians can provide mini facials. Chiropractors and massage therapists can offer assessments or chair massages.

Contribute to Your Community. One of the greatest ways to get noticed is showing that you care about a cause and/or contribute to the health and well-being of your community. It's a win-win for everyone. Arianna Huffington dedicates an entire chapter in her book, *Thrive*, to giving. She advocates to, "Use a skill or talent you have—cooking, accounting, decorating—to help someone who could benefit from it. It'll jumpstart your transition from a go-getter to a go-giver, and reconnect you to the world and to the natural abundance in your own life."

Victoria Markham, of Victoria Markham Productions, says, "Volunteer your businesses' specialty as a service for a charity function or, if you're a retailer, volunteer your time. A hair salon can do hairdressing for a charity fashion show; a tire salesman can be a waiter for a fund-raising dinner. You get the opportunity to mingle with guests and chat about your business. Your business card or promotional item may be placed at each seat or in gift bags. It's great low-cost exposure with tax benefits and you will be viewed positively by prospective clients!"

When we feel good about doing something nice for someone else, our spirit is enlivened. Then there is a ripple effect in play. Our innate creativity and problem-solving abilities are activated, and we begin seeing strategies to enhance our businesses.

Take the stage: Many companies are looking for great public speakers to fill their venues. Offering lunchtime talks on stress reduction, better sleep techniques—anything that can help their employees do a better job are just some of the topics that can be spoken about by wellness experts. Those in the beauty industry can also lend their wisdom by sharing tips for looking fresh for an important client meeting, dressing for success, easy hairstyles, and so much more. Take plenty of business cards and free samples. Remember to ask for the booking if anyone shows interest. If you don't have access to your schedule immediately, ask the potential client if they wouldn't mind receiving a call once you're back in your office.

Co-Market. One way to get your message out is to work with businesses who are not in competition with you and who have a large clientele base. Give them a sample of your work and then set them up on a bonus or referral program. One example might be for a salon to connect with a maternity shop and offer customers who purchase a nightgown, or some other outfit, a free makeover or a basket of sample products.

"Partner with a local coffeehouse and shoot your next video segment there," says Myles Miller of LeadUP.Biz. "Work out an arrangement with a coffeehouse to have free coffee provided for those in the video and promote the coffeehouse before, during, and after the shoot. This will also intrigue other people to inquire about what you are doing, and you can promote your business to a captive audience."

Use your existing clientele to up-level your business. Give your clients cards and have them put their names on it. When someone they refer comes in for a service, your clients will benefit by receiving a discount on their next service. Integrity builds the best referrals. Ask your clients to leave a testimonial on your Facebook, Yelp, or TripAdvisor pages. Make it easy for them to do by providing them with a link to all your social media on your business cards.

Endorsements: If you are in business in the beauty and or health field and you offer services by the hour or session, you can use that to get top mentors, celebrities, or tipping point contacts to help you spread the word and increase business.

Try to remember that everyone wants something from "celebrities," so do your best to serve to your absolute greatest potential. These individuals are smart, and if they want to help you, they will—however, they are cautious about who they align with. Be careful not to overstep your bounds or ask for too much. If these people have a major following, building a good relationship can take time. Be respectful and patient. No one likes to be used, so make sure that you can offer something of value to enhance their life. Remember, golden relationships are worth exactly that—gold.

Track Your Marketing. Some of the weakest links I've seen with wellness centers, chiropractors, and weight loss clinics are that they're missing the boat with marketing, and they're wasting a lot of money. Not only do they not see the value in marketing, when they do make any marketing moves, they're not tracking the programs that customers are purchasing.

By tracking your marketing efforts, you can put more effort or money into the ones that work and cut the bleed where it doesn't. Make sure to give a strategy ample time to play out before you make decisions on what's working and what's not. The key is to tweak the marketing until the number of "hits" on a particular approach increases. The golden formula is to expect to reach a 3X-5X return on the investment.

Survey Your Customers: One surefire way to failure is being the smartest person in the room. All successful people know how to ask for feedback. Create a survey for your customers and offer them a $20 gift certificate for giving you honest feedback on questions such as: What do your like about our place? What's the best service or product you ever purchased at our business? What keeps you coming back? What can we do better?

Patience and diligence is required. The right marketing formula will appear. It takes time and perseverance to drive all traffic to one funnel, build that list, and give your customers—or potential customers—value.

▌ YOUR EMPLOYEES MATTER

Business owners often wear many hats and feel they must be all things to all people. In reality, even when we are solopreneurs, we have members of our team, be it the accountant that does our books, the lawyer that draws up our contracts, or the graphic designer that perfects our web presence. However, as our businesses grow, we most often need to enlist the support of our employees to ensure our success.

Gamify the workplace. Whether you're providing direct wages to employees or splitting profits with independent contractors, create an atmosphere where goal-setting can be linked to some friendly competition. Reward your members for selling packages and/or for the number of referrals that they solicit.

If you have enough people, create teams and name them something fun like Racing Camels or Terrific Tigers. Track the daily, weekly, or monthly wins with a visually appealing chart. Reward the top performers with gifts and prizes that are appropriate for their contribution.

These few steps will prompt your team, who perhaps think merely of themselves as educators, into sales people as well. They'll also be more mindful of potential customers when out and about in other areas of their lives. And in a fun environment, members of your team will likely have your back when it comes to employee conduct.

Protect Yourself. Employee theft is one of the biggest reasons businesses go under. And theft goes beyond sticky fingers in the till. Employees will use product without thinking of the cost to the employer. A little bit of wax here, a little bit of color there, and the costs add up fast.

And of course, temptation may visit your employees around the cash drawer. It's unfortunate that some people may take advantage of their employers, but it does happen, more often than we want to admit. The best practice here is to monitor the area with a surveillance camera.

Then, there is the cost of time not spent wisely. An idle employee, wasting an hour a day for a week on Facebook or Instagram, is equivalent to six weeks of vacation a year. One of the biggest mistakes that employers make is expecting members of their staff to be self-starters. People with this talent are a rare breed. It's better to make sure that your full-time employees are working effectively and giving them two weeks of paid vacation each year. Granted, you can't be a watchful eye over every employee in every minute of the day; however, there are solutions to this problem. First, when assigning a task, demand that the employee tell you when they've started and when they've completed the job. This will ensure that the task is indeed completed.

Enlist the assistance of a Task Manager, as well. Here, you'll need a trusted employee who is a self-starter, who can oversee the team, and assign tasks. Many small-business owners tend to wear many hats to the detriment not only of the health and well-being of their bodies and minds, but their bottom line as well.

Find an Intern. Many students are looking for ways to learn more about their field of study and to have a foot in the door in their industry. Integrating an intern is one avenue to building your team without adding salary expenses to your budget. This can be extremely helpful in the start-up or expansion of your business. If you enlist three interns to work four hours a week, you'll have twelve hours a week of assistance that you don't have to pay for. It's important, however, to limit the number of hours they work to avoid their burnout. Taking advantage of anyone isn't the best business practice. You must also be providing the intern with new skills and added value.

If they do well, then you bring them on the payroll. An added benefit is that there will be little time needed for training, since they will already be familiar with your business.

▍ OPTIMIZE YOUR SPACE

One of the best ways to increase your ROI is to optimize every square inch of your business. Assess each of your rooms and look at the cost of your product and the cost of your labor associated with each room. Often when business owners put the numbers together for the products and technicians associated with the space, they find they are losing money. It's imperative to calculate the cost and demand of a service. If you are only making $15 to $30 an hour, you might want to see if that room can be better utilized by a product or service that has a lower cost but higher value. Even if you have only one room, the same tactic must be applied. It's often wise to integrate a specialty product or service into your business that makes your time worth more—and is of more value to your clients.

This is one of the reasons that I developed The Slimmer Silhouette® Body Sculpting System, which provides a number of benefits such as releasing impurities from the body, improved skin condition, look and feel; reduction in cellulite, and enhanced overall appearance. The "system" is designed to hydrate the body versus dehydrating. Body wraps have typically been used at spas, resorts, and high-end salons; however, they are designed to dehydrate the body in order to achieve the inch loss desired. The **Slimmer Silhouette® Body Sculpting System** has a very different approach, which applies micronutrients and minerals through the skin to help with tightening and toning. In my research, I discovered that over 85% of people are deficient in micronutrients and minerals because our foods are grown in mineral-deficient soils. Additionally, this deficiency also is attributed to drinking coffee and alcohol, and eating bread.

The added micronutrients and minerals in the body sculpting system contribute not only to the short term results, but also many clients are likely to achieve longer term benefits than with other wrap products in the marketplace. In some cases, in a series, we have seen similar results to liposuction in size reduction. With thousands of sessions complete, spa owners nationwide are seeing a higher ROI and achieving great results for their clients with the inclusion of this product in their lineup. One of the reasons to integrate services, such as The Slimmer Silhouette® Body Sculpting System is so that you're making more per hour—and providing your customers with a service that will make them look good and feel great.

▌ PUTTING YOURSELF ON THE TABLE

As service providers, we often focus on the people we are here to help—whether we're spa owners, hair stylists, chiropractors, or weight-loss experts. Yet, this requires us to walk our talk and ensure that our own health and well-being are cared for as well. When we do that, we'll have the energy and vitality to go above and beyond. We'll be remembered, and we'll leave the world in a better place than which we found it—by living our mission.

That's how I run my business and live my life—by owning my value and honoring my mission. My big "Why" is to help people find their value. For most business owners, value is the missing component in their world. I grew up feeling as if I had no value. When I found my value and my mission, my whole world shifted.

Additionally, the biggest lesson, I learned throughout my years in business is that money is not the purpose; money is a tool. If you have something other than money driving you—like adding value to someone's life, helping a customer solve a problem, relieve some stress, or feel and/or look better—then you will live a more meaningful, fulfilling life.

Building a business is not rocket science. It's connecting with other human beings with the intention of mutual support. As Albert Einstein said, "Only a life lived for others is a life worth while." The bottom line is that we're here to help each other.

Meggie Jones Hale

http://slimmersilhouette.com

Meggie Jones Hale's passion for health and wellness is founded in a 17-year medical background, including several medical certifications. Meggie left the health care industry to launch her own health and wellness spa, where working with biologists, and research and development doctors, to develop the Slimmer Silhouette® Body Sculpting System. She combined the natural healing formula she helped create with the body wrap concept.

By using her body sculpting system, along with diet and exercise, she dropped 120 pounds and did not have saggy skin. She was also able to reap the good side-effects from the micronutrients and minerals in the system. After witnessing the tremendous popularity and success of her system, Meggie realized the potential that existed nationwide and she began offering other professionals the Slimmer Silhouette® Body Sculpting System.

Meggie is currently in the process of launching healthyteens.org, a non-profit organization dedicated to helping teens "blossom from the inside out" through life and food coaching, personal training, and skin and beauty consulting.

PROCUREMENT STRATEGIES: BOOSTING SUCCESS FOR THE SMALL-TO-MEDIUM-SIZED BUSINESS

CARLOS SMITH SOARES

Excellence is an art won by training and habituation. We do not act rightly because we have virtue or excellence, but we rather have those because we have acted rightly. We are what we repeatedly do. Excellence, then, is not an act but a habit.

Aristotle

My main motivation to contribute to this book stems from fifteen years of working with clients to unlock the power of a well-defined procurement strategy, even in the smallest of companies. I've spent my entire consulting career helping small-to-medium-sized businesses improve their operating performance and grow their net profit through strategic cost reductions. I know that success is possible by integrating proven procurement strategies with proven operations excellence methodologies. Yet, so often my clients are under tremendous pressure to deliver EBITDA growth, usually at the expense of developing disciplined cost management. I'd like to give the C-suite, their executive teams, and business line leaders of these companies some perspective on how to overcome common issues and take advantage of basic strategies and techniques to help them improve their bottom lines, no matter what their size.

▌ THE PROCUREMENT LANDSCAPE FOR SMALL-TO-MEDIUM-SIZED COMPANIES

As small-to-medium-sized companies grow, they face many challenges, both internally and externally. Company culture changes as more employees are added to the mix, many of whom bring their own visions to the company. Products and services expand, adding complexity and straining processes built for a simpler portfolio. Policies and procedures, which may have been unwritten, are now unable to support the flow of work at all levels of the organization and potentially increase the risk profile of the business.

Customer demands also place tremendous pressure on a companies ability to manage and control costs. In a world where the concepts of more, better, quicker—and at a more competitive price—rule, companies are often scrambling to meet the expectations of their customers. The need to deliver results right away doesn't allow managers the luxury of implementing sound savings strategies in capacity constrained business lines.

Additionally, any discussion about procurement should never overlook the role that vendors play in a company's performance. They have a direct impact in the profitability of a firm, the quality of a product or service, and the satisfaction of your customer. However, vendors come in all shapes and sizes and have very different motivations, not all of which are completely aligned with your company's business strategy. As companies grow, a thoughtful look at the profile of your vendor base is also in order.

TOTAL COST OF OWNERSHIP

A key component of understanding the benefits of a well-defined procurement strategy is to understand the concept of Total Cost of Ownership (TCO). This means that the purchase price of a good or service is really only one piece, and often a small piece, of the total cost to own that good or service. For example, the costs of creating a PO, or paying an invoice, may seem trivial until you begin to ramp up your business and realize the manual efforts to reconcile your invoices are adding up. Other costs like maintenance, manufacturing, managing inventory, and the cost of missing service levels or revenue loss can all add up to drive your total cost of ownership. Depending on the product that you're buying, the vendor, and process you have for buying, these can become significant factors in the total cost. TCO forces you to ask questions like:

- » Can processes and procedures be improved that will help reduce these costs?
- » Have we over-engineered our products beyond what the customer is asking for?
- » What service levels are we demanding from our vendors that are driving up prices with little additional value?
- » What service levels are we not insisting on that could deliver structural cost reductions?
- » What are the return policies?
- » Cost of warranties?
- » To name a few...

The more specification and design built into the unit, the higher the costs and the more complex your SKU portfolio. The ability to standardize can generate huge savings as vendors are able to pass on efficiency gains or volume discounts. Although in many instances, there isn't much latitude to move these, for all the right reasons, you'll be amazed to discover how many products are over-engineered once you begin to question your initial assumptions.

For one utility client, we were able to engage the distributor of maintenance and repair operations (MRO) parts to make recommendations on how they would standardize the items purchased. After a few weeks of analysis, their vendors returned with a list of recommendations that would have saved anywhere from 10%-30% of the costs for managing the parts in question.

If your company is slated to purchase a fleet of vehicles, it is prudent to investigate various classes of cars and have a good understanding of how long they will last and what types of maintenance required over the life of that vehicle. Fuel efficiency is also a big-ticket item that must be considered. Fuel may be 40%-50% of the total spend over the life of the car. More recently the rise of electric vehicles has added not only to the cost considerations, but a marketing component to this purchasing decision. Tax credits often sweeten the pot, as do the impressions made in the minds of customers—both existing and potential—on the messages sent to them as your employees drive around town. Customer perceptions of your product and service may increase when you associate your company with environmental stewardship. All of these considerations could drive value to your business well beyond the unit price of the car itself.

For one retail client, we reviewed the cost of several types of equipment and tools in their stores. The objective was to find the best price for each of the product families. In researching compactors, we could have just gone by price. However, we delved deeper into understanding of the expected life and maintenance costs over the life of the compactor. We even researched ways to reduce the amount of cardboard system-wide, lowering the volume going through the compactor, and adding that much more life to that piece of equipment.

All of these are TCO considerations that need to be asked as you build your sourcing strategies. I recommend looking for areas of complexity in your business and those areas where your business is experiencing pain points. These offer great opportunities for process improvement, product or service standardization, and rationalization. Hold the business lines accountable for developing specifications that the customer actually wants and is willing to pay for. Do not allow canned responses from employees, like "It's what the customer wants," without actually testing whether the customer even knows the requirements exist, let alone whether they are willing to pay. If it doesn't impact the customer experience, or if they aren't willing to invest in the additional value you are putting into your product or service, then these specifications need to be eliminated.

A well-executed sourcing event will review TCO at the beginning of the process, creating a strong baseline and allowing you to explore opportunities for savings that would otherwise have been missed.

▍ THE IMPORTANCE OF A WELL-DEFINED PROCUREMENT STRATEGY

One way top-performing manufacturers stay on top is by focusing relentlessly on efficiency, whether that means constantly tweaking supply chains, implementing sweeping productivity initiatives, getting for growth and investing in differentiating capabilities, or looking for new ways to manage costs.

Retail & Consumer Insights, 2015 Financial Benchmarking

The financial benefits of an operationally excellent procurement department can provide strategic leverage for the company. Let's look at a back of the envelope calculation of the cash benefit of making incremental improvements in the TCO for goods and services purchased. If we were to take a look at a $1B company with an EBITDA of 20%, we'd arrive at $200M of cash flow. If you are able to impact the $800MM of conversion cost by a mere 5%, the resulting $40M is a 20% increase in EBITDA. Not only is that a huge figure, almost all of it is recurring. Do nothing this year, and you'll miss out on the $40M until next year.

But let's take it one step further. Assuming the market valuation of a small-to-medium-sized firm stands at five times its EBITDA, which isn't unreasonable, the total economic value of the $40M in savings is $200M. That's the cash generated if you were to sell a company at the new EBITDA levels.

Your company's particular situation will be different, but the math is the same. So I encourage you to put this simple calculation into a spreadsheet and begin to create your own assumptions. It will clearly reveal to you how small incremental changes in cost reductions (1%, 3%, 5%) can have profound impact on your total bottom line.

As a company grows, the ability to manage and control spend strategically, leveraging its purchasing power in the marketplace, becomes fundamentally imperative in order for it to compete effectively.

THE CHALLENGES

There are many challenges that a small-to-medium-sized company faces as they build a high- performing Procurement Organization, much of which is driven by internal factors that can reach deep rooted sensitivities. But there are external factors as well, such as customer demand and the behavior of vendors within your walls.

CULTURE

One of the things I've most enjoyed about working with small-to-medium-sized companies is their entrepreneurial spirit. Many employees are committed professionals with a passion for their work. There's a large sense of camaraderie that makes it a fun place to work. They are often given broad leeway to run their divisions as they deem best for their P&Ls, as would seem befitting a small organization who has no room for a bureaucracy. They are trusted to ensure that they buy the goods and services that best meet their needs and the needs of their customers, and rightfully so.

However, what is often overlooked is how growth can offer opportunities that cut across divisional or functional silos, which go unseen without a common view of the business. The purchasing of goods and services is one activity that can benefit tremendously from creating a common view across the organization through the implementation of a Procurement Organization. Initially, this may cause backlash from department leaders as the perception of losing control can occur.

It's also important to consider which activities are best suited by a procurement professional. These include, but are not limited to, the development of the sourcing strategy, spend analytics, communications with vendors and leading negotiations. Key stakeholders still define the requirements for the products and services they use, when they need their products, how fast they expect an order to be filled, at what fill rates they want/need, and other service levels. Also, as an integral part of the sourcing team, they have an influence in the final outcome of any sourcing event. It's important to reassure employees that they still have control of the requirements and services levels that impact their business.

According to researchers at the Center for Applied Purchasing Studies, "Participants in the CAPS Research Critical Issue Event identified five basic drivers behind the creation of the [shared] services center:

» Affordability—the opportunity to lower the cost of providing procurement services

» Commonalities—the opportunity to capitalize on common processes, policies and procedures

» Aggregation—the opportunity to aggregate spend

» Consistency—the opportunity to consistently manage suppliers that support multiple programs

» Efficiency—the opportunity to reduce the number of buyer-supplier relationships that must be managed and to put greater focus on each relationship."

The benefits of crossing silos can be felt immediately. Inevitably, you'll find opportunities to consolidate spend, as well as opportunities to price benchmark within your company and take advantage of pricing discrepancies, right away. You will also discover differing service levels and best practices, all before even putting out your portfolio to bid. Additionally, there's one other benefit that stakeholders in particular tend to forget: they can now put more focus on what really matters within their own business. This is very important to keep in mind.

According to Nancy Dearman, CEO and John Kotter, CIO at Kotter International, authors of "Leadership Tips for Cross-Silo Success," which appeared in *Forbes* online, "The very structure we have created to operate efficiently and effectively today gets in the way of what we need to do to innovate for tomorrow...[However], When your employees know 1) what needs to be done, 2) the right people who can help them do it, and 3) that they have permission to act in the company's best interest, they can help take full advantage of the opportunity facing the organization."

Pay close attention to, and plan for, the cultural sensitivities that a procurement transformation can trigger—and of the many benefits it will bring.

▌ COMPLEXITY

It is inevitable that as small businesses grow, so does the complexity of their operations. Product lines expand, new markets are entered, and capacity is stretched. Competitors also begin to take notice of your expansion. Further, customers may have unique requirements that require an ever increasingly complex supply chain strategy. Suddenly, those once simple tasks require a lot more attention, and the manual processes and offline tools that worked for you as a small business become increasingly strained, leading to longer lead times and greater fallout (mistakes and workarounds). All of these changes add variability into the process, which basically means that it's very difficult to produce your service or product, with the same level of quality and predictably. Although the final output may exceed your customer's expectations, the way in which you got there can take many different paths—and may be more costly if your procurement process had not been implemented.

The ability to meet demand and manage increasing complexity are not confined just to the core operations or service offerings, but also to all of the supporting business processes around it. Compounding this, as new lines of business are created, merged or acquired, each of these face their own set of issues.

So what does Procurement have to do with all of this? Actually, quite a bit. The complexity in your business can increase inefficiencies if they are not well managed, and these inefficiencies can drive your spend portfolio. For example, after an acquisition (or two), you may find yourself with multiple management workflows that do largely the same thing. Let's take an example: Perhaps your growth strategy lead you to buy the same products or product family from different vendors. One way to simplify your business is to reduce the number of vendors and standardize around fewer products. How do you do this without considering the operational efficiencies or cost per unit of all the vendors? Which one do you pick? What price will you pay for it? What are the performance metrics that you'd like the vendors to comply with? What types of discounts or rebates could be applied? How will you track those? As your operations and business process align, Procurement becomes a key capability to help you bring operational integration and provide a structured decision-making process—all of which could swing your bottom line in a favorable direction.

Additionally, participating in integrations is not the only way in which Procurement can support operational efficiencies. A spend and category analysis can often uncover process inefficiencies that must be addressed. For example, we recently guided a $3B electronics, appliance, and furniture retail client with over 1000 stores nationwide in the process of selecting third-party vendors to provide in-home repair services. Once a provider goes into a home and fixes an appliance with a new part, they must also try and submit a warranty claim with the original equipment manufacture (OEM). The problem was that there were approximately 300 small mom and pops that provided this service nationwide. Not all of them knew the process nor the unique warranty terms our client had negotiated with the OEMs, so there were many instances when our client absorbed the cost of the parts that should have otherwise been paid for by the OEM. Even though the client knew of this situation, and reported out the cost of this process breakdown to the P&L owners, nobody could come up with a solution to recoup those costs. That's where we stepped in. We discovered this process as we were touring one of their distribution facilities. Left alone, nothing would have changed and the company would have continued to lose money. We brought in stakeholders from finance, IT, retail operations, and the MRO group to redesign the process from end to end. During the solicitation process for third-party maintenance services, we included service level agreements to protect our client from paying for covered parts again. Providers were also educated on the new process, policies and procedures. This simple change was worth nearly $1MM, in addition to the savings for the unit cost of maintenance services.

Remember, complexity isn't all bad and some times it's why you are in the business you are in. But it's impossible to divorce Procurement from Operations Improvement particularly in a complexity driven industry. Though they can be managed differently, they ultimately must work together in order to maximize a company's strategic cost reductions efforts.

▌ COMPLIANCE

One of the trickiest issues a management team may have is the issue of compliance. And in the world of Procurement, this means buying off of a contract or master services agreement, or according to established policies and procedures (i.e. for P-Cards). There are several issues that make compliance a challenge:

» There may not be a contract or agreement to purchase from.

» If there is a contract, people may not know that it even exists.

» The process for buying off of a negotiated contract may be much more cumbersome than purchasing through some other vehicle. Peoples natural tendencies are to gravitate towards easier processes.

» The contract or agreement presents a greater price per unit than what others are finding as they go online, or from other sources. Travel is a classic example where you will find this behavior happening.

It's very common for most companies to have agreements with their direct suppliers—those that provide a product or service that is experienced by the customer (though it may not always be the case). However, with indirect categories—those products and services that a company needs to operate, but may not be directly experienced by the customer—there may be fewer and fewer contracts, and in some cases, none at all. This second scenario is very difficult to manage because it essentially allows buyers throughout the organization to select the vendors, possibly negotiate their own price, and make purchases. The downside of this is that the company has lost all purchasing power as common commodities are disaggregated across different vendors, at much lower volumes. The ability to aggregate your spend, and competitively bid out to a large group of vendors, is a classic opportunity for Procurement to add value to your company.

Once Procurement has properly negotiated a contract and gotten the best price available, buyers within your company need to know that it exists, and that they **must** purchase off of the contract. Otherwise, savings erosions occur. Think about the impact of a purchasing a product from an unauthorized source where you haven't negotiated a price or service levels. Likely, that vendor doesn't have a volume rebate that kicks in at a certain spend threshold; or doesn't have a return policy that would allow you to return products; or may not have a favorable warranty agreement, if anything at all. Just the cost of approving that payment, or paying that vendor manually versus through automated workflows can erode any price differential an employee might find elsewhere online. So it becomes increasingly important that vendor programs are communicated broadly and restrictions set on the ability to purchase outside of a negotiated agreement.

THE ROLE OF TECHNOLOGY IN COMPLIANCE

Technology helps you manage many different aspects in the procurement space, such as the buying process, the solicitation process, contract compliance (tremendously important for tracking levels of spend with a vendor and capturing service-level agreements in one place), as well as Sarbanes-Oxley compliance. It offers you the ability to quickly launch a Request for Proposal (RFP), reverse auction or request for quote, and manage the responses as they come in. For the nationwide retailer selling electronics, appliances and furniture, we had to manage the response from 300 third-party services companies. This would have been impossible to do without the use of technology, specifically an online solicitation tool.

But just as important as all of the functionality mentioned above, good technology will make it very easy for the organization to buy from a contract. Shopping is made easy and intuitive. The ability to allocate costs to budgets are automated. Purchase order creation and approval flows are streamlined so that the burden of making purchases are at their most minimal. All of these things help drive purchasing compliance.

Strong policies and procedures are excellent ways to control spend. For those that may already have one of the larger well-known ERP systems, such as Oracle or SAP, this is often a question of enabling the procurement/contracts module. However, there are several solutions that integrate very well with the big ERP systems and offer more functionality or flexibility, such as Ariba, Iasta, and Emptoris. Cloud-based solutions such as Coupa are able to do some very amazing things for the companies. So be open to the solution that best fits your strategy, and not the other way around.

Furthermore, in order to drive compliance, engage your leaders and hold them responsible for the proper execution of your strategy, processes, and procedures. Make sure that you have agreements with all of your strategic partners and providers. Build processes that are easy to follow, focused on what matters most, and let technology do a lot of the heavy lifting. If you are in the market for a technology solution to help control maverick spending, invest the time to envision your ideal best practice future state process, and use that to help build your requirements before making a final selection.

▌ CUSTOMERS

As you expand into new geographic markets, attract larger customers, introduce your products or services in different industries or different segments of existing markets, your ability to serve those customers becomes that much more critical and more difficult. Your Procurement strategy needs to grow with the changing demands of your customers. Top-tier Procurement Departments will have worked with executives in advance of customer acquisitions or marketing programs and be prepared to meet the new supply chain demands that growth brings.

High-performing Procurement departments must work with business owners to integrate customer's needs and offer alternatives that may be better priced or offer better terms. Having that feedback from the customer is a critical step in meeting and exceeding their expectations. Be proactive and ask your customer-facing teams about preferences, trends, and changing landscapes. Offer to talk about specific products that could help the customer. Speak to the customer directly and get their feedback, or survey them about what really matters to them.

▌ VENDORS

Probably the most significant competitive advantage a company can create, outside the value of its own products and services, are the strategic—and not so strategic—partnerships it builds with its vendor base. However, it's not always certain that vendors have your best interest in mind. They may well be happy to just meet your minimum requirements.

One of the things that I run into frequently, particularly with companies that don't have a well-established procurement strategy, is how embedded a vendor can become within an organization. I've seen vendors able to convince management that switching them out for a competitor would lead to catastrophic consequences that outweigh the risk/rewards of better pricing. Vendors many times fail to provide all of the information, particularly any options to mitigate risk, needed to holistically assess a renewed supply strategy. And companies often fail to ask the right questions.

However, vendors can also be your best friends. Good vendors jump through hoops in times of crisis. And if you ask, they can and often will, provide tactics for you to reduce your total spend.

In one solicitation for a $3B utility client where we were outsourcing their parts distribution, we asked the vendors to come up with strategies that would help the client improve their material management and reduce total spend. We had some very interesting responses, including ways in which to lean out the warehouse, remove slow moving products, move fast moving products to minimize travel time and motion, and rationalize SKU's. The effort accounted for 24% of the total savings above the unit price reduction, for a three-year period.

What's most important for a small-to-medium-sized company to keep in mind is that it's always a good idea to periodically test the market. It forces you to assess what you are buying and from whom, allowing you to consolidate spend and provide your vendors with the ability to gain even more business. It allows you to evaluate how you are buying, and it keeps you up to date on best practices, trends, and even innovative solutions you may have never thought of.

In short, the pressures on small-to-medium-sized businesses are unique. Leadership has to be innovative, flexible, responsive, and competitive in their decision-making. They have to offer the best products and services at the best prices, without having the purchasing power of their largest competitors. It's even more critical that they approach their procurement strategy with discipline, focus and urgency.

So now that you know all of this, what can a company with little purchasing power do?

▌ DEVELOPING A PROCUREMENT STRATEGY

Productivity is never an accident. It is always the result of a commitment to excellence, intelligent planning, and focused effort.

Paul J. Meyer, founder of Success Motivation International

There is a lot that the small-to-medium-sized business can do to structure and manage their spend optimally:

» Begin by defining your Procurement Strategy and understanding where your gaps are between where you are today, and where you need to be.

» Look to your corporate and business strategies to help you in designing your procurement strategy.

» Put time into thinking about what is the core value your business brings to your customers or industry.

» Ask the following big picture questions:

» Where do you need to be most competitive?

» What are the innovative products and services your customers are going to want in the coming years?

» What should you be doing in-house and what should you off-shore/nearshore?

» What are the strategic relationships that you need to have in place, what are the business relationships or tactical relationships?

The answers will help inform not only your procurement strategy, but also give you insight into your gaps. So if the idea is to be the lowest cost provider of a given product or service, then build your Operations and Procurement Strategy to do that. If it's to be the high-end quality provider, then ensure your Operations and Procurement Strategy are building relationships with elite vendors and that high-service levels are established. Every business strategy can be broken down into divisional strategies that support it, and Procurement is no different.

CENTRALIZATION

Centralizing core procurement functions will allow you to take advantage of your total spend portfolio. A centralized procurement function is critical to help get the end-to-end perspective that can drive out inefficiencies, strengthen your purchasing power, and drive implementation through the organization. There are several degrees of centralization, and there are some specific, category-level instances where local procurement can make more sense. But as a general rule, you would want Procurement to be responsible for the bulk of outside spend.

Expect resistance to this type of change, particularly from stakeholders whose own performance may well be impacted by the products purchased and vendor performance. They often perceive this as a loss of control, which is a difficult thing to do. Remind them that indeed they still do have control in very key aspects such as determining the specifications, requirements and service levels. Reassure stakeholders how critical their role is in getting the right products and services in the door, while reinforcing how Procurement helps drive the process, provides industry expertise, and can help test long held assumptions that unlock unknown value. This partnership is invaluable.

The procurement function also plays a key role in separating the emotions; after all, we are humans interacting with one another, above and beyond the numbers. Vendors and stakeholders can have very personal relationships that often extend outside work. What's really important to know is that Procurement can deliver the hard messages, do the analytical legwork, search and vet out vendors, provide unfavorable scorecards if need be, while the stakeholder focuses on what's right for the business.

Remember, the Procurement Strategy is critical to setting your direction in a way that brings the company that much closer to the corporate and business strategies.

MAKE IT A PRIORITY FOR ALL

Regardless of whether you are starting from scratch, restructuring an existing ineffective procurement organization, or boosting an already capable but underfunded procurement organization, you will need the support of all leadership. The business will be going through a transformation that touches on cultural sensitivities, changes policies and procedures, realigns roles and responsibilities, improves operations and business processes. Without a clear mandate it will be very difficult to be able to achieve the full benefits of what a high performing procurement organization can do.

█ BUILD A GREAT TEAM

For any service organization, the people are your products. Having a highly qualified team will be critical to the success or failure of your initiative. The Procurement organization will be measured and evaluated by the rest of the business based on the performance of your team. Building credibility early on helps the team establish themselves as the resident experts and lowers barriers and resistance from skeptical members of the organization. Credibility is built at every interaction, every phone call, conference call, or facilitated workshop. Recruit the best and brightest, with the emotional intelligence to withstand and overcome the barriers and roadblocks you can expect to encounter.

█ ASSESS

Conducting a spend assessment is a crucial step in streamlining procurement. Knowing what you buy, from whom, at what prices and terms, how you buy, and why you buy what you do, is a core capability of a procurement organization. Understanding is essential, and here are the three reasons why: Firstly and most importantly, you will base many of your most strategic decisions off of what you learn from your spend assessment. Secondly, it will help you develop your transformation roadmap, forcing you to prioritize and sequence your categories and, therefore, identify where to focus your scarce resources. Finally, it will help you take advantage of all of the operational and costs savings available to you.

If you do not have the infrastructure in place to quickly develop a spend analysis, then you'll have to invest the time and money to do so. But it will be well worth your investment. For smaller companies, this won't be such a daunting task, but the difficulty level does go up if you have a larger company with more divisions, or if you manage a portfolio of companies.

You'll want to begin with the general ledger where all of your spend data lies. If you have multiple companies that you are analyzing, then you'll need to centralize that data. You'll then want to remove any non-sourceable items like taxes, interest, and principle payments on debt, depreciation, and amortization. Basically, anything below the EBITDA line.

Once you've gathered all the data in one place, you'll want to categorize these items so that it's meaningful to you. The biggest challenge here is that the General Ledger (GL) may not have the level of detail that you may need. A lot of that depends on your taxonomy. Expect to spend time researching vendors, purchase orders, invoices and contracts so that you get a full appreciation for what is being purchased. Use the GL to help you focus your attention. Go to the biggest bucket first and work your way down. Or go where your strategic vendors are. Or, go where you think you will have the greatest opportunities. Spend assessments are crucial to improve your P&L.

Unfortunately, the worse your data is, the more time and money you will have to spend on getting it right. I've seen some very poor taxonomies for companies in the $1B-$3B range that require deep analytical support to get right. But again, it's very important to have good data at this point.

You'll also want to capture existing contract information and document key terms, such as when the contract ends, what the exit clauses are, renewal options, rebate structures, and the like. These will help you make some key decisions.

Speak with key stakeholders, and don't just focus on senior operations managers, but get speak with existing buyers and managers who can give you a deeper appreciation for the day-to-day experiences of working with a vendor, understand how you buy, lead times, and inventory strategies. The insights you glean from these discussions are invaluable.

As you are coming to the end of the spend assessment, you'll begin to get a sense of how your transformation is going to roll out. One of the most important factors that you'll garnish from the assessment, and probably most misunderstood, or disregarded is the sourcing strategy for which you are going to take a category through. There are many different ways to source your goods and services: RFP, RFQ, reverse auction, 3-bids and a buy, consortium, and direct negotiations are the most common that you'll run into. The method you choose can drive your return on investment. All too often I've seen companies over-engineer their sourcing strategy in favor of a more cost-effective approach.

A well-designed roadmap will tell you what categories to source, in what sequence, and how. There are some constraints that will naturally push categories into certain phases (or waves as commonly known in the industry), such as when a contract is up for renewal. Early on you'll want to take advantage of quick hits and those categories where you know there are tremendous savings to be had. For example, you might find that you are buying the same product in different divisions at two different prices. A simple call will likely help you attain a less expensive product and maybe even a rebate for past purchases. Moreover, you also have to consider where your larger more complex categories will fall. Much of this is about resource balancing, but it's also a lot about cash flow. Remember the EBITDA discussion at the beginning of this chapter.

As the procurement function begins to mature into a top performer, you will have established the infrastructure that allows you to conduct spend analysis with much less effort. Getting to data that is useful to help you with this plan is important to get right. So investing time and effort is money well spent.

▌ EXECUTE ON THE PLAN

Now that you've got your roadmap, you're ready to execute on the plan. Everything you've done to this point has been to lay the groundwork for a successful implementation. Some keys to success here are to make sure that you show some early wins, communicate often, keep the momentum going, be flexible and adaptable, and grow.

A good roadmap exercise will have laid out for you the opportunities that you have to address in the short-, medium-, and long-term. Be sure to consider the short-term gains because those will be the ones that you can point to early on the process to demonstrate the success of your program. Even if they are small wins, they are important wins that prove your hypotheses correct.

Communicate to the rest of the organization what you are doing and the success you are having. Your success will breed further success and provide important information to employees throughout the organization. It will help finally explain the things that you can do, the benefits that you can bring, the way in which you work with other organizations, and it will most importantly build credibility.

Additionally, transition quickly from the assessment phase into execution. You've already invested political capital, resources, and probably some money, with little to show for it (hence the importance of quick wins). So quickly set up your cross-functional teams and begin your sourcing processes. Gather your invoice level data, conduct your interviews, design your category-specific sourcing strategies, and drive home the savings.

CLOSING THOUGHTS

The only constant is change, continuing change, inevitable change, that is the dominant factor in society today. No sensible decision can be made any longer without taking into account not only the world as it is, but the world as it will be.

Isaac Asimov

Flexibility is key. As you get into your sourcing processes, details will emerge that may require you to be adaptable. What you thought could be a quick win may have a bigger payout if you increase the scope. What you thought you would have to put through a long drawn out RFP process can be quickly negotiated. Whatever the myriad of cases that could happen, your ability to be flexible will be important to getting your sourcing events over the finish line.

Always improve. No matter how many years I've been doing procurement transformation work, it ceases to amaze me the new techniques, technologies, products and services that emerge. Continue investing in your organization and the people in it. Push the envelope of what Procurement can do for the broader organization.

Last but not least, have some fun. There will be some very hard times, some low lows, and some high highs. Maintaining your perspective, sense of humor, and your focus will help you move through any challenges that will be thrown your way, so have some fun while you are at it.

Remember, every journey begins with the end in mind.

CARLOS S. SOARES

2897 N. Druid Hills Rd., Suite 283

Atlanta, GA 30345

CSoares@TheProkurGroup.com

www.TheProkurGroup.com

404-545-3359

Carlos Smith Soares is the Managing Director of The Prokür Group, with fifteen years experience helping senior executives design and implement sustainable transformation initiatives. Carlos has successfully integrated core principles of both the Procurement and Operations Excellence disciplines to develop a methodology that delivers above-market results for his clients in the manufacturing and service industries. He earned his B.S. in International Studies at Drexel University and an MBA at the University of Virginia's Darden Graduate Business School. He hikes and travels internationally when he can; however, he mostly treasures time playing with his kids and grilling for friends and family.

SELLING SUCCESS

AMY SIMATOS

When you hear the words 'sales' and 'selling', what comes to your mind? For many, thoughts such as "I can't sell", "I don't want to sell", "I have never been good at sales", or "Sales is full of rejection" pass through our mind. We may have an image of a pushy salesperson trying to convince us or pressure us into buying something or forcing us into a corner with no way out. It's no secret that the thought of selling for many of us brings up unwanted thoughts or emotions. It's almost as though the idea of sales is something many of us avoid.

But what if sales was fun? What would it be like if we had the right skills and processes in place in our business to be experts at selling? The good news is you have that opportunity. After having spent over 20 years in sales prior to becoming a sales trainer, I can tell you that in my experience that selling can be one of the most rewarding skills to learn personally, professionally, and financially. Yes, it can be fun, too!

As a sales trainer, a question I like to raise during my sales skills sessions to business owners and entrepreneurs is "how many of you are in sales?" As barely half of the room raises their hands and the other half looks at me like a deer in the headlights, I always say "if you are in any business, whether you are an employee, entrepreneur, business owner, professional, or consultant, you are in sales!"

So for those of you that started to look at the title of this chapter and/or started to glance and the pages and thought "I don't need to read this; I am not a salesperson", think again! Whether or not we are in a selling role or not, we are all selling every day. We are selling our ideas, vision, and strategies, whether internally to colleagues or externally to clients. We are always marketing our products or services.

After we think about what our opinions are about selling and what level of sales skills we have, the next thing to consider is the selling environment today. It's no secret that the way people and businesses make purchasing decisions today is not the same as it was a yesterday or years past. I often compare the way we buy today and the way we sell today as being similar to fashion or technology trends. In other words, what was 'in' yesterday is quickly 'outdated' today. There lies the risk and one of the key focuses of this chapter.

As a seller, we must adapt to the new buyer today. What we did yesterday is no longer effective today. Having spent over two decades in business-to-business including medical capital equipment sales, I can say the bigger challenge is that some sales organizations and 'selling styles' are not keeping up with the changing buyer. Fortunately, most organizations I represented were Fortune 50 and made the investment in sales training to keep the sales team up-to-date on sales methodology, which kept the sales force 'ready' for the new buyer of today.

As a sales trainer today, I often raised this question to my training audience: "How many of you came from an organization with a formal sales training process, or better yet, sales training program?" It was common to see about 2/3 of the room raise their hands. The remaining 1/3 are evidence that companies are not keeping up with sales methodologies. Could it be that we dislike the idea of selling because we never received the proper training? Or our business has no formal sales process in place? As an entrepreneur, we know we need to sell, but we just don't know how or where to start?

Another challenge we face when it comes to selling is that there is definitely more complexity in the process today than yesterday. The challenge this creates for you as an entrepreneur, or professional seller, is that your job just got much more difficult than it did yesterday, too. Amidst the buying trends that have changed, there are many other changes to consider as well. The economy, downsizing, and 'doing more with less' all add to the challenges you may face in selling your product, consulting, or service this year.

I still remember when I was new to healthcare sales. It seemed as though I could easily do a product demonstration, get the clinical staff and hospital nursing unit manager's acceptance, and then be directed to purchasing to pick up a purchase order. In other words, it was a quick, simple, easy, and often repeatable process in many of the hospitals and accounts I called on. I did not have to spend as much time, energy, and effort in closing the sale. But over the years, more people, more internal processes, additional sources of approvals, and let's just say 'red tape' came into play. What once seemed simple no longer is.

The process was very similar when I was in business-to-business sales, too. When I was selling payroll services to mid-size businesses, the process seemed fairly simple. The business manager could meet with me a couple times, I would ask questions on the first appointment, determine the right service for the business, and then I would bring in my proposal during the second appointment. I would handle objections, answer questions, and then get the agreement of the business owner to move forward with the proposal. Once again, the steps were often repeatable, and there was not much complexity in the process. In other words, it was rare I would encounter any roadblocks or issues before I made the sale.

Therefore, the purpose of this chapter is to educate you on the value of keeping up with the most current buyer behavior and selling trends to drive results in your business. I will also share the value of investing in sales training for yourself as well as your business. There is a return on investment it can provide to your business' bottom line as the solution to the challenges in the selling market. I will share the latest trends of why sales training brings a solid return on investment and demonstrate what has changed in the eyes of the buyer and strategies to overcome this through selling insight and improving the sales experience for the buyer.

The value to you is to understand how sales methodologies, buyer behavior, and selling strategy must be aligned today to succeed, whether you are an independent entrepreneur, business owner, or employee. The best way to stay current on sales trends, skills, and buyer behavior is to invest in sales training with a qualified sales trainer. This will impact sales, revenue, and the success of your business.

We will cover the following in this chapter:

- » How training is an investment in your business' growth and sales skills development
- » The latest trends in the way businesses buy today that will impact you/your sales team's performance
- » The top challenges that you will face this year as a sales leader and how to overcome them
- » The key drivers of customer loyalty: Four strategies to drive sales growth in your organization today
- » What you need to consider before you invest in a sales trainer consultant

HOW TRAINING IS AN INVESTMENT IN YOUR BUSINESS' GROWTH AND SALES SKILLS DEVELOPMENT

Companies that fail to invest in training jeopardize their own success and survival. Like many businesses, you may think that investing in training is costly and expensive. Training may not be at the top of your priority list. It may be something you have never considered investing in as a new business owner. I invite you to look at this in a new way: Sales training is a wise investment. In one study, it was revealed that businesses whom invest in sales and sales development training experience an increase in their profit margin by over 24% and sales by up to 6%. Businesses that invest in $1,500/per employee per year in training also have lower employee turnover, which is associated with higher customer satisfaction (according to *ASTD: American Society for Training and Development*).

In other words, investing in training and development drives better skills, knowledge, which in turn drives employee loyalty. Companies that fail to invest in employees jeopardize their own success and survival. In another study, IBM determined that a company loses 10-30% of its original capabilities each year. Within 3 years, companies lose 41% of their staff. It is clear that you must invest in sales training and employee skills development!

THE LATEST TRENDS IN THE WAY BUSINESSES BUY TODAY THAT WILL IMPACT YOUR/YOUR SALES TEAM'S PERFORMANCE

As I had mentioned earlier, the selling environment has changed dramatically over the years. There are many factors that have impacted the fact that the selling environment today is different than the selling environment of yesterday. Let's take a look at the top factors that have shifted in the buyer/seller environment. The following are the top factors that have changed in my experience of being in a selling role over the past 20-plus years, as well as some research that has been conducted to examine what has recently changed in the buyer/seller market:

The first trend is that the customer knows as much as the salesperson. Today people and businesses are doing more of their own homework about you, your product, or service well in advance of when they reach out to you. Information is everywhere: the internet, social media, newspapers, magazines, TV, colleagues, your competition, as well as information from others that may have done business with you in the past.

The challenge this creates is that the buyer can more easily make comparisons between you and the competition in advance of your first meeting. They may already have beliefs or judgments about you, thus reducing the opportunity for you to educate them at your initial meeting or contact. The beliefs that the buyer has about you or your business could be true/false, negative/positive, and correct/incorrect. I often saw this dynamic in my sales career. The toughest part of this was when a customer would reveal some misinformation that they had heard about my company, product, or service as to when I asked why I didn't win the sale.

The second trend in the buying environment to consider is that it takes more than one person to make the final purchasing decision. The days of getting a single person to "OK" a purchase are long gone. Today, people are not as willing to risk their political capital to say "YES" to you, your product, or your service without getting agreement from others in their group. According to the Corporate Executive Board (CEB), on average in complex sales, the number one item senior decision makers look for in making a purchase decision is support from their entire team before proceeding with a large purchase. This means that even if you win the approval of the key decision maker, they are not likely to move forward without first consulting with others within their business.

This can also put you at risk if you get opposition from any of the team members making the final decision, and they are able to dissuade your key decision maker from moving forward with your solution. I often saw this when I was selling. I would have the key decision maker ready to move forward with the purchase. Then, they would direct me to go meet with several others in the organization who were also important to them in the decision making process. This also could slow down or even stall the momentum of the sales process in many cases.

The third trend is that the buyer contacts the seller later in the purchasing process. We previously discussed that today, the buyer does more research on their own without you in advance of contacting you, the seller. In addition to this, the other dynamic that occurs is that this also delays the buyer contacting you for your expertise on your product or service. On average, the buyer is 57% complete with their internal purchasing process by the time they reach out to you, the vendor, according to the CEB. The buyer waiting to contact you later in their decision making process can put you at risk in the fact that the buyer may not be as open to changing the course they have already begun about the purchasing process. Also, we do not have visibility to what buying criteria or factors that the buyer has decided they are most interested in as they make their purchasing decision before we are involved. We may be left having little to no influence on their internal process.

I would sometimes see this happen when I was selling. The prospect would contact me and let me know they were looking at my product or service. Once I became engaged in the buying process, it became clear that the business had already determined their 'buying criteria list'. The list usually would include price. It could also include criteria that was specific to my competition, which also meant I was at risk as they had already gathered information about the competition and were leaning toward them. To me, that was always evidence that they had created a criteria list well in advance of contacting me, the seller.

The fourth consideration with regard to buying trends is the consolidation of businesses. Today, businesses are merging, being acquired by larger businesses, and with that comes restructure, uncertainty, and organization as well as process changes. I had seen evidence of this when I was in healthcare sales. Smaller hospitals were being acquired by larger hospitals and IDNs (Integrated Delivery Networks or hospital groups). With this dynamic, standardization of product, centralized purchasing decisions, and seeing a key decision maker or 'sponsor' you were working with can suddenly shift to a new role or leave the organization. Budget cuts and cost reduction focus can also be a result of mergers and acquisitions. Sometimes if the shift was to a larger business, they may have a pre-existing relationship with another business or supplier that may also be your competitor. In other words, it is almost as though you are locked out of the process due to their consolidation of businesses.

The last buying trend to consider is that your biggest competitor is not your competition, *it is inaction!* In the past, the biggest competitor was just that: the other vendor or supplier selling a product similar to you trying to get the same account that you are targeting. Today, the real competitor is inaction or lack of decision. Why is this occurring you may ask? As the complexity rises within the organization to make a purchasing decisions, based on all the factors I listed above, often there are times the complexity can lead to the buyer simply deciding 'no change is okay for now'. Not only is this a waste of time, resources, and energy for the buyer, you are now at risk as your product or service has been put on the back-burner. This inaction can be either temporary, indefinitely, or forever.

I often saw this occur when I was in medical sales. The buying process would be moving along and things seemed to be proceeding well. Then, usually at the point where the key decision maker would need to gain others' approval in the organization to move forward, there would be a stall. This would then be followed by the decision maker becoming silent and non-communicative with me. Once the communication resumed, it was usually followed with "we just can't seem to come to agreement internally so we are going to put this on hold for now" with regard to their internal purchasing process.

THE TOP CHALLENGES THAT YOU WILL FACE THIS YEAR AS A SALES LEADER AND HOW TO OVERCOME THEM

If you are not prepared to handle the new buying trends we just reviewed, your business success could be at risk. In addition to the the selling environment being more complex, there several additional factors to consider when it comes to the sales success in your organization. As we review these additional challenges, I invite you to ask yourself: Am I prepared to handle these trends and changes? If you are not prepared, you can fail. Let's review these additional selling challenges and later, we will reveal how you can overcome them and succeed.

For those of you within a business with a dedicated sales leader and/ or sales team, you probably agree that it is common for the star sales performer to get promoted to be the Sales Manager or Sales Leader tomorrow. This is exciting as one of the best ways to recognize great performance is to promote someone, assign additional responsibility, and also to delegate more leadership and decision making power to the person. I have witnessed this many times when I was in front line sales. It was very common to see promotions from within the organization. The good news is the person moving from a sales representative to sales leader position already knows the product/service, the company's internal processes, and the internal politics much more than someone that could be hired from outside into a sales leadership role. Also, the personal has already established relationships with both internal and external customers, and there is a level of trust with the sales team that they will be leading.

As we just reviewed, front line sales managers were 'promoted' from sales representative positions. On the surface, this sounds like a great opportunity. There are challenges that the new sales leader who was just promoted into the position will face. First of all, they typically do not receive the leadership training required to lead a team. I frequently witnessed this dynamic within organizations I was working in. The 'once sales representative, now sales leader' has an entirely new responsibility on their plate-leading others. Many times, they are not equipped with the right skill sets to be an effective people or team leader. Some can adapt and learn as they go along. However, others never can achieve the leadership skills they need on the job to be effective as a sales team leader.

I once had a sales manager who was promoted to be my sales' team director. His style was more similar to a tyrant than an inspirational leader. It was clear he lacked conflict/resolution skills and was often coming across too strong and aggressive to the sales team. He lacked emotional intelligence and the encouragement skills of coaching others towards success. In less than a year, the sales leadership team became aware of his lack of team leadership skills, as well as the fact that his style was not inspiring sales results and performance. He was later eliminated from his position.

The area the most often overlooked by sales managers is 'coaching' their team toward results, as I just described in my personal experience. There is the dynamic of tactical 'deal' coaching, in which the sales leader is mostly fact-finding about who the decision maker is, what the $ value of the deal is, when will it close, etc. I often think of this as transactional coaching. Yes, I know that as a sales representative, it is critical that we hold ourselves accountable for results. But, it takes more than solely focusing on the numbers to be successful. It takes strategic thinking. What is often lacking is how to coach the sales rep toward success in the deal, or, in other words, the development of critical thinking.

When it comes to selling any product or service, I think we can all agree there needs to be a strategy in place. When I was in medical sales, for instance, the average sales cycle could be anywhere from six months to three years in length, involving millions of dollars and many decision makers. I know there are some sales leaders who only focus on 'tactical' coaching and others, very few, focus on 'strategy' coaching. Out of the four sales leaders I worked for in medical sales, only one of them truly coached me on 'critical thinking and deal strategy'. I would suggest that there is definitely a gap here.

Why is coaching for results between the sales leaders and sales representative so important? Typical turnover in a sales organization is caused by breakdowns in communication between sales reps and sales management. I have seen this for myself. Most of the times when I left a sales position, it was because of a lack of relationship or poor relationship with my sales manager. I often ask others that leave a sales position why they are leaving, and they all too often cite there is a breakdown between them and their sales manager. The sales representative has not been coached for success. They have been coached on tactical deal components, which all too often also can be interpreted as 'micro-management'. I once had a sales director that would consistently ask me the same questions about the same sales opportunity, "when is it coming in...can you bring it in any sooner?" or "how much is it worth?" I do agree we must all focus on the results in selling. I think it is often overlooked that some effective strategic coaching can go a long way in helping sales representatives be more successful, and then, they can teach this to their future sales team.

There is a cost to your business when you lose sales talent. On average, sales organizations invest over $30,000 to hire and bring on-board a new sales team member. The cost comes in the form of new hire training, administrative fees, and the fact that it may take time to ramp up sales production for the new hire. This doesn't take into consideration the amount of time that you as a sales leader invest in teaching and spending time with the sales new hire, helping them to get up to speed on the product or service they are going to be selling. As it has been said, time is money.

In my sales training role, I have seen another impact that is detrimental to losing a sales representative on your team. You will often need to play double-duty by continuing your role as a sales or business leader and also you will be given the added duty of covering the now open territory that the sales representative who just left was covering. Managing an open territory in addition to your daily leadership duties is not only challenging, it can put the territory at risk. If you are not in the territory consistently and managing the accounts, the competition will have an easier time penetrating the accounts. I recall this happening time and time again in my years of experience. Territories can be open for a long time and customers can become frustrated if they are not getting the attention and focus that they did when the sales representative was in the territory.

Are you prepared to handle these challenges? If you are, that is great! If you are not, there could be an opportunity for you to invest in not only effective sales training for your team but a leadership development training program for you sales team and future sales team leaders. This training should include coaching skills, effective sales strategy, sales process, and a component on emotional intelligence, or crucial conversations. The training should not be a one-time event. To be effective, the training should be ongoing. It should also have to touch points during the new hire and early coaching process, additional training for the later tenured sales representative, and then future leadership skills development.

Another concept that worked great in my medical sales career was the concept of 'Field Sales Trainers'. This is a great opportunity for your rising star and future sales leadership to have an opportunity to mentor a new sales team member. Not only does this give them leadership experience, it is giving you an opportunity to build you future sales leadership bench. This can also give your field sales team experience in development of the sales coaching skills that are often lacking in new front line sales managers. In other words, it can give the field sales representative a taste of what sales management is like. Also, it can take some burden off of the sales manager to have a field trainer also help with training the new hire.

Overall, I can say having been a field sales trainer myself that not only was it rewarding for me personally and professionally, it was a great way for me to reinforce the good selling and business habits I had developed by teaching the concepts to someone else. It also gave me recognition and visibility within the organization. I have never met a sales representative that was not hungry for recognition! Businesses today that invest in field sales trainers and sales & personal/leadership development skills will not only retain talent, but they will have an edge on the competition.

KEY DRIVERS OF CUSTOMER LOYALTY: FOUR STRATEGIES TO DRIVE SALES GROWTH IN YOUR ORGANIZATION TODAY

When it comes to being successful in selling your product or service, what do you think really drives customer loyalty? What is your sales force selling toward? Company and brand impact? Product and service delivery? Cost? Sales experience? What really drives customer loyalty may surprise you...

Over the years, what drives customer loyalty has changed significantly ("The Challenger Sale," Adamson/Dixon):

1. Sales experience (53%)

2. Product and service delivery (19%)

3. Company and brand impact (19%)

4. Cost [value to price ratio] (9%)

I know if any of you are like the way I was in selling, I always thought the most important focus for the customer was the price! I discovered over much time and experience that I was wrong! It is the Sales Experience that the customer sees as the biggest driver in doing business with you. Yes, product and service delivery along with your company brand impact are important, but these factors may not be as important as you think. Price is the least important consideration for the customer.

Let's focus on the first sales strategy, the importance of the buyer "Sales Experience." What exactly does this mean? As an example in my sales training sessions, I often ask the participants to share an example of a great sales experience they were involved in as the buyer, as well as a horrible sales experience they were involved in as a buyer. On the positive side, many will comment that when they made a large purchase, (e.g. - a car, house, major appliance) they thought the sales representative was a 'consultant', looking out for their best interest. The sales representative was not as focused on making a sale and knew the competition and industry to the point that it was impressive.

On the negative sales experience comparison, one example I have often heard is the 'vacation home, time share' sales experience (I don't mean to offend anyone reading this that sells time shares, but maybe this is a concept to consider). The participants commented that they were told it was "an opportunity to win a free vacation if they attended a brief session." What happened was quite different and they were often mislead in the sales experience. The participants commented that they felt like they had been held hostage for over an hour and were tricked into attending the session. They had thought it was an opportunity to win a vacation, but instead it was a one-hour vacation home purchase sales pitch. The environment was tense to the point they were frowned upon if they left the presentation. That is what we mean by a comparison between a positive and a negative sales experience.

How will you train your sales team to be more effective in the 'right' areas to drive customer loyalty and satisfaction? Is your salesforce driving the right sales experience for your prospects and customers today? Hiring a sales trainer consultant that can educate your team on driving a top 'sales experience' is critical. What do we mean by 'sales experience'? According to the CEB, it means the following: Offer unique, valuable perspectives on the market; Help the customer navigate alternatives; Help the customer avoid potential landmines; Educate the customer on new issues and outcomes.

The next strategy for sales growth is "don't ask, teach!" Today, one of the biggest shifts in sales methodology is to teach your customers something they do not know about their business. In the past, certain sales methodologies focused on 'asking' many fact finding questions, in other words, SPIN selling (Rackham). I don't want to imply that asking questions in not important: this is very important during the discovery and needs analysis phase of the sales cycle. What really resonates today is that customers' expectations are that you will be a consultant and help them identify the blind spot that they are not seeing in their business that could cost them future pain and money. You are there to help them set the buying criteria versus them setting the buying criteria themselves, which can be focused on price, your competition, etc. as we discussed earlier. Remember that your prospects are doing more fact finding on their own before they contact you!

Also, the way that they are going about making the purchasing decision may be based on criteria that is irrelevant and could actually lead them to make a bad decision long term. This is outlined in my book *"From Zero to Sales Hero: How to Double Your Sales and Income in 90 Days"*. I know that teaching is critical because when I did that in my medical sales career, it compelled the key decision makers to take action.

I once had a hospital I called on reveal to me that the reason they were going to purchase from me was because they had some funds available to spend. The funds were $25,000. After I did more discovery in the account, I identified that the hospital was out of regulatory compliance on some new medical safety standards with some of the devices they were using. I also revealed to them that there were risks in patient care if they continued to do what they were doing. The 'teaching' compelled the customer to take action, as I had revealed something they didn't know about their business. The result was a $500,000 purchase order and a sale that was closed in 21 days. Teaching will not only increase your success, it can increase your sales value and shorten your sales cycle, as I experienced in this example!

The next sales strategy to drive results this year is to follow the process. In my over 20 years of selling everything from telecom, business-to-business and medical capital equipment sales, there was one consistent recipe for success: Follow the sales process! I expand on this in my aforementioned book *"From Zero to Sales Hero"*. Every company I ever worked for had a sales process. Typically, it begins with discovery, which includes finding out about the customers' business before the first appointment. From discovery, it is targeting-prioritizing where/what accounts I will spend my time in. Once we identify the target, it is about needs analysis-finding; a 'Why' for the customer. Next, it is about finding the right decision maker or sponsor. Then finally, it is about presenting the solution, which includes helping the customer assess the solution (negotiations, internal assessment), confirmation of solution, and then commitment (closing).

There are many risks to not following the sales process. First of all, I think it is one of the many reasons the sales profession and reputation of selling has a bad rap. If we do not follow the sales process, we usually go in and lead with our product or service. In other words, we come to the prospective customer and begin to tell them everything they will ever need to know about what we are selling. Telling someone about your product or service before you have earned the right usually results in the prospect not inviting you back for a second meeting. Or if they do, you will have a tough time getting a commitment from them to purchase at the end of the process. This is all because you don't understand their business, there is no 'why' (buying reason for the customer), and you have not taught them anything new. This is how we lose sales and also how our sales opportunities can stall. Of all the steps of the sales process, discovery is the most important!

The final strategy to use is to remember, it's all about insights! Insights are everywhere. They are what inspire customers to take action. An insight can be something specific to an industry. It can also be something internal to a customer's business. It can be a new trend. Today, insights sell and they also give you the opportunity to be a consultant. I shared an example earlier of how I used an insight (safety regulations) to compel a certain hospital to take action by resolving their lack of device safety compliance through an insight I revealed to them.

Also as we discussed earlier, it is all about the sales experience. If you can create an experience where you are helping your customer to think outside the box, you are more often seen as a consultant instead of a pushy salesperson trying to make a sale. Insights are interesting, and they also are a reason you must stay current and up-to-date on the product or service industry you are representing. Our customers today expect us to know the industry as well as their own business better than they do!

WHAT YOU NEED TO CONSIDER BEFORE YOU INVEST IN A SALES TRAINER CONSULTANT

In summary, I have shared the value in making an investment in sales, leadership, and personal development skills for your business as well as your sales team. We have discussed how the buying and selling environment is constantly changing and also that what worked yesterday is no longer effective today when positioning our product or service. We also discussed the importance of keeping current on sales methodologies and how creating a world class sales experience is critical today. I have suggested the importance of investing in ongoing sales and skills training, not just a single training event. If you do not already have a full-time sales trainer on staff, there is value in outsourcing training and investing in the sales trainer consulting service.

Before you hire a sales training consultant, there are many questions you may have on your mind. Specifically, how can you set yourself up for success by investing in a sales trainer consultant? What questions to consider before you hire a sales training consultant? I put together a list of the most important questions to ask before you invest in a sales training consultant or program from a third party:

» Experience: How much time has the sales training consultant spent in the sales and training industries?

» Sales Methodology: How current is the sales methodology that the sales training consultant will train your salesforce on?

» Industry Experience: What types of industries has the sales training consultant had experience in (e.g. - business, consumer, product, service, and complex sales process)?

» Sales Process Knowledge: What knowledge does the sales training consultant have of sales process?

» Customization: Will the sales training consultant customize a program for my business needs or take a 'one size fits all' approach?

In closing, I would like to leave you with one final thought: There are many training companies, consultants, programs, theories, sales methods, books, and ideas you can invest in when looking to improve your salesforce performance. It can be overwhelming when you consider all of the options available to you today. How can you ensure that you will get a solid return on investment on whichever sales training consultant you make as your final selection? We can help you determine which path is best for you to drive top sales results for yourself or your business!

Amy Simatos

AIM Training and Consulting, Inc.

"Fortune 50 Sales Training Without the Fortune 50 Price Tag"

www.aimwithamy.com

www.fromzerotosaleshero.com

amy@aimwithamy.com

847-630-2334

Amy began her journey as a Sales Trainer, Keynote Speaker, and Business Consultant over 25 years ago. Amy is a master at public speaking, a member of Toastmasters for almost a decade. She is a Distinguished Toastmaster Award Honor (DTM, achieved by 3% of Toastmasters). Amy has also presented at the Toastmasters Leadership Institute and District Conferences, 2008-Present and served as an Ambassador for Area 1, Chicago District 30 Toastmasters. She has over 2 decades of experience in business and healthcare capital sales and has been recognized as a fortune 500 top sales performer and international sales trainer. She has trained hundreds of entrepreneurs, sales professionals, and teams on sales skills, public speaking, presentation skills, sales process, and negotiation skills. Amy's business, AIM "Action-Inspire-Motivate: Fortune 50 Sales Training without the Fortune 50 Price Tag," Training and Consulting, offers sales training, business consulting, and program facilitation. She recently became an Amazon #1 Best Selling Author with her book: "From Zero to Sales Hero: How to Double Your Sales and Income in 90 Days."

COMPANY CULTURE – THE UNDERAPPRECIATED ELEMENT OF HIGH PERFORMANCE

A.J. TOZZI

Businesses are constantly engaged in the struggle to beat the competition and win in the market place. With competitors and customers coming from across the globe, at no point in history has this challenge become more difficult. To thrive in this super-competitive environment, many companies are turning to the implementation of continuous improvement programs. While there are many "systems" that are used as the foundation for these programs, the most popular today are Lean and Six Sigma. There is also the combined system of Lean Six Sigma.

These programs promise breakthrough levels of performance improvement by solving the process problems that create waste, quality problems, low productivity, poor cash flow and low profitability. With these kinds of promises, and the success stories that fill our business publications, the excitement to implement these programs is understandable. The sad truth, however, is that there are many more failed implementations than there are success stories when it comes to the results being produced by these programs.

In fact, the majority of my new clients contact me to come in to help them "fix" their failed implementation. As I begin the process of assessing the needs of a new client, I inevitably hear the same old stories about how much training they have received, how many kaizen events they have done, how many Six Sigma Black Belts they have, and how many projects they've completed. This is rapidly followed by a litany of excuses about why these programs have failed them and not produced the promised results.

So why do some companies seem to achieve outstanding results that propel their business to new heights while other companies seem to struggle and achieve very little, if any, substantive results? The principles and tools being implemented are the same. Why don't they yield the same results? The difference comes down to COMPANY CULTURE. It is the cultural aspects of how people are encouraged to become engaged and passionate about continuous improvement, or not, that actually determines whether the program will be successful.

Let's explore how to build a positive and enabling culture while avoiding the common pitfalls of negative cultures. Let's also explore how to integrate these cultural aspects into your continuous improvement initiatives.

THE FIRST BIG MISTAKES

Continuous improvement programs get started in many different ways. Sometimes they are commissioned from the executive level, driven by the pressure to improve performance. Sometimes the need for an improvement program is identified by the middle management team and is "sold" upward to the executive level.

In either case, often the first course of action is that the executive leader(s) "delegates" the implementation to a middle manager, usually to the Operations or Quality Manager. This action generates the first two common mistakes.

The first problem with this action is the failure to recognize that achieving performance improvement requires the engagement of the **ENTIRE** enterprise, not just the Operations or Quality functions. Value to the customer is created *horizontally* through all the functions of a business. It is not limited to operations and quality. By delegating the program to this limited scope of the company, the executive has just sent the message, perhaps unintentionally, that the performance improvement required is limited to the operations and quality teams and the rest of the business need not participate.

The second problem with this action is that the executive leader(s) don't just delegate the program, they actually abdicate and absolve themselves of any responsibility in its implementation by failing to personally engage in the process, believing that this is a level of detail in which they need not participate.

We will revisit these decisions and outcomes later. But for now, let's look at the next steps in the typical implementation.

▍THE TYPICAL IMPLEMENTATION

The typical continuous program finds its roots in Lean or Six Sigma (or some other similar discipline). These systems usually are focused on improving the delivery of products and/or services to the customer. This is where many companies start (and end) their implementation. Many times these efforts involve significant amounts of training in the principles and tools employed by the selected program with an aim to create "subject matter experts" (Green Belts, Black Belts and Master Black Belts) to lead the effort.

Then employees are trained in the foundational principles and tools. With Lean, for example, employees are trained to identify and eliminate waste in their processes. They are trained in the principles of process flow, 5S, and standard work (for starters). Six Sigma has its similar set of foundational training that practitioners need to go through before the improvement efforts get underway. This training includes the fundamental structured problem solving process as well as varying levels of training in the statistical tools needed to employ the Six Sigma system.

Then, as the opportunities for improvement are identified and the improvement projects are launched, process changes are identified, teams are formed, and process changes are executed. This is where the fun starts!

Improving the results of any process requires that the process be changed. We've all heard the definition of insanity, "doing things the same way and expecting a different result". So, in order to improve performance, the process must be changed. When processes are changed, obviously, this changes what the **PEOPLE** in process must do to perform their work.

Changing what people actually do and how they perform their jobs is not as simple as implementing the technical aspects of what seems to "make sense" based on the principles and tools defined by the improvement system. The changes require the people to believe that the changes will work and will improve their lives AND then the people must actually modify their behavior, AND these behavior changes must be supported throughout all levels of the organization. All of this must take place before any changes can be successfully implemented and sustained.

Now we find ourselves squarely in the realm of human behavior modification, something that is not addressed in all the lean or six sigma training that the experts received. Since this area is not normally part of the preparation for the implementation, it is generally ignored, and the process improvements end up being forced upon the people that need to perform the work. This almost always results in failure, even if the process change was the right thing to do!

Figure I
Lean Impact Group Business
Transformation System™

WHY SUCCESSFUL COMPANIES ACHIEVE BETTER RESULTS

Successful people and companies leave clues to their success. Having participated in and led hundreds of implementations, some successful and some failures, I have observed that there are 4 key factors that determine the level of success a company will achieve.

1. **Vision, Goals & Strategy** - establishing a clear vision and direction, and having a robust process for communicating, focusing & executing the strategy

2. **Winning Team** – attracting and retaining the best people, and ensuring that all employees are in the right roles

3. **Positive Culture** – policies, procedures and behavioral norms that define and govern how things get done

4. **Creating Value** – driving customer satisfaction by being the best at delivering products & services

These 4 Factors have become the foundation for the business transformation system that I use with my clients (See Figure I – The Lean Impact Group Business Transformation System). Successful companies have learned to focus on improving and achieving balance across all four of these factors as they seek to transform their business results. The less successful companies fail to understand the interrelationship of these four key areas of focus and fail to achieve successful balance across these areas. What's worse is, they tend to focus only on implementing tools rather than taking a cross functional and systematic approach to improving their performance.

Furthermore, successful companies recognize that they need to undergo a *transformation* and not just implement a set of tools. Transformation is so much more than a "Continuous Improvement" program. Transformation is not about just changing a few processes. Transformation means changing nearly **EVERYTHING** so that the enterprise becomes something completely different in terms of how they behave and operate as a company. They become completely different in how they behave in the market place. They become completely different in how they attract and retain the best customers, the best suppliers, and the best and most talented people. Ultimately, they become completely different in their level of performance.

It is this balanced approach across all 4 Key Factors that delivers the outstanding results. Since the principles and tools (lean six sigma tools) are the same in both the successful and the unsuccessful implementation, the difference must lie in a combination of the other three areas. In my experience, the most critical of the three is the cultural aspect.

DEFINING COMPANY CULTURE

So when we talk about company culture, what exactly does that mean? More importantly, how does a company's culture effect the ability of the business to achieve high levels of performance?

Webster's dictionary offers two definitions of the word "culture" that fit here; 1) all the knowledge and values shared by a society, and 2) the attitudes and behavior that are characteristic of a particular social group or organization.

With those definitions in mind, I would suggest that company culture is the formal and informal set of rules, policies, procedures, values, beliefs and behavioral norms, that determine and govern how people behave, how decisions are made, how problems are solved, how priorities are set, how people communicate and how work gets done every day.

As we have discussed, performance improvement is dependent upon making changes to all aspects of how work gets done, how problems are solved, etc. Therefore, the act of making any changes in the organization will run squarely up against the backdrop of the cultural norms that currently exist.

IDENTIFYING THE CULTURE

Now that we know what company culture means, how do we determine what the culture is within a company? I use a "6 Question Culture Quiz™" as part of my process for working with clients to improve culture and performance.

The 6 Question Culture Quiz™

1. **What are the "Rules"?**

2. **Is There a Practice of Blaming?**

3. **What Results Are Rewarded?**

4. **What Does Communication Feel Like?**

5. ***Are There Any Sacred Cows?***

6. ***What is the Tolerance for Risk and Learning?***

Underlying each of the six questions is the constant theme to identify the behaviors and values that are displayed and communicated in each of these six key areas. I have found that these answers and behaviors speak directly to the core of the culture within a company. These answers and behaviors will also determine the level of performance the company can achieve. They will set the boundaries and limitations for growth, profitability and competitiveness in the market place. Ultimately, they will determine the level of success that is possible for the company. Let's explore each of these 6 Questions more deeply and look at the effects they have on the behaviors within the organization. As we will see later, the behaviors within the organization will have a direct impact on company performance.

QUESTION 1 – WHAT ARE THE "RULES"?

It is important to identify the basic set of common "rules and expectations" that have become established practice within the organization. Rules and expectations help to define the basic boundaries and guidelines for how and when things get done as well as how people communicate and behave. It is important to identify both the "written" and the "unwritten" rules and expectations. Then it is necessary to observe the behaviors that occur when the rules are broken, ignored, or adhered to closely. The system of reward or punishment will then begin to present itself.

For example, let's say that there is a "rule", or a policy stated in the company handbook concerning tardiness, being on time for work each day. Let's also say that there is a prevalent behavior in the organization for people to be late for work and this behavior is not addressed in accordance with the handbook. Clearly, since this rule is ignored, it actually ceases to be a rule. Furthermore, the leadership within the organization is sending a very clear message to the employees that "being on time to work is not important to us". This sets up the dynamic where each individual employee will create their own rule which creates inconsistency in the organization. Inconsistencies like this always result in feelings of animosity, frustration, resentment, and anger within the organization.

By contrast, let's say that there is an expectation for the "Daily Sales Report" to be printed and distributed every day by 9:00 am. If you observe that people are punished (yelled at, demeaned, "written up", etc.) or if there is a verbalized fear of punishment for not delivering the report on time, then this is a rule or expectation (perhaps unwritten) that has been identified as extremely important. However, "getting yelled at" sends the message "make sure you never make a mistake again, I don't care what your reasons were for not meeting the expectation, just do what I tell you to do, and make sure you never let that happen again". This not only sets up an atmosphere of fear surrounding the specific rule in question but it also will project this fear to other "rules and expectations" within the organization. This fear also can create a paralyzing effect where people will become blind followers of rules at the exclusion of using their creativity to find improvement opportunities.

Clearly, the above are simplistic examples of rules, both written and unwritten. It is important to "unearth" the rules by observing the demonstrated behaviors that define how work gets done and which work gets done. Then, it is important to observe whether or not the associated behaviors are positive and supportive or negative in nature, in other words are the behaviors rewarded, punished or ignored?

▌ QUESTION 2 – IS THERE A PRACTICE OF BLAMING?

In this area, I look to see what the responses are when something goes wrong, someone makes a mistake, an opportunity is missed, a deadline is missed, a key performance metric is off track, etc. I look to see if the response in the organization is to place blame. Do they blame specific people, departments, or the ever present "they"? I also look to see how prevalent this practice is. Is it often the first response, is it wide-spread or is it limited to certain departments or groups?

When there is a prevalence of blaming in an organization, there is also a tendency for "shaming" people within the organization. I have seen the placing of blame and shame done very openly as well as quietly, behind closed doors or in the classic "water cooler meeting". In any of these cases, if placing blame is prevalent, clearly the behavior of blaming is rewarded, condoned and, therefore, it becomes the accepted practice.

When people are blamed and shamed, especially when it is done openly, people feel demeaned, unappreciated, unsupported, and often will begin to question their own competency and lose confidence in their ability to contribute positively to the organization. This also creates an atmosphere of fear. People will now retreat into a space of self-protection and self-preservation and will use blaming and shaming as a mechanism to protect themselves, further proliferating the practice and limiting creativity and innovation.

Blaming, the act of deflecting accountability somewhere else, results in people failing to take responsibility and accountability. When there is a lack of accountability, people fail to learn and grow, both personally and professionally. This is because the root causes of problems or issues are rarely recognized and addressed. Lack of accountability also results in missed deadlines, tasks that are forgotten and go uncompleted, and goals and objectives become meaningless. All of this leads to poor performance.

Another critical issue is the effect that all of these behaviors have on the high performing people in the company. High performers thrive on accountability, challenging the status quo, and meeting deadlines. Since their key motivational factors are not supported by the culture, they will have a tendency leave and go elsewhere, limiting the company's ability to attract and retain the best people.

On the opposite end of the spectrum, if blaming is not present, what behaviors take its place? Usually I find that companies where blaming is not common, there tends to be a focus on what went wrong with the process, the policy, the procedure, the information flow, etc. Problems are treated as opportunities to learn and improve, unlocking the creativity of the employees and creating a sense of accountability. This type of atmosphere breeds collaboration and mutual support. When something does go wrong, the organization rallies together and supports each other in solving the problem.

QUESTION 3 - WHAT RESULTS ARE REWARDED?

Remember the old adage "what gets measured, gets done"? I look for which results are rewarded. This is the work, the tasks, the results, and the performance metrics that actually get talked about, supported and funded within the organization. I look for how and where people are spending their resources. If time and money are put into certain activities, then you know that these are the results that are important.

I then look to see if there any disconnects between what is said to be important and what is actually rewarded. Where there are disconnects, there will also be confusion, error, mistrust, and dysfunction.

For example, let's say that there is a strategic objective to penetrate and drive top line sales in two new market segments and that this objective supports the overall sales objectives for the company. As these strategies are deployed and implemented, suppose that the overall top line sales numbers are consistently on target but the mix of that revenue is off track with respect to the penetration into the two new market segments. If the result of this situation is celebration of hitting the overall sales targets and missing the sales targets for the two new market segments are never discussed, what is the message that Sales Team hears? Right, the two new markets are not important, what is important is hitting the monthly total revenue target. So, what do you think the resulting behavior will be? Right again, the Sales Team will take the path of least resistance for achieving the overall revenue target and disregard the strategic objective to penetrate the two new markets.

There is a clear disconnect between the strategic objective and what is rewarded. This not only puts the strategic plan for the company in jeopardy, but it also sends conflicting messages and creates confusion in the organization. Engineering, for example, might be heavily engaged in developing new products to launch into the new market segments. But if the Sales Team isn't working to develop new customers to use these new products, all this work is wasted. Not only will this result in resentment, criticism, and animosity between Engineering and Sales, but Engineering will also be resentful of upper management for not staying true to the direction that was given. This also creates significant trust issues within the organization.

Sometimes I find cultures where results and performance are secondary. I call this the "country club culture". In the country club culture, as long as fun is being had, stress is low and the company is not losing money, then all is well. In this type of culture, the mere thought of even measuring performance let alone working to improve it could be exceedingly uncomfortable. Even when the business leader has identified and communicated the need to affect change and improve performance, overcoming the ultra-laid back cultural norms will be a challenge!!

▌ QUESTION 4 - WHAT DOES THE COMMUNICATION FEEL LIKE?

How "open" or "guarded" is the level of communication within the organization? What is the response to constructive criticism, challenging the status quo, discussing problems openly, or providing feedback? Are these behaviors rewarded or punished? What is the nature of the reward or the punishment? Do these behaviors even exist or are they totally absent?

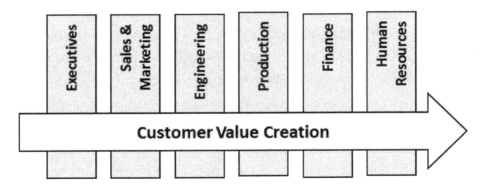

Figure II
Enterprise Value Creation

I not only look for clues in meetings and during the course of normal work but I also look for what happens behind the scenes, behind closed doors, or in the "just between you and me" discussions that take place.

To understand the effects of poor communication in an organization, we first must recognize that Value to the Customer is created **horizontally** through the organization. However, most companies are structured **vertically** by function (See Figure II – Enterprise Value Creation).

If the behaviors of constructive criticism, open discussion of problems, and challenging the status quo are discouraged or punished, the message being received by the employees is "mind your own business", "stay inside your own silo". Therefore, people will stay inside their silos and cross-functional communication and collaboration will be reduced or non-existent, limiting the ability to create customer value across all functional areas in the company. This will clearly place limitations on how competitive the company can be as market trends, customer needs, and competitive pressures change over time. This will also frequently create "turf wars" and animosity between functions and departments. This will often create or fuel "blaming and shaming" behaviors that we discussed earlier.

Sometimes, even within a vertical silo or function, open communication is discouraged. The message being received here is "don't rock the boat" or "just do what you're told". Again, this will create behaviors where people withdraw, fail to think creatively, and fail to provide much needed communication and feedback necessary for good performance.

▌QUESTION 5 –ARE THERE ANY "SACRED COWS"?

"Sacred cows" and "legendary stories" are the policies, procedures, behaviors, and "stories of lore" that seem to be "untouchable" or "deal breakers" within the organization.

I look to see what happens when these are challenged, who fights to keep them intact and how hard they fight. I also look to uncover the reasons or issues behind the attempt to preserve the legend. There are usually two general responses when a sacred cow is challenged: 1) Open hostility; or 2) Covert subversion.

When open hostility or threats of severe consequences is the response to a proposed change, the desire is to produce fear in order to squelch the attack on the sacred cow. The open hostility response manifests itself in behaviors like extreme resistance, inappropriate personal attacks, complete close mindedness, and the always present "there will be hell to pay if you want to change that one". When fear wins the day, people will not only revere the sacred cow going forward, they will also have a tendency to begin to view all policies and procedure as sacred cows and refrain from, or be fearful of, using their creativity to make changes that will improve performance.

The other behavior, covert subversion, occurs when people in the organization allow changes to the sacred cow to go ahead and then subvert the change later. The subversion is usually demonstrated in one of two ways. One way is the "tattling" behavior. Rather than directly confronting and protecting the sacred cow, defenders will bring their fear to a higher authority so that person can squelch the revolt. The second way is, once the process has been changed and implemented, the defenders will completely ignore the new process and continue to follow the old process, preserving the legend and the worship of the sacred cow. These subversive behaviors always result in some combination of fear, animosity, frustration, resentment and anger.

I usually find that sacred cows tend to be knee-jerk reactions to something that happened long ago, under circumstances that many times no longer apply and did not address root cause and solve the problem. Sacred cows almost always create more work and wasteful activities. But nonetheless, the sacred cow has been lifted to a status where no one in the organization can challenge it without fear of rejection and reprisal.

QUESTION 6 - WHAT IS THE TOLERANCE FOR RISK AND LEARNING?

The two ends of the spectrum here can be an environment of extreme conservatism, or "anything goes – damn the rules!"

Companies that have a tendency to be overly conservative will usually get stuck in over-analyzing and endless talking about what should be done. They take very little action and project timelines tend to continually shift to the right. Improvement initiatives move very slowly, if at all, and the ability to sustain improvements is virtually guaranteed to fail. Being overly conservative is the result of the fear that a change may not work as planned and produce blame, shame, or worse. This fear typically comes from demonstrated behaviors in the past whenever something new or different was tried and didn't work as expected.

The overly conservative culture does not value learning, growing and reasonable risk taking. This type of culture is doomed to remain in past and achieve the same results they have always achieved.

Again, high performing people do not fit well in this type of culture. High performers are action oriented and continuous improvement minded.   Attracting and retaining high performing people will be a constant challenge for a company that is too conservative.

On the opposite end of the spectrum, the "anything goes" culture can be very risky, lack a sense of discipline and can be out of control.   Even though the behaviors of trying new things and challenging the status quo are supported and seem to be rewarded, the behavior of being results oriented is often out of balance.   Therefore, people do not learn and grow because getting to root cause and corrective action is not the focal point.

THE TWO TYPES OF CULTURES – POSITIVE AND DYSFUNCTIONAL

After making the observations from the Six Question Culture Quiz, you will have a foundational understanding of the prevalent behaviors and environmental factors which define the culture within an organization.   Now let's look at how the culture impacts performance.

I have observed that there are two basic types of cultures; the **Positive Culture**, and the **Dysfunctional Culture**.   The Positive Culture tends to accelerate performance levels while the Dysfunctional Culture will tend to slow down or even completely derail the ability for a company to achieve its goals.

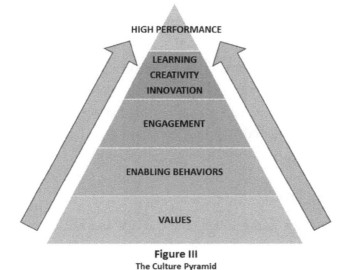

Figure III
The Culture Pyramid

THE POSITIVE CULTURE

Companies with a positive culture have been able to create a system of Values, Enabling Behaviors and Employee Engagement which then enables creativity, innovation and learning. This system is shown in Figure III – The Culture Pyramid. As we have explored earlier, performance improvement can only occur when process and policy changes are made. The life blood of making these changes is **Creativity, Innovation and Learning**. Creativity spawns new ideas and new ways to do things, innovation puts them into action, and learning continues the cycle as people experience the results of their efforts and continue to solve problems and improve based on what has been learned.

Employee engagement is the fuel, the very reason that creativity, innovation and learning exists in an organization. Engaged employees genuinely care about their work, the success of the company and are driven to continuously improve. So what creates this engagement? I believe that engagement is created by a solid foundation of clearly defined and supported Enabling Behaviors which are created and supported by positive **Values**. There is also a noticeable lack of fear in the positive culture. Finally, these values and behaviors are linked to the company's Vision, Goals and Strategy (refer to Figure I – The Lean Impact Group Business Transformation System).

In this type of culture you will find that behaviors such as open communication, giving and receiving of constructive feedback, challenging the status quo, and teamwork are all consistently demonstrated and rewarded. And even when negative behaviors are demonstrated, employees are corrected immediately and with dignity, as this too is viewed as an opportunity for learning and growing.

THE DYSFUNCTIONAL CULTURE

Disengagement is the killer of creativity, innovation and learning. The dysfunctional culture creates disengagement in its employees. Let's take a look at how this happens.

Reflecting on the examples discussed in the Six Question Culture Quiz™, we observed behaviors such as blaming, shaming, inconsistent application of rules, guarding the "sacred cows", and limiting good communication. All of these behaviors lead to negative emotions such as fear, animosity, resentment, anger, loss of dignity, and confusion.

When these behaviors and emotional responses are prevalent, people will tend to retreat and remain silent in order to survive within the culture. They disengage and just try to protect themselves from these emotions, which in turn destroys the creativity, innovation and learning needed to drive performance improvement.

FIXING THE DYSFUNCTIONAL CULTURE

Because culture is the direct result of the behaviors that create the emotional climate within a company, changing the culture requires behavior modification among all the employees in the organization. I start down this path by leading the client through a series of workshops designed to create self-awareness of the current culture, define positive and supportive values, and generate the actions required to replace the dysfunctional behaviors with new enabling behaviors Ultimately this process helps them define what the new culture would look like.

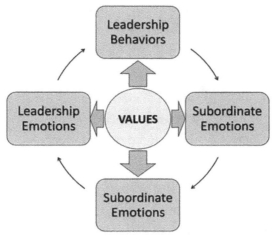

Figure IV The Values – Behavior – Emotion Cycle

The organization may not even be aware that their behaviors are limiting their performance and creating disengagement among their employees. Exploring this highly emotional world within a company can be a daunting task for the people in the organization. There is often a lot of "baggage", hurt feelings, animosity and resentment that has built up over time and addressing these areas can be painful. Having an outside person to help navigate through these sensitive areas is perhaps the safest and most productive way to open lines of communication and help solve long standing problems.

Understanding the "system" of values, behaviors and emotions is an important step. Another way to visualize this is shown in Figure IV. Leadership behaviors create emotions within the organization. Those demonstrated behaviors also serve to define the true values that the company lives by. The people in the organization then have an emotional response which in turn generates their own set of behaviors, either positive or negative. These behaviors have an impact on the emotions and feeling among the leadership team, generating another set of behaviors and so the cycle continues. This cycle feeds the foundational aspects of the system shown in Figure III – The Cultural Pyramid.

In the dysfunctional culture, this system creates the negative emotions and outcomes described earlier and continues to feed on itself, becoming more and more negative over time. Breaking down this system is a critical and often difficult task. Changing behavior requires that new thought patterns and habits be developed and implemented to replace the old ones. This takes repetition, coaching and holding people accountable for making the transformation stick. This is not easy work! It takes commitment, patience, and perseverance.

Another key ingredient to fixing the dysfunctional culture is to ensure accountability. While the primary responsibility for establishing and sustaining company culture falls squarely on the shoulders of management, it is important to note that every person in the organization is accountable as well. Every person plays a role in defining and sustaining the culture through their own beliefs, actions and behaviors.

▋ SUMMARY & KEY LEARNINGS

We started this discussion by observing that implementing continuous improvement programs does not always produce the desired result of sustainable performance improvement. High performance can only be achieved when employees are engaged and creativity, innovation and learning are prevalent, resulting in substantive changes in how value is created in the organization.

We talked about the two common "First Big Mistakes" when implementing a continuous improvement program: 1) failure of company leaders to engage the entire organization in the program; and 2) failure of the leadership team to be engaged in the program themselves. Company culture reflects the values and behaviors of its leaders. If the leaders are disengaged, the employees will be disengaged. If the leaders don't understand the tools and principles of the system being implementing, it is not possible for them to be engaged and support their employees. Employees will see this and become disengaged, killing creativity, innovation and learning and virtually ensuring failure of the program.

In the end, the culture of the organization, the values, behaviors and emotional climate, must be viewed as an integral component of the company's strategy, goals and objectives. By creating these linkages leaders will be better prepared to develop a system of enabling behaviors that drive engagement, creativity, innovation, and learning. It is this culture, teamed up with a structured continuous improvement approach that will deliver what we all want.........***HIGH PERFORMANCE!***

A.J. Tozzi

The Lean Impact Group, LLC

109 Russo Drive

Hamden, CT 06518

Website: http://www.leanimpactgroup.com

Email: ajtozzi@leanimpactgroup.com

Phone: 203-645-4714

Since 2004, A.J. Tozzi has owned and operated The Lean Impact Group, a consulting firm dedicated to helping clients transform their business performance. A.J. uses a balanced approach focusing on Vision/Goals, Winning Team, Positive Culture and Value Creation, along with simple, highly effective and proven principles and tools rooted in the Lean and Six Sigma disciplines to achieve sustainable breakthrough results for his clients.

Prior to establishing The Lean Impact Group, A.J.'s twenty three year career in manufacturing culminated in a role as Director of Operations at Danaher Corporation where he polished his business leadership and lean six sigma skills. A.J.'s educational background includes a BS in Manufacturing Engineering from Brigham Young University and a Master of Business Administration from The University of New Haven.

THE BIGGEST THING SMALL BUSINESS OVERLOOK THAT ENDANGERS THEIR BOTTOM LINE

MARNI SPENCER-DEVLIN

There is a new world order. People are becoming more self-aware. Words like passion and purpose are now part of everyday business vernacular. Employees choose meaningful work over higher pay. Conformity has been replaced by a need for authentic expression.

This demand for authenticity has had far-reaching consequences. Consumers shop differently. With the rise of the information age markets have changed from regional to global, making authenticity and ethics even greater priority. Consumers refuse to be treated like a number and businesses must be responsive to this demand or face the consequences. The game has changed and those who would remain the same will go the way of the dinosaur.

▊ NO MORE BUSINESS AS USUAL

Many companies, from small and local business to large international concerns, are finding themselves struggling and they're not sure why. They're doing what they've always done; they're following tried and true business practices but the results are no longer the same. They blame their rising costs and shrinking profit margins on the economy but the argument falls flat in the face of many other businesses, which are experiencing exponential growth in the very same economic climate.

Companies like Apple, Amazon and Zappos; even grocery stores Publix and Trader Joe's are easily outpacing rising costs and are showing profits that are through the roof. What are they doing differently? The brightest minds are clamoring to jump onboard with these firms even though oftentimes the hours are longer, the pay is not necessarily higher nor are the work environments better. In-'N-Out Burgers, a privately-held, California hamburger chain that was on the forefront of the new business trend, actually has a waiting list for new employees – and we're talking a fast food type establishment!

Yet these employees do not require special management tactics and incentives to spur them to higher performance. They are self-driven, eager and passionate about their work. The eagerness and passion is rooted in the new way of doing business.

There's a new sheriff in town. The old way of doing business is taking a hit and those in charge, whether solopreneur or large corporation, would do well to take heed the warning signs. The only difference between small businesses and the big guys is that that the big guys can sustain the downward trend a lot longer; for the little guy it's lights out.

▋ CUSTOMER EXPERIENCE IS THE NEW BLACK

Big or small, there's one thing all businesses have in common: They all need customers. It matters little how wonderful or life-changing the products or services are if nobody ever tries them. It won't matter how well trained the staff or how beautifully appointed the offices if nobody ever walks through the doors. Without question clients are the most important component of any business because without them…. there *is* no business.

Hence one would think that it would be top of mind for all businesses to ensure that their customers are absolutely deliriously happy before, during and after the transaction. And one would be wrong. Of course, all companies want their customers to be satisfied but customer satisfaction is considered sort of incidental to the transaction. Customer satisfaction is seen as the byproduct of a good product. The idea is, if the customer got what he came for he'll be back. This effectively leaves the most important component of a business, the component that keeps the business alive, in the realm of faith. And as it turns out, this faith is not always rewarded.

A 2011 Harris Interactive report on the impact of customer experience, commissioned by RightNow, found that 82% of consumers who stopped doing business with a company did not do so because of a poor product or a bad service. 82% of customers left a company because of a poor customer experience. It turns out that, while, of course, a good product or a great service is important, it's not everything. If the customer experience during the transaction is lousy 82% of your business may walk out the door and never look back.

▌ STAYING ON YOUR GAME

The Harris report also found that 1% of customers died and 3% of customers moved away or simply stopped needing the product or service; underscoring the constant need for new sales because a certain amount of attrition is normal and natural.

9% of business was lured away by cheaper pricing. This deserves a closer look. When profit margins are shrinking, as they will be with the old way of doing business, the temptation lower pricing in order to lure customers arises. It may seem harmless, even prudent, in the face of the momentary sales increase. In the long run, however, the short-term gain is short-sighted and foolish.

Pricing is controlled by business model; and that was determined long be business ever opens its doors because the business model determines every aspect of how a business is run. On one end there is the discounter business model and on the one end of the scale there is the high-end, luxury brand model; naturally you can also fall anywhere in between but wherever you fall determines your brand and that affects every decision from the cost of ingredients, the quality and experience of employees all the way down to the look of your marketing and the décor of the offices.

You must be clear and consistent within your business model. One simply cannot offer both quality products at discount pricing. Something's gotta give. If you want to be able to compete on price your services, products and ingredients have to reflect that.

Conversely, you can't create high-quality products using cheap ingredients or experienced employees for minimum wages. If your business model is luxury brand you simply cannot skimp on quality anywhere and your pricing has to reflect it. Then, if a client asks for a lower price you can confidently explain about the high quality ingredients and the experienced service professionals you employ. The client then has a point of reference and can either feel good about paying your higher prices – or walk on down the road to get something cheaper.

Pricing is clear-cut; it should always be a business decision and never an emotional one. The temptation to sell costly items at discount pricing for short-term gain in the long run creates a loss far greater than the 9% attrition of the price-shopping customer.

▌ LISTENING FOR THE ECHO

The Harris report further determined that 5% of customers were lured away by a friend's recommendation. This was not included in the 82% customer attrition due to poor customer experience. However, if it is possible for your clients to be lured away at all, then the customer experience simply was not what it should have been. There are no excuses here.

Out of the 82% of preventable customers attrition, 14% left due to insufficient follow-up. Imagine 14% of your business – that's more than most people's profit margins – gone, simply because there was no communication after the transaction and possible problems were never addressed. Your follow-up directly communicates how you feel about your customer.

Far too many businesses are unaware that a sale consists of three components. Like everything else, a sales cycle has a beginning, middle and end. There is the initial contact when contracts are signed or business is otherwise agreed upon. Then comes the actual transaction and third is the follow-up. Without follow-up the whole transaction feels inauthentic.

'Wham Bam Thank you Man'. It's not something that makes anyone feel too good about doing business with you. Far too many businesses miss that there has to be conclusion of the transaction. They feel that they are done when the transaction is done. That's fine if you don't care whether you ever see that client again but if you want any hope of repeat business, or a referral, then you best have an authentic conclusion in place.

I'm not talking about sending off a pre-printed Thank You card. Might as well save yourself the postage! In fact, it probably works against you because it smacks of inauthenticity. Put yourself in your client's shoes. Think about how you would want to be treated and then do that. Find an authentic way to let the client know that you truly appreciate their business and find out if they felt the same way! In my company, a designated employee called every single client the day after their job went out. We gave them all the pertinent details of the transaction.

It gave us a valuable opportunity to thank our clients for their business but even more importantly we were able to ask if there was anything we could have done better – then we shut up and listened. It is essential to provide space and opportunity for the client to express their feelings and opinions. Most people don't like to confront. They won't tell you outright if they weren't happy about something. They'll just leave and never be back. Whenever we learned that there was indeed something we could have done better we showed huge integrity and generosity in fixing the problem. We turned many clients into life-long believers simply because we originally screwed up and then showed ourselves extremely generous in fixing it. So I'm not saying, make mistakes intentionally but I am saying that a mistake doesn't have to be the end of the world – as long as there is follow-up. It can even be a huge opportunity for you to shine!

IT'S NOT WHAT YOU THINK

Harris further found – and this is the most shocking percentage! - that 68% of customers stopped doing business with a company because they felt that nobody cared about them. Sixty-eight percent! - I could start a whole new company with those numbers! They walked away simply because of lousy customer experience!

In the wake of this poll many companies began trying out all sorts of methods and manipulations to make their customers *feel more cared about*. Some companies tried *incentivizing* their employees to give better customer service. One company actually gave everyone bonuses for the week if there weren't any customer complaints.

You will notice that these days, when you're on hold for an hour calling, say, your insurance company you are not waiting for the *Customer Service Department*. These days you are waiting for the *Customer Care Department*. Does it make you feel more cared about? Probably not! All these methods and manipulations to make customers feel more cared about don't work for two reasons. First, everyone can tell when they are being manipulated and nobody likes it. It doesn't make anybody feel more cared about.

The main reason, however, why these strategies don't work –and this is the biggie! - is that customer care really has very little to do with how much you care about your customers. Customer care has everything to do with how you care about your company. It has to do with how your staff feels about their jobs. It has to do with the atmosphere of the company. It has to do with the culture.

▌ LOVE WHAT YOU DO AND IT SHOWS

It's a no-brainer, really, if you love what you do it shows. If your employees love their jobs you can see it and feel it. Happy people – whether leadership or staff - are more productive, more innovative, and more knowledgeable. They instinctively look for ways to improve because they care about the outcome. Happy people automatically create a better experience for the customer.

You can feel it in the air and it's the type of atmosphere that customers instinctively respond to. Have you ever noticed that in TV commercials people are always smiling and having a great time? That's because human beings are wired to respond to that. The commercial could be telling you about the most horrific side effects of some drug but the people look so happy and they have such a great time that we want in, regardless.

It is very compelling to walk into a company where people love their jobs. They are smiling and you can feel that it's genuine. They are eager to help. They are passionate and knowledgeable about the product or service they're selling. It's infectious and it makes you feel good. You look forward to doing business with them again next time. And you want to tell all your friends about it.

For example, I buy my coffee at Starbucks. As you know, there are about a billion Starbucks's all over the world and they all sell the exact same product. There are three stores in my immediate vicinity. One would think that I would drive to the closest one to buy my coffee but I don't. In fact, I drive to the one that's furthest from my house. Why? I look forward to walking into the place because everyone is always so cheerful. They love their jobs and it shows. They are knowledgeable about their product. They go out of their way to be helpful. It's just a great, fun atmosphere to walk into. I know it's genuine. They don't need to employ *customer service strategies to make me feel cared about.* They don't need to pretend they care about me. They have fun and I am automatically included in that when I walk in the door. And it feels great!

In the other two stores the employees seem like they don't want to be there. They are always grumpy. They make me feel like I am a burden, one more thing that takes them away from what they really wanted to do. It's very off-putting. So I simply drive a little farther to buy a product that I could have gotten closer. Yes, I am only one customer but no company is too big to fail is the long run. Customer experience makes the difference between success and failure.

▌ "CULTURE EATS STRATEGY FOR BREAKFAST!"

Companies like Apple, Amazon and Zappos got that and they made customer experience not just an important focus of their business; they made it their main focus. They proved that when authentic customer experience is your number one goal the streets are literally paved with gold for you.

Customer experience makes your bottom line and it comes from having a joyful atmosphere; it comes from a happy work environment. Customer experience is about the culture in your company. And it's not something that can be faked or strategized or incentivized. Peter Drucker, famous management theorist and recipient of the Presidential Medal of Freedom, said it best. "Culture eats strategy for breakfast!" It's the new way of doing business and companies must adapt or be left behind!

Here is where I usually get 'the look' from clients. The look that says, "Yeah well, that's all very nice but I don't pay my employees to be happy; I pay them to work! If they're happy, sure –bonus! - but I have to worry about the bottom line not a "joyful work environment - otherwise we're all out of a job! When I get as big as Apple or Amazon then maybe we can afford the luxury of operating that way. Show me the money first then I'll worry about our company culture!" But that kind of thinking is a fallacy. It's culture that creates the customer experience and it's the customer experience that makes your bottom line.

CULTURE MAKES SMALL BUSINESSES BIG. REALLY BIG!

Here are some examples of companies that started very small but they made customer experience their number one focus and ended up as 800-pound Gorillas.

Most famously of course, there is Zappos, which started with two guys who had a little idea of selling shoes online. They weren't doing too well in the beginning and they found themselves scrambling. In order to stay afloat they had to find a way to distinguish themselves. That's when the idea was born to place their entire focus on customer service. Their business was no longer about selling shoes but about offering the best customer service ever! Their new slogan had nothing at all to do with shoes; it became 'Delivering Happiness'.

The story of Zappos is famously immortalized in Tony Hsieh's book, 'Delivering Happiness – A Path To Profits, Passion And Purpose'. Tony divulges that there were many detractors who argued that focusing on customer experience instead of on selling shoes, while the company was in peril of going bankrupt, was preposterous. "Tell people you're selling cool shoes and let's fix the delivery problems we are having." Instead, they spend time and money on building their internal culture.

The strategy was so successful that today they are giving company tours at Zappos for which it's necessary to make reservations to get a spot. Amazon bought Zappos for 1.3 billion dollars. Amazon was big then but nowhere near as big as they are now. They were happy to spend such a large sum to buy Zappos because they realized that they could facilitate their own continued growth by adopting the secrets that were hatched at Zappos.

Trader Joe's grocery stores started as a little Mom-and-Pop store in Pasadena, California and grew to 456 stores nationwide with total revenue of 9.38 billion annually, all because they discovered the secret of passionate engagement. Trader Joe's has an almost cult-like customer following. They offer really great products at really good prices but what makes Trader's so irresistible is the atmosphere. It's easy to see that their employees are happy and truly proud to work there. They are excited about their work and knowledgeable about each and every product and so the public is excited to shop at Traders. Recently, the first Trader Joe's opened in Fort Lauderdale. They required police to handle the traffic from the massive onslaught of customers during the entire week of Grand Opening. That's what's possible when your customer experience is exceptional. Customers follow you like a cult!

In-N-Out Hamburgers started with a little Mom & Pop hamburger stand. At face value it does not appear to be a particularly great way to amass a huge fortune - but here is another who company found a way to take passionate engagement to a whole new level. They started in 1948 and are still family owned but now they bring in a cool 575 Million annually – not bad for a little hamburger stand!

So what did these companies do that you can do, too? How can you create a thriving atmosphere in which everyone benefits and your customers become raving fans that refer you to everyone? Let me tell you that it is possible. I did it with my first company in 1990. I didn't know then that it was called 'creating culture'; I only knew that I had created a goldmine.

In a relatively short time my company grew from a tiny two-man-shop to a multimillion-dollar firm with seventy, happy and proud employees. In order to tell you how I came to create such an incredibly successful company though, I have to tell you a little about my story.

▌ ROCKY ROAD TO SUCCESS

You see, I had a pretty rough start in life. For the first ten years of my life, my brother molested me. Then, when I was just a gawky kid of twelve I was raped. This sent me into an emotional tailspin and I started hanging around with a bad crowd, and when I was fourteen, I was raped a second time.

When I was seventeen, it looked like things might be looking up. I was discovered as a professional model and I married my high school crush. My new husband was so proud that his young wife was a professional model - until he realized that this meant that other men would be looking at me. He became insanely jealous and he cooked up a diabolical plan: With full knowledge and foresight of what he was doing he got me hooked to heroin. Yes. Intentionally.

The plan was to control my heroin supply in order to control me. The plan backfired. I got away from him eventually but I was in so much emotional pain from all I had already been through that I could not find a way to get away from the drugs. For the better part of ten years I struggled with heroin addiction – with all it entails. And it got pretty ugly! You can read all about it in my #1 bestselling book, Crawling Into The Light. Without wanting to spoil the ending for you, if you read it, remember she survives in the end. You see, it's not always clear.

My absolute breaking point came when I finally ended up homeless on the streets of LA. A broken-down VW bus outside of a junkyard provided a roof over my head. Things were so dirty all around me and pitch-black in my soul. But in all that darkness I became aware of a tiny spark within me that said, "Whatever you might have done wrong in your life - you deserve better than this!"

Perhaps it was the first time in my life that I felt I *deserved* anything good. I decided - and it was a flash decision - that I would have a better life. I turned myself in to the authorities hoping for a slap on the wrist so I could be free to start my new life. Instead, I was sentenced to two years in state prison. I was scared out of my wits but I remained steadfast. I wanted a better life. I decided to view my prison time as my rehab. I read and studied and I exercised and by the time I was released I was healthy and strong and a new person. Someone gave me a chance and gave me a job in marketing – and I loved it. It turned out that I was really good at my job and some three years later I opened up my own company.

Why am I telling you all of this? What is my personal story doing in a book about business? It's important to know that you can't divorce yourself from your past and neither should we try. Almost everyone has experienced adversity; very few get away unscathed. Instead of trying to bury the past I urge you to look for the treasure that is always hidden within it. Painful past experiences can become the catalyst that catapults you into the future you are meant to have. My horrific experiences were the catalyst for me. It turns out that they were the reason that caused me to structure my company in a way that created its massive success.

▌ THE THREE PILLARS OF SUCCESS

The reason my company became so insanely successful was because it was based on three simple pillars that were rooted in my past. These were **vision, clarity** and **respect** and those were born out of my past experience.

Vision translates to personal clarity, which is the first pillar of success. The decision, made in that wrecked VW bus, to have a better life sparked in me an intense vision for the future. I was passionate about my vision and this passion fuelled my endeavor. When you are absolutely clear on what you want it can manifest but only to the extent that you are clear.

Company clarity is the second pillar. I was passionate about my vision and I there was no way I would let anything stand in my way. *Pie-in-the-sky* was not going to take me there. I had to have a clear path and a clear plan of action.

Respect translates to team clarity. I had been mishandled and abused all my life and it was for this reason that it was supremely important to me that everyone who worked for me would feel respected, valued and heard, both as a human being and as a professional. I made sure that every voice was always heard. Team clarity third pillar of success.

Our team was invested in the vision of our company and personally engaged with their valuable input in taking us there. Together, we created an atmosphere of absolute thriving. Everyone truly cared about making the company grow. It was a great place to work! For twenty years I truly loved going to work – that's a gift in itself!

Our employees were passionate about their jobs and you could feel it! We were so successful, that headhunters were constantly calling trying to recruit our people away from us. My employees would actually come to my office to tell me about it! "Guess what - just got another call from a headhunter and I told him what I tell all of them – not for a million bucks would I go to work anywhere else!"

Our people cared and they did their all to be knowledgeable and do the best job possible – so as a result our clients were passionate about working with us and they told others about us and so our business was a goldmine. All our business came from referrals. For the first fifteen years in business we didn't even have any sales people!

I didn't know it then but the principles I was using that turned my company into a goldmine were the same used by Zappos and Trader Joe's and In-N-Out Burger. So here are the three steps you should be taking to turn your company into such a goldmine.

PERSONAL CLARITY

Steve Jobs said that the only way to do great work is to love what you do. But in order to love what you do you have to know what you love.

We all have certain desires for our life, things that are important to us or that we are passionate about. Most people have never taken the time to be clear about what that is for them. Awares or not, those desires still smolder deep down underneath. When those needs and desires clash with the demands of the business stressors are created.

For examples if family and your children are important to you but your work demands 60-hour commitment, you will always be torn. You will perpetually walk around with this vaguely uncomfortable feeling; like you left something on the stove. When you are at home you'll be worrying about the company; when you're at work you'll be missing the kids. You're never really comfortable; your head's not fully invested in either game. Eventually something has to give. Perhaps your body will give out and you'll get sick. More likely, however, the company will simply not perform to the extent that it could or should. You're frustrated; you're working hard, doing all the things you should be doing but you're not experiencing the success you envision.

No business can outperform what's between the ears of its leaders. It is essential for the success of a company that all those in leadership are deeply aware of their personal feelings and beliefs about money and success. An astounding number of people in this country grew up with a subconsciously belief that money is the root of all evil. They adopted this concept from the grandparents and parents long before they were old enough to know what it meant. Unquestioned, it became a subliminal part of their paradigm and still affects their unintentional decision-making abilities today. If such a person is in a leadership position the company's success will be negatively impacted.

It is possible to create synergy between personal and professional objectives but only if everyone is absolutely clear about what matters most to them, personally.

CORPORATE CLARITY

There simply is no competition when you are clear about what makes your company different from others. A company's unique value is more than just its products or services. It lies in the unique blend between its offerings and the personal passions, abilities and strengths of leadership as well as staff.

For examples, there are 62,000 realtors in the South Florida area alone. Every one of these real estate professionals basically does that same thing – they help people buy and sell houses. That's a lot of competition! Upon closer examination, however, each one of them provides their services in a slightly different way simply because they bring themselves to the table. The key lies in cultivating their differences and, based on that, attracting a specific target audience. By cultivating what makes them unique they will have no competition whatsoever.

It is also absolutely essential to have a clear company plan of action. What are the financial projections of a company and what will it take to achieve those goals? Are the company's offerings appropriate for their target audience. Is the target audience able to fulfill the financial projections? Is the branding appropriately directed toward that target audience? Does the brandling align with marketing strategies and online process? Finally, when the company is ideal what will it look like in every area? What is its mission? Out of this, a clear-sighted, step by step action plan can be created.

TEAM CLARITY

According to 2014 Gallup poll slightly more 68% of American employees are not engaged at work. That means they show up and do what they absolutely have to in order to get a paycheck.

You'll remember that number from the top. It's not a coincidence that 68% of customers stopped doing business with a company because they felt that nobody cared about them. And they were right! They were being services by the 68% percent of employees who don't care about their jobs! Disengaged employees cost a company big money!

Yet, employees don't want to be disengaged. Human beings innately seek meaning. People want to know that their contributions make a difference. Time and time again polls have shown that people value meaningful work over a higher paycheck. Disengagement is simply defense mechanism human beings use to protect themselves when they find that their contribution is not valued.

Teams must discover their personal passions and their goals for an ideal professional life. And they must tap into their personal internal motivators for high performance. Then they can be enlisted in the company's ideals and mission and engaged in the action plan. This creates a high-energy atmosphere of passionate engagement. When everyone is onboard the same boat and everyone rows in the same direction it is astounding how fast and how far a company raise beyond all expected projections.

Those two guys who started Zappos didn't have a concept of what 1.3 billion dollars looked like – they can now!

Marni Spencer-Devlin, CEO Passion4Profit, Inc.

250 Pacific Ave, Ste 204

Long Beach, CA 90802

949.315.0475

http://Passion4ProfitInc.com

Marni@MarniSpencerDevlin.com

Marni Spencer-Devlin is founder and CEO or Passion4Profit, Inc. certified business consulting, a company that offer clients a unique brand of service that increases profits through corporate happiness & authenticity. The program offers personal & professional clarity for the leadership, followed by analysis of the unique corporate contribution & branding, which is used to enroll and engage staff.

Marni Spencer-Devlin was also the founder and president of ocdm marketing, Inc. a Southern California direct mail advertising, marketing & fulfillment company she turned into a multimillion dollar enterprise with seventy employees, before selling the company in 2009.

Marni is also author of the Amazon #1 bestselling autobiography Crawling Into The Light, which speaks of unspeakable adversity she overcame before becoming a successful entrepreneur. Her second book is entitled, The Iceberg Principles – the Truth about the Universe and Your place in it, which offers a metaphysical look at the purpose & meaning of life.

THERE IS ALWAYS A BETTER WAY: OPTIMIZING MANUFACTURING PERFORMANCE TO MAXIMIZE YOUR RESULTS

LUIS RAMOS

With over twenty-five years operational expertise transforming manufacturing and distribution organizations by improving their business processes, lean sigma manufacturing, project management, sales management, technology training, and supply chain management, there's one thing I've learned: No matter how efficient and profitable a business is *there is always a better way*.

In fact, in many, if not all cases, I say, if it's not broke then break it. In an ever-changing global economy, companies must remain on the cutting edge of organization process, employee satisfaction and development, and customer service to create profitable teams. Those elements are behind the Somar Business Improvement Basics™ (SBIB) process.

SBIB was developed for the end purpose of optimizing manufacturing performance and exceeding bottom line expectations. It is a customizable tool that utilizes many of the continuous improvement elements available from Lean, TPS, Six Sigma, and more. Each are tailored to the organization, by selecting the tool(s) that will best suite a company's available resources, and that will be understood and accepted by all employees.

Our thinking is that it doesn't make sense to implement the Toyota Production System or Six Sigma for a business that lacks the internal resources to undertake the demands of said systems. The process needs to be keyed to fit the size of the business and its resources for it to work. And when that's accomplished, success is assured.

One of our clients, who we will refer to as Company X, underwent a $1.8 million investment for a complete facility rehab and business operations improvements. Within three years, they managed a $4.1 million Return on Investment (ROI), increasing profits from 8% to 19% and the capability and capacity to support new business growth. They became poised to maintain their position in the industry with a more efficient, satisfied workforce. The improvements we designed included the development of planning, manufacturing engineering, quality and tooling departments, and employee training and the creation of processes and procedures. The results were astounding:

» Efficiencies were increased from less than 70% to unprecedented 98%

» Labor was reduced $1.1M or 15%

» Non-exempt salaries Reduced $200K or 13%

» COQ was reduced by $910K, from 4.9% to 1.4% of sales

» Inventory cost reduced by $975K, increasing turns from 3 to 6 annually

» Tooling outsource cost reduced $250K

» Savings of $665K were realized for cycle and set up time reductions

» Culture change, employee empowerment, and moral improved and happy customers—Priceless!

Throughout the following pages, I explain the SOMAR Business Improvement Basics and Phases. The Basics are outlined in Figure 1 and the phases are noted in Figure 2. Additionally, I will refer to Company X to exemplify how SBIB can be implemented. Keep in mind, however, that this is not a cookie-cutter approach. Customization is vital and begins with initially establishing the lay of the land, so to speak.

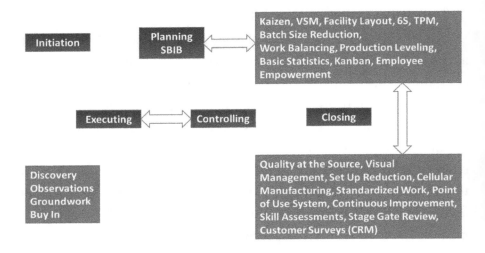

Figure 1

THE FIRST STEP: DISCOVERY

For any business transformation plan to be implemented, discovery is essential. Here, observations must be made on organization structure and cleanliness of operations, the utilization of metrics and procedures, employee morale and initiative (or lack of), and the overall culture of the business.

When working with Company X, we determined that there were no metrics in place to measure operations. Nor were there processes or procedures in place. Outdated software further complicated the situation. Employee issues were far and wide, including the lack of employee training and unsafe working conditions created by chemical odors and the lack of ventilation, which was exacerbated in the hot weather. They were also treated miserably by management, and hounded about productivity issues that were more the result of the processes or lack of the process not the people.

In situations such as this, kaizen events assist in the development of processes, procedures, and documentation used to guide the transformation process. Often times these events need to be scheduled in a manner not to disrupt the production of product. Furthermore, management participation is essential. Top-down buy-in is the only way to create lasting change. Leadership must lead by example and often that requires a change in their mindset. Once that is accomplished, employees will get on board with implementing changes—or even being open to the fact that changes must be forthcoming for the overall improvement not only of the production process, but other factors that affect their physical and mental health and well-being.

Leadership can initiate employee involvement by building a sense of community and belonging. When employees have a sense of community and belonging, they are encouraged to contribute to the process. They come to think of themselves as part of the business and become thinkers, making valuable contributions to their company. This is when they also take their responsibilities more seriously and to new highs as they take pride in the company brand. This in and of itself often has beneficial impacts on speed, quality, and production costs.

In Company X's case, I scheduled meetings with management and employees to gain an understanding of how they viewed the company and where they thought the problems lay that they were experiencing. We reviewed how orders were taken and entered into the existing system. I also familiarized myself with the operation of equipment and the production process to better assist employees to improve their processes and ensure that they were adequately trained. A well-educated workforce is the best way to enhance any process and procedure. As is often the case, skepticism can thwart any intended changes, which is why it's essential that management wholeheartedly buy-in.

With Company X, I met with upper management and presented to them a pro-forma P&L and a present state map and a future state map, displaying what could be the outcome if changes were made. I also stressed that if nothing was done, they would continue as is or fail. Success would come if they were willing to make changes to culture and made an investment, financially in the infrastructure and in their employees training and basic needs. After about a month of back and forth questions and answers, they decided to take the gamble (as they called it) and allocated the money and agreed to employee development. I was happy and excited for them to accept the proposed change. I had broken the leadership barrier and communicated the importance of change to improve an organization that was in need of a fresh perspective from the top floor to the shop floor.

Change is important and no company should ever accept a status quo, because there is always a better way. All companies should have a mindset to live by: "If it isn't broke-break it, you can always make it better." And implementing SBIB is one of the ways to make any operation better.

▌ IMPLEMENTING SBIB

SBIB is essentially eight phases, outlined in Figure 2, and which provide the transformational structure to increase speed, improve quality, and reduce costs for nearly any business. These steps include Data Integrity, Metrics, Continuous Production, Point of Use Logistics, Cycle Time Management, Production Linearity, S & O Resource Planning, and Customer Connectivity.

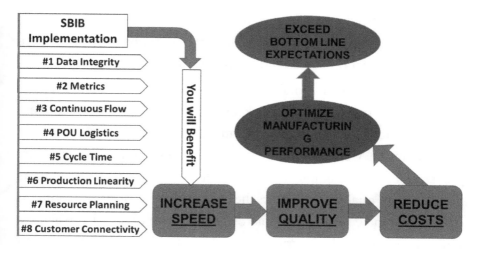

Figure 2

DATA INTEGRITY (DOCUMENTATION)

In this phase of improvement, we address the documentation available for everyone to work with. We look for how BOMs are structured. The availability and accuracy of standards, routers, processes, and procedures are reviewed as well. For optimal results, data must be accurate, timely, controlled, accessible and understandable by every member of the team—from the CEO to the floor worker.

Establishing the departments to create and manage, documentation and develop processes and procedures is the start to data integrity improvements. For Company X, we generated a quality manual, standards for production, processes, and procedures. We ensured that everyone involved had understood the missing elements that made it difficult to have structure in their workplace. We addressed the flow of an order, from entry to receipt by the customer in order to institute the processes and metrics required to meet expectations.

The documentation for each process was crafted by the operators, quality, planning and manufacturing engineering. In the spirit of collaboration, we even enlisted the graphic arts department to create a blueprint of products that were to be printed on the production floor for all of the company's customers. The artist's involvement was key to having the correct processes and procedures in place.

Accountability by the total workforce was crucial. This shifted their mindset, resulting in better work experiences. Jobs that once were deemed difficult and impossible became achievable when the data and documentation were implemented. Additionally, controlling relevant processes became credible and believable. Today, management admits that getting a quality product in the hands of the customer on-time is truly under the control of the factory people and that if the executive staff was eliminated, the factory would not skip-a-beat! Now that's success!

▌ METRICS (MEASUREMENT)

Metrics are a basis for continuous improvement, as we cannot fix what we don't measure and a lot of times we are measuring what will not help. We need to establish standards that are measurable and achievable. We don't need to establish a metric for every process we do, just the processes that need augmentation.

In this phase participative goal setting, benchmarking, balanced scorecard, basis for continuous improvements, data accessibility, measurement clarity, program commitment, and process ownership are established as SBIB objectives.

With Company X, metrics were developed by the establishment of manufacturing engineering, quality, planning departments, and making the graphic arts department the engineering department. This assisted in identifying performance internally and perhaps most importantly, how the customer perceived the company. As we all know, when customer satisfaction is increased, our bottom line increases as well, and here quality is key.

By addressing the quality of product printed, through establishing metrics and procedures—and properly training the workforce, everyone that touched a component was aware of the requirements, both location and color, and date required by customer. Training required that the set up persons and operators knew how to interpret the sketches and a Pantone color chart.

We developed metrics and processes for planning and quality. Standards, BOMs, and routers, were created for production to measure speed, quality and cost, we also established a friendly competition for lines and support functions. The workforce developed a mindset for measurement, and a balance scorecard was implemented to track progress. To boost employee contribution, weekly and monthly achievement awards were given for on-time delivery and quality, meaning no returns or complaints, to anyone involved in the product.

Optimally, every department involved in the process of a product developed its own balanced scorecard to measure customer satisfaction, operations, planning, and finance performance. Goals need to be set in place to know what's been achieved and what hasn't. This is very effective in making positive things happen in a difficult manufacturing work environment. The more a company uses Real-time data (RTD) to perform situation analysis and to establish and track corrective actions, the more comfortable and effective they became at interpreting and applying data-on-the-run.

For Company X, developing metrics resulted ultimately in a reduction in labor from 375 to 320 employees, and costs by $1.1M or 15%. Non-exempt labor was reduced from 45 to 39 employees, and cost by $200K or 13%.. Quality costs were reduced by $910K. All in all, these facts are a good reminder that metrics are an important element in a performance measurement system. It is the ability to capture relevant data that will provide a valid assessment of how the process is being performed.

To this end, establish ownership of the processes by everyone involved and then establish and sustain an appropriate method of performance measurement. Without this happening, there will be no worthwhile commitment to goal attainment. And remember, without data, your ideas are just another opinion—and you can't fix what you don't measure.

CONTINUOUS PRODUCTION (SELF-DIRECTED TEAMS)

Continuous Production (CP) is when a process is not interrupted by waste, such as moving parts, waiting, etc. and the part is handled in a continuous flow (One Piece Flow). In CP, teams must be given the tools to be self-directed and empowered to act in order to ensure that they can produce the specifications and demand of their work cell.

Here the SBIB objectives include: challenging everyone to buy into the changes, creating self-directed teams, cell layout, cell work flow, line balancing, enhancing workplace integrity, improving total quality, and reducing waste.

Training the entire staff on how One Piece Flow improves production and quality is imperative. Additionally, employee buy-in is a must. This is where the development of self-directed work cells come in. These cells must be accountable to assure that product is manufactured on a timely basis and quality is no longer just good enough. It must be stellar. Everyone in the cell is held responsible and accountable for the quality of their output and delivery.

Accountability was lacking across the board at Company X, from customer service to the production line. Shipments were often late, as many ignored due dates. To make matters worse, the quality of the product was rarely checked, resulting in poor customer satisfaction.

We addressed this by eliminating the habit of supervisors picking easy orders to fill first, and they were trained to understand the importance of due dates. 100% of orders were dated and had to be where the customer requested, when requested. Previously, the company often picked up the tab for express shipping methods.

Training and establishing new process flows often results in a company culture that encourages and supports the team concept. Prior to changes of processes, a small order would take a three-day lead time and after the changes, an order would have one-day lead time. Sufficient time for adequate skills training and team development increases the willingness for team members to take risks and improve team leadership.

Changing the way employees at Company X worked was a challenge. They first had to be educated, then shown the benefits—not only to the company but to themselves—of the proposed changes. They were guided to acceptance, and finally they had to be asked for their total commitment. Without their commitment, little of the accomplished would have been possible.

Self-directed work teams operate best in organizations that have flat or horizontal structures. Environments that require inter-organizational cooperation and have high levels of workers expectations of participation also optimize performance. When people share purpose, process, involvement, communications, commitment, and trust the production and quality are increased and waste minimized. All contribute to the goals of increasing and exceeding bottom line expectations.

▌ POINT OF USE LOGISTICS (JIT)

Point of Use Logistics ensures that parts are at the right place at the right time and in the right quantity. It is a Kanban, a just in time system, that supports a continuous flow of parts through the facility. This contributes to the object of eliminating the need of a staging area and lowering overhead costs. Integrity for schedules is also a high priority. Additionally, key supplier development must also be considered.

Company X had to overcome the lack of logistics in their workflow. Components were picked by stock employees and delivered to the staging area. However, the staging area was nowhere next to production and this space was used to unpack and then repack components after printing. This process made no sense and created a lot of confusion. Parts travelled all over the factory and were often damaged or misplaced before arriving in shipping. Our solution was to eliminate the staging area and required that every item had to be placed on the scheduled line. With the development of 5S established, everyone knew to always keep components and tools in their place. Improvements in all areas of workflow followed.

It would have been ideal to eliminate the warehouse and move all products to the shop, but due to the high turnover of production for printing, we did not know what processes would be used for parts to be printed, so we could not eliminate it completely. The same component could be required to be printed in one color or multiple colors and/or printing in multiple locations, which would change the process. Lines were developed according to processes; however, even with these considerations, we managed to eliminate staging area. Additionally, we partnered with our offshore suppliers to provide printed components for large orders, helping reduce in-house inventory cost by $975K.

Having the correct inventory data and processes in place to measure improvements, and suppliers willing to print large orders, we were able to increase inventory turns from 3 to 6 annually; as they did not need to move or print parts for large orders.

▍CYCLE TIME MANAGEMENT (SPEED)

Long cycle times lead to poor performance in speed, quality, and customer satisfaction when a company is constantly fighting to meet a schedule. This section addresses the need for finding ways to reduce cycle times from order entry to customer receipt. When we reduce set up time, we reduce cycle times, inventory and on time delivery. Simultaneously, dynamic teams are developed by educating the workforce through individual and group coaching, further driving the reductions.

Here the SBIB objectives are to improve productivity as well as increase speed and agility. On-time delivery improvements and inventories reduction must be included in the mix of goals. Line balancing, team dynamics, and management's coaching role are also considerations.

As we have mentioned throughout, developing documentation and standards to help measure progress are imperative. As with Company X, we established the requirement to change the way an order was processed through the factory in order to reduce cycles. To meet this end goal, we instituted continuous production methods, one-way flow. SMED (Single-Minute Exchange of Dies) improved set ups from over an hour to under fifteen minutes for multiple color printers and five minutes for one color printers. Schedules were implemented according to processes required to print and based on process standards.

All manufacturing businesses must be familiar with the 8 Wastes of Manufacturing (see Figure 3) and training for all employees ensures cross-company participation to develop ways to eliminate waste. Company X enacted self-directed work teams to ensure that all required parts were printed as per specifications. This improved the process where lack of communication created flaws in the production line and required duplication of efforts more times than not.

With the improvement of processes and reduction in set up and rework time, changes were made to the express offering—moving from a three-day turnaround for 1000 parts or less and only one color and one location to same-day service for these processes as long as order was received prior to 1:00 P.M. This again increased customer satisfaction. Improvements in cycle time and set up times were realized as order cycles were reduced from three days to one day, and set up time was reduced from one hour plus to under fifteen minutes—for a savings of $665K. Again, when we optimize manufacturing performance, the bottom line has nowhere to go but up.

Remember, this was only made possible because the teams controlled every aspect of production, including the continuous elimination of waste and the improvements needed. Perhaps, however, the biggest change can best be experienced through shifts to the business culture where managers learn to back off from micromanaging the people and adopt a coaching role (think: no more badgering).

Types of waste	Effects of Waste
Overproduction	Producing more, sooner and faster than required by the next process
Transportation	Any movement that does not add value to the product
Inventory	Maintaining excess inventory
Processing	Doing more work than necessary
Waiting	Operator or machine idle time
Correction	All repairs to product to fulfill customer requirements
Motion	Any wasted motion to pick up parts or stock parts. Also wasted walking.
Unutilized Talent	Encourage employee creativity

Figure 3

▌ PRODUCTION LINEARITY (TEAM WORK)

Production Linearity calls for tools such as daily progress reviews, waste reduction methods, reviews of the effectiveness of MRP/ERP, checks for resource availability. The use of these tools lead to reduction in scrap, rework, overtime, and late deliveries—all elements for optimizing the manufacturing process and increasing the bottom line.

Continuous production is one of the important processes relative to achieving production linearity. The challenge for Company X was to keep daily pressure on the critical path of scheduled tasks such as artwork, screen or cliché, ink, materials, and print. To address this challenge, we initiated an organized and focused assault on production flexibility, speed, quality, and costs via daily progress reviews. The planning and manufacturing team became sensitive and proactive in the execution of early production planning details to be sure up front planning and execution would yield results and lead to profitability. We also initiated the use of a magnetic board to schedule daily production planning details and monitor production linearity. By doing this, the workforce was able to focus on details, corrective actions, and recovery planning and quality issues. Additionally, shift meetings were held every day, prior to start of shift, to status the prior day's or prior shifts progress on the magnetic board, and to establish the daily challenges and assign team actions—and they were always provided the tools to get the job done.

By planning everyone's workdays around the production schedule, management was assured that required personnel were present daily and where needed. There was a focus on cycle time reduction and setup times, preventative maintenance, workplace integrity, visual scheduling, and worker flexibility.

Again total employee involvement and empowerment is called for the execution of any transformation. With Company X, empowering employees was key, as the efforts led to a mindset of continuous improvement and collaboration for the entire organization. *There is always a better way* became the thought of the day, every day. It made nearly everyone aware of capabilities they never thought they had or trained for. After they were shown a different way of looking at things, many experienced an awakening that would continue as they reached for the stars.

This awakening also shifted the mindset of employees about who their "real" boss was. During my meetings, I would ask employees who was their boss and I got every answer except the "customer." Afterwards, nearly everyone was walking around asking each other who was their boss, which turned into an obsession for the entire organization. "The Customer" became the echo from the top floor to the shop floor. Management was assigned the task of doing walks (gemba) through the factory and coach on anything they saw wrong or out of place. They had effectively learned to replace their old habits of badgering with empowering techniques designed to uplift their workforce, adding to the investment in customer satisfaction.

A company needs customers to stay in business and if they do not commit to focus on satisfying the customer, someone else will. We all know that a company without customers is not going to stay in business to long. If there is no business, then there are no jobs. Once that epiphany is reached, everyone will take care of the customer every day.

Moreover, respect for others and collaboration are important for any objectives to be achieved. The phrase "good enough" should no longer be part of anyone's vocabulary in any organization. Good enough denotes disrespect for one another—and the customer. If all employees take ownership of their work and do not settle until results are achieved, that will exceed the expectation of the customer, success is assured—and that means the customer is satisfied. Company X experienced customer satisfaction of on time delivery and quality of printing at 98%. Customer complaints and returns became a rare occasion!

For a make-to-order business, production linearity measurement displays the time-phased schedule for each customer order. The importance of this method is that it presents a daily status of achievements and provides a target for daily corrective actions. With this approach, companies can have as much focus on action at the beginning of the day as they do at the end—and that is the key to linear production! Adopting this tracking method eliminates such elements of waste as overproduction, excess inventory, and correction and again unutilized talent (see CTM).

▌ S&O, RESOURCE PLANNING (COMMITMENT FROM EVERYONE)

A good sales forecast leads to exact capacity planning and will harness workforce stability and create cost effective materials management, by tracking the skillsets of employees in order to determine where weaknesses exist. It calls for the utilization of a Stage Gate Review process that allows for everyone's up front involvement in the introduction of new products or changes that allows for on time completion of projects.

Here the SBIB objectives include increased customer responsiveness, workforce stability, flexibility and retention, cost effective materials management, make/buy decisions, sales forecast management, people value and skills training, and capacity planning.

The goal for Company X was to determine what resources would be required in order to maintain a stable workforce. Historically, they were using the roller coaster approach, increasing and decreasing the workforce dependent on the demands of production. They also relied heavily on contract employees, hindering the full buy-in for any changes. After all, temporary workers hardly are comfortable being loyal, knowing at any moment their contracts can be terminated.

A stable workforce also demands employee training—something I emphasize over and over—not only here in the chapter, but in my work with clients. Onboard training is essential for new hires so that they don't feel as if they've been thrown off the ship without a flotation device. With the correct training, they'll have the skill necessary to navigate the new waters on which they are sailing.

When new processes are developed, employees must be trained— and their skills must be measured. Emphasis is required on customer value training, so that the needs of the customer are never far from the minds of employees as they go throughout their workday. As Company X discovered, employee training improved morale significantly as the employees saw the opportunity to improve their processes. Contract hires were also able to fully inhabit their roles as they became permanent members of the workforce. Ultimately, these actions led to improved customer responsiveness from everyone.

As employees were given the opportunity to be hired full time for the company, their morale was lifted to a sense of community and belonging. They were no longer afraid of being replaced. With training their skills became more proficient and a skills inventory system was developed and implemented to measure not only their progress, but how well they were trained. The company became more conscious of equality in pay and to assure that an equitable "pay for skills" review process was in place, a technique to assure equity was developed and reviewed on an annual basis. Employees started to think out of the box and continued to offer ideas to improve their processes and skills. This resulted in multifaceted changes including the adoption of manufacturing tooling in house and the establishment of a tool room. This yielded a savings $250K annually.

Furthermore, the over the wall syndrome was eliminated and product launches were ahead of schedule with the right resources and tooling, with adequate time to do print testing as stage gate review was implemented.

Any manufacturing company should know that the development of the system that tracks and records the skills of people and monitors progress in acquiring the five primary skills are required to assure worker flexibility. It can be used throughout the organization, not just on the production line.

▌ CUSTOMER CONNECTIVITY (CRM)

In this phase, it is everyone's responsibility to have a customer focus and reach for total customer satisfaction by meeting customer demands. The entire objective is to become the supplier of choice by every customer.

As everyone that is in business knows (or not), a business without customers, is not a business, it's just an expensive hobby. As I mention to all I touch, no customers-no business, no business-no jobs. If we have happy employees and quality parts, we have productivity and most important happy customers. This ideal is created through establishing an environment of product and service leadership. Additionally, everyone "walks the talk," to create superior customer treatment, with a focus on speed and quality. Ultimately, this leads to becoming the preferred supplier of choice.

The icing on the cake is to change the customer's perception of a company. For Company X, this occurred during the course of a few years, from the perception of poor quality and service to one of superior customer satisfaction.

Any company can achieve such results when efforts are focused on not only providing speed, quality, and competitive prices, but also on assuring that their true value is communicated to their customers through many channels of the organization. In this way, they would become again their customer's preferred supplier of choice.

Customer feedback is vital in this process. Company X implemented an "Are You Happy with Our Products and Service" program where they would include a card in each shipment and also had individual business function solicit their customers for feedback to be used in their customer connectivity training programs. The company made it a point of training their employees in customer relations and courtesy. They started to plan and implement proactive projects that breakdown the communication barriers that create unwanted perceptions by customers.

Initially, the company ate a lot of humble pie, and in the end they became better and stronger. The customers loved their same-day service offerings and used it in many cases to test if they would come through in order to return for good.

As progress for improvements were made, we recorded the present cycle times as a measure of improvement from 19 days to 8 days for 10K orders. This was done for all processes and order quantities of 1000 to 10000 pieces.

Customer connectivity represents a set of business processes touching on all aspects of the company. Customer satisfaction is a great deal more than the clichés "getting close to customers" and the motto "the customer is always right." As Company X learned, all processes of business operations must be in line with the real boss—the customer, from the top floor to the shop floor.

▌ FINAL THOUGHTS

This is a quick take on how the Somar Business Improvement Basics™ can help any business make the necessary improvements to stay competitive. You don't need to spend a lot of money as the system can be tailored to make improvements that will help you succeed. What is required is commitment to employee education and empowerment, customer focus, and a willingness to make change. It is based on lean, TPM, continuous improvement, Six Sigma and strides to teach kaizen, improving a little at a time.

As Thomas Edison always said, "There is always a better way." And there is.

Luis Ramos

282 West Main Street

Milford, CT 06460

lramos@somarassociates.com

(203) 640-5470

Luis Ramos has over twenty-five years operational expertise transforming manufacturing and distribution organizations by improving their business processes, lean sigma manufacturing, project management, sales management, technology training, and supply chain management. Luis' experience includes operational responsibilities, lean implementation, continuous improvement, change management and serving in a variety of management roles. He was general manager of an OEM manufacturer, managing all aspects of business management and company operations including strategic planning, staffing, new business development, marketing, sales and customer service. Luis led the company through a successful transformation helping to increase sales by 40% while leading a lean manufacturing initiative, increasing employee productivity by 35%.

He has also worked with companies to start up and or relocate their facilities, while managing all manufacturing operations and serving as project manager for new product development and lean initiatives. As a management consultant, Luis implemented lean initiatives in eight different facilities for a container manufacturer. He has provided facility layouts to improve process flow and implementing best practices for consumer goods, distribution and OEM manufacturers. Luis has had the leadership role in the implementation of ERP systems (SAP and Made2Manage). Beginning his career as a tool & die maker, Luis has a BS (Mechanical Engineering) from University of Puerto Rico, Mayaquez (CAAM), and a MBA (International Business) from the University of New Haven. He is also Lean Six Sigma Black Belt Certified. In 2012 Luis Co-Founded Somar Associates LLC a project management and continuous improvement consulting firm.

WORKPLACE WELLNESS CONSULTANT: REDUCING STRESS IN THE WORKPLACE

FORREST WILLETT

As workplace consultant's we are often welcomed into the workplace and not always with open arms. Most businesses will hire a consultant when change is required and it is in many cases not a welcome change from the employees view. We as consultants are not always welcome and the number one reason for that is a lack of trust. I have found that in most companies the breakdown in communication all starts with a lack of trust.

With a lack of trust stress is often present. Stress costs company money right off the bottom line, which starts with time off. Insurance premiums may reflect this time off. There is also the loss of productivity when stress holds back the skills of clarity, creativity and especially cooperation within the work environment. When stress is present across various departments, the basis for a negative culture is present.

To reduce stress in the workplace I often start with trust building exercises. Building trust right off the start will reduce stress and resistance of change. I always start off by sharing my own personal story of overcoming stress and resistance of change in my own life and work environment. By being authentic and honest with the people you are working with you will immediately build trust and that in turn will reduce the amount of work necessary for the change required. How vulnerable and how fast you are able to become vulnerable will determine how soon you are welcomed into the work community.

Here is my story I share with workplaces and explain the stresses and change I have overcome in my own life. I only speak on topics I am passionate about, and those topics are reducing stress and creating mental wellness in your life. If you do not speak of topics that you know firsthand people will see right through you and your ideas will not be welcomed.

October 6, 2002 I lost the most important person in my life in a horrific car wreck, it was not my wife or my son, I lost myself. Yes I'm the man who lost himself. I lost who I was as a husband, father and friend. I lost my ability to read, write and speak fluently. I was a two-year-old child in the 31-year-old body everything around me was new and extremely frustrating. I could not even control my balance while walking I looked like a baby deer on a frozen pond trying to stand up straight. Early on this caused me to fall down a set of stairs breaking my leg. I often wondered what went wrong why did this happen? Just weeks ago I was a successful entrepreneur with offices in eight cities and 23 employees, now I was unable to even count change to buy a coffee.

At the time of the accident I had my car for sale and a gentlemen wanted to test drive the car, I gave him the keys and I sat in the passenger seat and that's all I remember. Later through the police investigation it was revealed that the driver was speaking to his son on a cell phone and lost control of the vehicle at a high rate of speed. The accident scene was one of confusion as the car came back registered to myself, the police and people on the fire department who were there to extricate us from the car knew that it was not me driving as I was on that fire department for 10 years as a volunteer, I knew every person on that department personally. They knew I did not have a moustache or glasses and the person in the passenger seat was unrecognizable swollen, bloody and unconscious with no personal ID. My left arm was flopping around broken in several places. I can't believe how devastated they must have been to see me in this unrecognizable condition, even my good friend Lorus who was one of the several paramedics on scene later told me that he could not believe it was me. Yet just hours before I was at the fire captain's house visiting with my son feeling I was on top of the world.

My first memories were 10 days later waking up in the hospital they were very foggy memories as I slipped in and out of consciousness, the only thing that felt familiar was the constant ringing in my ears and the sound of the blood pressure monitors "beep beep beep" my first thought was what happened to my arm? I could not move it, and why is my mouth full of stitches inside and out? My wife Julie walked in to the hospital room with my then two-year-old son Hunter, although I recognized them I was frustrated that I didn't remember their names as a matter of fact I didn't remember the names of many of the people I had known for much of my life. If you have ever known anyone with Alzheimer's disease you know that losing your memory is one of the most devastating things in life and here I was 31 years old losing mine.

Although I new what I wanted to say my no's were yeses and my yeses were no's I would ask for cream in my transmission "coffee" is what I was thinking. People had a hard time understanding me and I had an even harder time understanding them. So often I would just stare at them with that deer in the headlight look and nod my head as if I understood. I have so much compassion for people who come to North America from all over the world and do not know the language, I have felt the pain of knowing what I want to say but the words just don't come out and the words that do come out do not make any sense to the people I was speaking with. So for a long time I would remain speechless.

Through several MRI's and Neuropsychological assessments I was deemed to have a catastrophic brain injury through the Glasco outcome scale if you're not sure what that means don't worry I did not either. It had to be explained to me by several different doctors because I did not want to do believe what the first or second doctor told me. In a nutshell what they had told me was I had a permanent loss of 55% or more of myself as a human being mentally and behaviourally. An example of a catastrophic injury that would be easier to comprehend is the loss of two arms, two legs or both your eyes. I was in denial and in shock. How could I have lost so much? Looking in the mirror other than several scars some broken and missing teeth I was still the same person. I don't know who I was trying to kid maybe I thought I was in a bad dream and it would just go away when I woke up one morning. That did not happen unfortunately it was a bad dream from which I would not wake for a long time. I had to face reality. The reality was I have changed, and I have lost. What people don't understand is the total absolute frustration of this injury, the things you take for granted every day like getting out of bed jumping in the shower washing your hair and brushing your teeth then sending some emails were gone I couldn't do it without the help and assistance of someone else.

How lucky can one person be? Very few people are given a second chance in life I was grateful to be given a third chance. Yes a third, you see this was my second traumatic brain injury the first one occurred when I was two years old and I fell down the basement stairs and acquired a subdural hematoma which is caused by extreme bleeding to the brain usually brought on by blunt force trauma increasing the pressure inside the skull, my skull did not split open to relieve the pressure so my lifeless body was taken to the hospital for surgical intervention where they drilled a small hole in my skull the size of a nickel and then removed a small triangle shaped piece of bone beside it where they were able to evacuate the blood clot. I have been reminded of this injury and how lucky I am everyday as I wash my hair and run my hand over the area where the bone was removed. I would have to say that growing up seemed just as normal as any other kid because I did not know myself any other way. Fast forward 30 years and I could see huge changes from the way I was.

Everything in life had changed, friends would stop over to visit and say to Julie and I that they had gone boating for the weekend at the cottage, what have you guys been up to? Julie would then share the events of our week, Forrest learned to brush his teeth and shave on his own this week and he did not cut his face once I'm so proud of him. And next week he will be working with his speech therapist on a grocery list and if he's feeling up to it he may actually go with her to the grocery store and try to complete the list if his anxiety does not stop him at the door. As friends and visitors would come to the house they could not help but notice large laminated signs on the fridge, stove and doors. They were reminders for me not to touch the stove, to remember to put things back into the fridge and also contact someone before I go outside. We also had another person in the house, a rehabilitation support worker, who I called my babysitter. As I was to have 24-hour attentive care to keep me safe from my own actions on the advice of my team. Many people have experienced the frustration of coming out of the mall and forgetting where your car is, I would walk just a few blocks away and forget where my house was, we were very fortunate to live in a small community where everyone knew everybody so if I was lost neighbours would kindly direct me home or sometimes walk with me. This must have been unbelievably difficult for Julie I don't know why she stayed with me but I am grateful that she did, she herself has transformed from a go-getter to a go-giver.

I had a whole team of professionals working with me daily some of them where neurologists, psychologists, psychiatrists, surgeons, physiotherapists, speech language pathologists, occupational therapists and the list goes on and on. Close your eyes for a minute and just imagine if you had a dozen or more of the top professionals in their field whose full-time job it was to help you get from where you are to where you want to be, working with you and your goal tirelessly day after day year after year and unfortunately not reaching your ultimate goal. How would you feel?

I started to spiral into deep depression and anxiety disorders, the feeling of hopelessness and helplessness was the flavour of the day. And my favourite activity became lying in bed all day in between my therapy sessions. I also became dependant on prescription medication, anti anxiety pills and painkillers such as oxycodone, Percocet and anti-depressants they were my crutch. At the time it did not register with me that after all my surgeries were over, the casts and wheelchairs were gone but I was still taking these pain relievers daily just to cope through the day it had become a habit. Years later I now see that the pain relieving effects of such drugs also soothes the pain of a broken heart and broken dreams, I can also see how not having the ability to create a future can get people hooked on these drugs by chemically removing all fear and anxiety.

This was a letter written from my family doctor to the treatment team one and a half years post accident. "I have known Mr. Willett for over 20 years and I have watched him grow from a young boy into a very successful business person. As you know, he had a major motor vehicle accident October 6, 2002 at which time Mr. Willett was a passenger in the car that was involved in a single vehicle rollover. He suffered a major traumatic brain injury at the time and was unconscious at the scene, had facial trauma that knocked out several teeth and fractured left humerus. At the present time, he presents as a pleasant handsome gentleman who is able to carry on a superficial conversation. However, I have major concerns regarding Mr. Willett and that he has trouble with his attention span and cannot hold onto thoughts for a sustained period of time. He has certainly lost a substantial part of his judgment and his ability to speak fluently has been substantially reduced from what it was. My understanding of the notes from the speech and language pathology assessment is that he has major problems with reading comprehension and short-term verbal memory. This is well documented in the literature. This gentleman, certainly at present, is unable to function in his job as an entrepreneur at the head of a fairly large and complex company. He certainly does not show the wit and depth of thinking that he had prior to the injury. It is my opinion that he will never be able to go back to the level of work he was doing prior to the injury.

I have concerns that when something like this happens it often leads to breakups in families further down the road and major depression that will further impact on his ability to function as a person he once was.

It is strongly held in my opinion that this gentleman has a psychological and/or mental impairment that will affect his life at least 55% or more his ability to function as a father, to make a living and enjoy life has been changed." Dr Richard Coutts Feb 12-2004

Just two and a half years after the date of the accident, a neuropsychological assessment that spanned over four days of testing had concluded that I had plateaued, this means I have reached 95 to 98% of my spontaneous recovery and not to expect any further spontaneous recovery. The doctor said I should just be lucky to be alive, I wasn't so sure about that. 2 1/2 years that's all they give you? 912.5 days, hope has to last longer than that.

This recent news would be yet another blow not only to my recovery but to my now disintegrating self-esteem. I thought to myself how many times can a human being be beaten down and continue to get up? With all of the diagnosis from the doctors it may look like I was a modern-day Frankenstein. Catastrophic brain injury, clinical depression, several anxiety disorders, Post traumatic stress disorder, mild aphasia and I could go on. I had many thoughts of what's the use, why even try anymore. I could not get excited about anything for the fear of failure was ever looming, I was a real mess. The days and months went up and down with new hope and a zest for life one day and suicidal thoughts the next and in between all of that was just a grey numbness. No emotions and no control over my own life other than breathing and eating. I felt like a puppet on a string being toted it around by well-meaning doctors and therapists, do this, do that, try this, go here. And like a timid little puppy afraid of getting into trouble I did just as they said, although I still felt as if I was getting nowhere until my favourite hobby of laying in bed finally paid off big-time one morning. I felt as if I had won life's lottery.

We all have days in our lives that we will never forget, something so significant happens you remember the exact time and place you were such as the day JFK was shot or the day the twin towers fell in New York on 9/11 you remember where you were who you were with sometimes even what you are wearing.

My significant day came as I was lying in bed with the blankets pulled over my head waiting for the world to go away, when I heard the morning show host on television say coming up next is Jack Canfield with his new book the Success Principles how to get from where you are to where you want to be. In my head I thought this is probably more crap, until the commercial was over and they introduced Jack, he claimed that his book the Success Principles can help transform anyone to get from where they are to where they want to be, it doesn't matter what your current circumstances are or your past situations if you apply these principles you will transform your life. I have to say for the first time in years I sat up and pulled the covers off my head. I remember the words clearly that Jack had said "If you could do anything in life and there were no limitations, what would you do?" I remember chuckling to myself and saying if I could do anything in life and there were no limitations "I would take my biggest disabilities and turn them into assets. Not only would I learn to read and write I would become a best-selling author, I would also overcome depression and anxiety and help others do the same and not only would I learn to speak fluently again I would become a professional speaker." I then chuckled again thinking "Ya right" and then called my wife to come into the room and write this guys name down because I wanted to buy this book.

Julie looked at me confused and said "you can't even read your son a night time story how are you going to read such a book"? Julie does not sugar coat anything. I exclaimed "yes but this guy said if I do this, this and this I can transform my life." Julie entertained me and brought me to the bookstore to purchase the book only for one reason, she said she had not seen me that excited about anything in years, I finally had that spark back in my eyes, that was until I presented the book to my speech therapist and told her that if I read this book and applied these principles I could write my own book and become a professional speaker. I don't know if she was gasping or choking when I told her my exciting news. I was waiting for the drink of tea to come out her nose while she tried to contain her emotions. Once again I told the story of this fellow on TV who said if you apply all of these principles in this book you can change your life. My speech therapist explained a few roadblocks I may run into, one I could not read very well or comprehend what I was reading, at that time I was just learning to read a child's book to my son. The second roadblock was the immense size of this book over 450 pages. The children's books I was reading at the time where 8 to 12 pages and would take multiple readings to comprehend them. I would read a book to my son at night lying in bed and my son would say "that's not what it says daddy". You see my wife would read to him every night the same book he knew the words in the order they were to come in and he would spend no time letting me know when I had made a mistake. This would bring up a series of considerations, fears and roadblocks in my own head, seriously how could I write a book when I have not yet re-learned the basics of spelling? And the thought of being a professional speaker, I was nervous to say the least considering that when we rarely went out for breakfast I would just get Julie to read me the menu and I would order OOrange J J J J J J J J Juice. Whenever my anxiety would arise my stuttering was out of control and the thought of speaking in front of people brought on anxiety. Kids are honest and the truth hurts sometimes, I remember one of Hunters friends saying "your dad talks funny" his reply was "that's how he talks".

I was determined to read this book and change my life. I knew where I wanted to be I just did not know how to get there. My speech therapist and I made an agreement that I would give myself one year to read this book and if I did not finish the book or gave up due to difficulty that I would not beat myself up emotionally as I've done in the past. I was now motivated more than ever not only to learn how to read and comprehend but to show everyone there is life after brain injury and depression.

We created many strategies to read the book such as highlighting, underlining and using a white envelope to slide down one line at a time so I would not skip lines and get confused.

The first principle felt like a kick in the stomach take 100% responsibility of your life. "Who me?" I thought they must mean for everyone else not me! I wasn't responsible for what happened to me it was the guy that was driving the car, I would think to myself.

The concept of taking 100% responsibility for my life did not kick in for a few months until my son's birthday when I discovered that baseballs don't bounce. "The title of my first book." One of his friends gave him a present as he ripped the wrapping away and threw it on the ground his face lit up with excitement, he was given a big white softball in a black leather glove that looked four times too big for his hand yet he was still excited, he dropped the ball to the ground and looked at it confused he then picked it up again and dropped it, at that point his friend shouted "baseballs don't bounce" those three words hit home very hard. I had to go in the house as I broke down crying, here was my son growing up and someone else had taught him how to skate and ride a bike. I was missing his childhood while I was hanging out in the awe ain't it awful club telling all the poor me stories. At that moment I realized I had to give up all my excuses and poor me stories and take 100% responsibility for my life if I was to get where I wanted to go.

Over the next week I did a really big life review going over areas in my life that I had not taken 100% responsibility in and there were many.

For starters my family and then my rehabilitation, I would lay around in bed all day waiting for the therapists to show up and "make" me better, not realizing that I was to do the work especially while they were gone. Somehow I just thought that it was their job to get me better. I realize now that it's not the case. Just as Jim Rohn says, you can't hire other people to do your push-ups. It now totally made sense to me that if I was to be better I am the only person responsible for that, not my family not my therapists, me. Yes they were all there to assist me yet I was the one in the end that was responsible for doing the work. We are all self-made people yet it is usually the successful people who will admit it. It took a lot for me to admit to myself that I have created this life I was living. It was time for me to get down to work and escape this self-created prison I was living in. It was time to "Take action"

I soon started to apply the success principles in all areas of my life and to my amazement life was becoming easier as I was able to release the brakes and accept life as it unfolded.

It was then I made the choice to be a mental health advocate and consultant!

There are so many Success Principles that have made massive changes in my life I would like to share a few of them. Principle number 15 Experience your fear and take action anyway. This one principle would help me overcome so many limiting beliefs and roadblocks in my life. Starting with my social anxiety disorder and depression I was at the point where I would not go out in public or speak with people that I've known for years. Somehow my anxiety grew so powerful that when I tried to speak to people my throat would close up as if a professional wrestler was holding me off the ground with his arm around my neck. Or if I was able to talk my voice would start to crackle as if I was about to cry, I would have to take anti-anxiety medication just to go outside that is if I wasn't too depressed to go out. So I decided to go out in public and start volunteering. My occupational therapist set me up with her friend who ran the recreation department at a retirement lodge where I met many wonderful people. Tim Nesbitt was one of the first people to introduce himself and we have since become close friends we were both born in the same week in the same town exactly 50 years apart. Tim was a proud World War II Air Force veteran as I got to know him he revealed to me that he had suffered through many of the things I was, such as depression and Post traumatic stress disorder. It was a relief to know that I wasn't alone over the next several years I would spend 3 to 4 hours a week with Tim and the more we spoke of how we felt the better we both felt. I felt very comfortable with Tim as he was with me, we said we would adopt each other as he never had a grandson and I never had a grandfather in my life. When I first felt the fear and anxiety of going to volunteer I backed out several times. I am so glad now that I felt my fear and took action anyway. Who ever would have thought that I would talk my way out of depression, in those early days of volunteering at the retirement lodge I thought it was going there to help people, as it turns out they were helping me. Tim really taught me how to be a class act even though he was retired and 93 years old every day he was well dressed and clean-shaven, he once told me something that will stick with me for the rest of my life "when you make agreements keep them." he told me in August of 1947, I married my wife Joan after returning home from war and we made the agreement "till death do us part". And Tim kept that agreement, Joan passed in 1988 and Tim stayed single until his recent passing April 16, 2014 and I am grateful to have been with Tim at his bedside holding his hand the morning he past.

Principle 13 Take action. This is another principle that has allowed me to make massive change in my life, as I was recovering in what seemed like leaps and bounds I was asked by many organizations to share my story and for quite a while I turned them down until the day I decided to take action. The March of Dimes is an organization that helps many people with physical and mental disabilities, they were having their annual conference and one of the speakers backed out so they asked if I would be willing to share my story of success and triumph over adversity. Although I agreed I thought in my head "Oh my God what have I gotten myself into, I am not a professional speaker" and I only have 10 days to prepare. It was time for me to "act as if" this was my big chance to reach one of my biggest goals in life and I wasn't about to let it slip through my fingers. I prepared a speech on paper with the help of my speech therapist and read it over and over again for several days and on the day of the speech I walked into the convention center to see a room of 287 people, this was the first time in over a year that I wish I still had an anxiety pill, sweat rolled down my back like an April rain shower and then I stood up at the podium my hands were shaking so bad I could not read the paper so I set the paper down to a deep breath and said to myself " this is it, I am finally here." I looked around the room and started with a joke. I told the crowd that I was shaking so bad I could thread a sewing machine while it was running. Their laughter put me at ease and I was able to share my story without the paper. After it was over, I was given a standing ovation. I have never experienced that in my life. It was a rush of feelings that I cannot explain. After the talk was over I was approached by several people who wanted me to speak at their organization. I was on cloud nine just a few short years ago I could not speak fluently or put a full sentence together that made much sense and now people want to hire me to speak all over the world, wow.

In my commitment to constant and never ending improvement I decided if I want to take this professional speaking to in the next level that I better get some training to be a professional speaker, the following February I started on my journey with Jack Canfield as my personal mentor in his Train the Trainer course. And just like anything in life came the fears, considerations and roadblocks. On the first day of the course I thought to myself, what am I thinking? I'm not a professional speaker. What if all of these people I am surrounded by find out that I could not speak fluently just a few short years ago? I was given the opportunity to share my story on stage with all of these amazing people and to my surprise only good has come from that day forward. I also wanted to improve my consulting business so I contacted the experts in that field at the Business Consultant Institute where they helped me hone my craft and flourish my business. I have now been invited to speak in many different places all over the world. This year I will be traveling to Switzerland and France, it is truly amazing what can happen in life when you decide what you want, believe in yourself, set goals and take action.

The greatest transformation in my overall well-being came from applying three principles together daily, Principle number 11 Visualization. Principle number 22 practice persistence and Principle number 23 practice the rule of five. Through my recovery one of my biggest obstacles was fatigue the feeling of constantly being tired and this affects every aspect of your life from relationships to your work life and your everyday well-being. The reason I was fatigued is that I was getting very little sleep at night, tossing and turning awake all hours of the night worrying of what the next day might bring unable to slow down or turn off the thoughts going through my head. I was sent to do overnight sleep studies in the hospital on three occasions and each time the only result was a heavier prescription sleeping pills. I turned this around by making a list of my top five priority actions that I would do the following day towards my goals. I would then visualize the whole next day as if it were a movie playing in my head, the actions I would take, the activities I would be doing. It didn't happen overnight but my sleep improved tremendously over the coming months. I did have a slip up as I thought I had very thing under control I began to slack off on the visualization and rule of five thus falling back into my old sleeping patterns it was then I realized that I had to practice persistence with patience if I wanted the change to be long-term and I did. As my sleep improved so did my relationship with my wife and son and when that happened I no longer felt as depressed. I went to my doctor with the goal of getting off the medication that I was told that I would likely be on for life. I exchanged the pills for exercise, diet and applying these Success Principles. I have been off all medication completely since August 2007 with no symptoms of depression or anxiety and I am still happily married over 20 years.

I have not only reached the goals I originally set out for myself I have exceeded them, I have learned to speak fluently and have become a professional speaker and not only have I learned to read and write I have written a number one bestseller!

True transformation cannot occur with hope and willpower alone we need specific tools to make lasting change this book gives you the tools you need for that change I am living proof of that. My transformation did not occur overnight it took a long time reaching one small goal after the other which eventually turned into a massive change. If I am able to overcome all of these obstacles in life and succeed at my goals imagine what is possible for you.

Building houses for most of my life I know that a solid foundation is the most important part of a solid home if you don't have that everything else is out of whack. When I hit rock bottom I needed to start over and The Success Principles would be the solid foundation on which I would rebuild my life, and an extraordinary one at that.

As you can see I share all information in my life with my clients as an open book with nothing to hide and when you can be this open you can build trust that will last a lifetime. By being open and vulnerable with the people you are working with it will allow them to do the same and that is when real change happens. I believe this is the reason I am hired back repeatedly by many of my clients all over the world. I am grateful to be able to share this information to many different corporations such as Dubai airports, Emirates Airlines, Clark's inn's India, many school boards throughout North America and India as well as hospitals, police and fire departments.

I have transformed many workplaces as well as myself I am a two time #1 bestselling author Featured in the New York Times Bestseller the Success principles by Jack Canfield I have also been named one of the top 50 difference makers in the world by Defyeneurs magazine for 2016 alongside Jack Canfield.

Forrest Willett

www.forrestwillett.com

Forrest Willett is an international keynote speaker and mental health consultant who increases productivity in the workplace through positivity.

Forrest's unique trust building exercises greatly reduces the stigma of mental health issues such as depression and anxiety which is the number one reason people miss work and extend time off on stress leave. Through addressing the elephant in the room " mental health" and building trust among coworkers, Forrest's workshops will rebuild the workplace atmosphere as a place to enjoy and look forward to each day.

Forrest has worked with many fortune 500 companies such as Dubai airports, Emirates airlines, BP oil, Central bank of the Philippines

Forrest is also a #1 best-selling author of two books and is featured in the #1 New York Times best-seller The Success Principles by Jack Canfield. Forrest along with Jack Canfield have been named two of the top 50 difference makers of 2016 by Defyeneurs magazine.

LESSONS LEARNED FROM PROFESSIONAL ATHLETES TO HELP YOUR BUSINESS THRIVE

DR. LAVERNE ADAMS

You can only imagine how amazing it was for me to receive an email from Rick Warren, the lead pastor of the Saddleback Church with over 20,000 members. He is impressively the author of *The Purpose Driven Life* which sold over 30 million copies. He wrote to commend me for my transformational work. He had just read an article that I had written regarding strategies for resurrecting dead places. He was searching for help because he was invited to be the first Caucasian pastor to preach the annual memorial message in Dr. Martin Luther King's home church in Atlanta, Ebenezer Baptist. He wanted my advice on what to say ad he considered the opportunity as one of the greatest privileges in his ministerial career. He considered Dr. King as his hero. I had come to realize that he turned to me as a trusted advisor because he believed that I had the capacity to give him what he needed at one of the most important times of his life.

I was extremely honored that such a great man would ask for my assistance, and the biggest take away for me was that it doesn't matter how successful you are or how far you have come in life, you can learn something from anyone. More importantly, you must be willing to reach out to those who can best help you with what you need, if your goal is to be able to perform beyond your current capabilities.

After almost 25 years of experience in ministry, and consulting and advising high profile professionals, including radio personalities, politicians, pastors, and great leaders, I am completely convinced that you will not manage to achieve and maintain success without some form of assistance. The biggest challenges that come with being highly successful is that 1) it is difficult to find someone to match your level of competency, 2) being able to recognize the need for a coach to help you sustain and maintain success.

This is why I developed the Total Life Transformation system, filled with powerful strategies based upon scientific research designed to produce amazing life changing result which are especially helpful for high profile people when they are searching for meaning answers to life's complexities. This system offers a guided roadmap to peak performance and includes a supportive coaching relationship to assure the accountability needed to facilitate transformation in every area of life.

As a result of my research, I stumbled upon some valuable information regarding the coaching relationship with a professional athlete that can show you how to be successful in business and thrive!

▌ LESSON 1 - LEARN THE RULES OF SUCCESS

In the United States, 1,121,744 boys play high school football but the average person is unfamiliar with the level of dedication and discipline that it takes to become a professional athlete. To get a better understanding of just how brutal this discipline needs to be, here is some statistical information that proves that desire is not always enough to get into the pros:

» 1 in 40 high school players will play in college

> » 1 in 1,010 high school players will be drafted to the NFL

> » 1 in 325 college players will be drafted in the NFL

Even though many players start in high school, the real opportunities for instruction on the game begins when some kids are old enough to walk. For many, the pathway to the NFL starts when players are as young as 5 years old. This is why little league football is a booming boutique industry for coaching these young courageous contenders. It has been found that the players who have the best performance at the high school level, will earn conference and state recognition for their play and have the best opportunities to be recruited by colleges. So it stands to reason that the player with the most bravery and experience early on, has the greatest chance of going further.

But the daring football player would not even begin to be successful without the instructive direction of the Head Coach who is responsible for training in all aspects of the football program. It is the attributes of the coach that translates into strong leadership in the player and staff. It is the work of the coach that helps to foster and character development and value of athletics that inspires the desire for the player to perform at the highest level. A good coach will instill a fearless attitude, appreciation of good sportsmanship, and a sense of pride in self, team, school, and community.

And it is primarily the same with business. A good business coach will introduce you to all aspects to the game of business. They will help show you the ropes and the rules of the game. They will show you how to produce an appreciation for entrepreneurship and strategies to perform at the highest levels. You can try to do all this on your own but you will only get but so far.

For example, I knew that if I wanted to be a winner in business, I had to learn the rules of how to play the game! I knew that I needed training. Even though I possessed an entrepreneurial spirit, there was so many things that I did not know about starting a business, let alone running a successful one. So I positioned myself to acquire all of the knowledge required. I built my endurance by spending all of my waking hours consuming all the instruction on business that I could handle regarding plan development, marketing, financing. I sat in classrooms with attorneys, accountants and other business professionals. I invested in every on-line course I could find to help me understand all the basics to starting and running a successful business.

But I quickly realized that wasn't enough. All of this staggering information that I had acquired was useless unless without implementation. I had learn how to put all of this eye-opening information into action. I knew that if I wanted to be successful, I had to create a devoted discipline of continuously working on my business. I spent one hour before I went to work and four hours when I came home every evening. I listened to business recordings during my lunch hour. I would think about business techniques when I went to bed at night. I became my business and my business has become my life.

When I realized that I went as far as I could go on my own, my only hope to surpass my personal limitations was to hire an experienced business coach. I soon discovered that the business of starting a business is a complicated process. My business coach helped me make sense out of all of the information that I had recently been introduced to and where to put all the pieces. She also helped me understand how to apply all of the strategies that I just learned. I knew that if I wanted to possess the winning edge, I needed someone to coach me who had experienced a level of success and understood the rules of the game in business. Although it seemed miraculous at the time to have a great coach, what was even more thrilling was not to have to try to figure everything out on my own.

I knew that it was absolutely essential that I recognized the need for someone else to take me to levels that I could not take myself. There were dimensions in business I had yet to reach and I needed someone to show me how to improve my business model and develop marketable products, while learn new selling skills. In addition, I had to continuously apply the information that I had learned in all of my training, as well as implement creative business strategies. I knew that it was time for me to invest in myself and get a business coach to inspire me stretch and reach for higher goals and advance in my business. From experience, I knew that coaching helps you be more productive, improve your outcomes and help you perform better because you feel supported in your efforts. The results from using a coach were stunning! I soared far beyond my own expectations. But don't just take my word for it, the powerful outcomes of coaching can be found in the research done by the International Federal Coaching* which has reported the results of coaching as follows:

» Increased Productivity - 70% improved work performance

» Improved Self Confidence - 80% improved self confidence helps to better face challenges and demands,

» Improved Relationships - 73% improved relationship interaction

» Improved Communication Skills - 72%

» Improved Life Work Balance - 67%

» Guaranteed ROI - 86%

*http://coachfederation.org/need/landing.cfm?ItemNumber=747

These statistic, no doubt also apply to business coaching. I can gauge because, I had previously started a business before and failed. I did not want to repeat the same mistakes so when I finally got up the courage to start my business again, I decided to do whatever it takes to make my business successful from the onset. I invested in myself and my business by securing a dynamic coach to help me assess my weaknesses and developed a plan to strengthen those areas so that I could advance and succeed in my business.

So what does all this mean for you and your business? You can do as much as you can to prepare for success. Develop a discipline to do the things that you hate doing like paperwork and paying attention to the little details. But don't make the mistake of trying to succeed on your own. Steven Covey puts it this way: "Begin with the end in mind." It is absolutely critical that if you want to have success in your business, you have to plan for it from the very start! Some people just want to go into business because they don't want to work for anyone else. But that reason alone is not going to help you succeed. When you work for yourself, you work harder than you do for someone else because everything depends upon you. When you go to work for someone else, they are responsible for all the details that it takes to maintain a successful business. You get to go home and think about something else, while they spend all of their waking hours thinking about how to be profitable.

In many cases, when you work for someone else, you can walk away... but the true entrepreneur can never be separated from their business. They sleep, eat, and drink their business...all day and all night. They dream about it in their sleep and any extra time is spent on how to advance the business. Those that are not willing to make these kind sacrifices will always be at the mercy of mediocrity in business and could face the probability of failure.

Athletes train hard to become the best. They devote a lot of time and energy to build strength. But regardless of how much work they do, they will never be able to surpass their own limits without the skillful assistance of a coach. With that being said, if you are going to do all of the work that it takes to be in business, you might as well investing in the tools required for success. This is not a fantasy that I am talking about but a strong intention to triumph and achieve victory. Planning for success in business is a complex science that begins with your initial concepts regarding your business ideas. You would do well to conquer your doubts and fears and involve the experts from the onset. Simply put, just like the athlete, acquiring a coach will help learn the rules of the game of business and help you to go beyond your own limits if you implement the strategies for a successful endeavor.

If you were like me, you started a business before. I thought that it was just that simple. I would sell some books and run the speaking circuit all my life and then ride into the sunset. I was not aware of the plethora of components needed to sustain a successful business and quite frankly, I did not want to take on the responsibility of the investment of time, money and energy. I learned the basic system of meeting all of the local, state and federal requirements. But if I can be honest, it wasn't because I didn't want to be considered an official business. It was because it was just too much trouble! I tried, of writing a business plan, it was like learning another language. I bought a computer program to help me, but it did no good. It was all like Greek to me. I did open a separate bank account to make my business official because I expected the money to just flow in! You can only imagine how disappointed I was when it didn't.

In retrospect, the main reason I failed is because I tried to figure it out all by myself. Although I received all of the information I needed to have a successful business, what I lacked was accountability to the strategies that I needed to implement and execute. But once I decided to get the help I needed and get a coach, I learned some of the rules of business and my business model started to take off! Here are 10 Rules To Build A Wildly Successful Business*

1. "Build something you believe in — because that's the first step to building a great brand."

2. "Don't aim for 10% improvement. Make it radically better and different."

3. "Prepare to be copied. Don't start unless you'll survive imitation."

4. "Build up reserves of money and energy for bad luck and mistakes."

5. "Never, ever give up control — until you sell."

6. "Don't compromise on the big things — compromise on everything else."

7. "Figure out how to achieve your goals on a tiny budget — then cut that number in half."

8. "It's a marathon, not a sprint."

9. "Take care of your family, personal and spiritual health — if you aren't laughing or smiling on a regular basis, recalibrate."

10. "Build the enterprise and the brand as if you'll own them forever."

http://www.forbes.com/sites/ericwagner/2014/01/14/10-rules-to-build-a-wildly-successful-business/#7649483ce287

LESSON 2 - SUSTAIN YOUR SUCCESS

It is not a mystery that the football players who get noticed by college recruiters are the ones who triumph and rise to the top of their high school conferences. You can be sure that this takes a great deal of hard work combined with skill. These players consistently executed what they learned from their coach to eliminate any margin of error and virtually presented themselves as winners. Time and time again, they come out as victors.

College programs look for the players who appear regularly in national prep football headlines. These players become all-league, all-state or all-American and attract a great deal of attention from college teams. Even though the college recruiting process can be difficult, the best players will have multiple options. Players that are in the middle will receive offers from smaller colleges, but they will have to work harder to sell themselves.

Their hard work continues as college players consistently perform at the highest level while also maintaining national media attention. Players who succeed and win collegiate awards, are placed on all-conference and all-star teams. These players have the advantage to be considered as potentials for the NFL Draft and the league's 32 teams. It takes three years after a player graduates high school to be eligible to declare for the NFL Draft. By that time, many of these players already have an idea where they will rate in the draft. That's because every step of the way, for them, it's been a calculated process.

The NFL Draft process helps us to see why planning in business is important to constantly perform at the top of your game and sustain your success. It is the job of the coach to give you the basics on how to play by the rules of the game. It is up to you to stay on top and in the game by continuously implementing strategies of sustainability. A lot of what a coach can teach you, can get you noticed by your potential customers. But it will take a lot of hard work and little imagination and creativity, to get your customers to buy. Your business career builds on every one of your previous wins. It is important to keep track of your progress and consistently play to win!

Most business success can be tracked by numbers... and numbers never lie! You will always be able to measure your success with your numbers so make sure that they are accurate. This is the most precise way to understand where you are in the game. You may need to get professional help with this but once you understand this concept you will never forget it. Your success is always about the bottom line.

At Total Life Consultancy, LLC, we observe a wonderful mission oriented triple bottom line that puts people first, then the planet, then profits. It may seem a bit out of order for the average profit seeker, but this is the order and by which we measure our success. This formula positions us to maintain our business achievements. These positive intentions is what makes us to stand out and separates us from the crowd of other similar businesses who are simply motivated by monetizing every encounter and focus simply on increasing their bottom line. If you are going to be sustained in business, it is imperative that what you do in business benefits people and is kind to the planet. It is this continued focus that will make you profitable in more ways than you can imagine.

The lifestyle of an NFL athlete also teaches us that you can never rest upon the laurels of your previous success. And just like the athlete who develops an early track record, all of these historical records must be consistently leveraged to increase business credibility. You have to consistently strive to make what we do better, delivered faster, and more economical. Quality, delivery of service, and resources must consistently be updated and improved in order to repeatedly get the attention of your target audience.

When looking for a coach, it is important for you to look for someone who is uplifting and possesses the ability to keep a positive gaze on how you will sustain yourself in the future. Like the NFL Coach, a good coach can help you go well beyond your own limitations. A coach will help you make realistic projections that you can achieve as well as avoid making too many estimations. A coach can also help guide you to the information available to help you narrow your target market even if it is a unique niche. Seek ways to maximize every moment with your coach to help you develop a strategy that will help you accomplish your goals one day at a time.

Once you develop your goals, a coach can recommend that you effectively research and analyze the market as well as your competition. When you adequately understand the landscape, you can develop a marketing strategy that includes efficient target channels or no one will know that you are out there. A coach can help you to remember to engage in advertizing and promotion and not to forget to develop a plan that involves networking with the community. This type of interaction will stabilize your business over the long haul. Putting benchmarks in place will help you create a point of reference to know that you are hitting the goal. You will be grateful for the kind of coach that can reveal one of the worst things that you can do in business -- making assumptions. So be prepared to research the trends of your future customers. Learn what they need and give it to them and create your business practice around them.

If you are just starting a business, you might be thinking: "This is a lot to think about!" But this is where your coach comes in. Your coach will help you to develop and implement these strategies as well as help to guide you through to execution. Just like the young football hopeful who just wants to have fun, you too may want to fun with your business, as you should. It is the coach's responsibility to reveal your true talent, and also to guide you, the player, to understand the rules of the game of business and how to play with valor and distinction. Once you understand the rules, then and only then can you learn to play to win...and enjoy it!

Just like the high school football player, your coach will become your backbone and help you think about and plan for your future. For example, a coach can help you think through what legal business structure is right for you such as: Sole proprietorship, partnership, or a corporation. All of this will be determined by the kind of business that you will be doing, the products and services you provide as well as the tax implications. Even if you are a sole proprietor, you should never try to make business decisions alone. Defiance of this rule of thumb will produce costly mistakes. This can be avoided by getting trusted advice early on, so do your homework and seek the counsel of a coach.

Now that you considered all of these factors, how will you finance your business? Will you use your savings? or will you take out a loan? Perhaps your coach will have the skills necessary to help guide you in financial matters. This person should be well versed in the financial systems that can help you build a successful business like software, bookkeepers, accountants, etc. Why would you try to figure it all out when someone else has already "been there and done that"? Sharing their experience and expertise with you could help keep you from wasting a lot of time and money. This way your investment in a coach will more than pay for itself several times over. If your coach has no expertise in this area, feel free to engage one that does. Who says that you can't have more than one coach? Collaborations are powerful because they synergistically get more done in less time. With this in mind, consider building an alliance with more than one coach to thoroughly meet all of your business and personal needs.

You might as well face it, it is virtually impossible to be successful in any kind of business alone. We all need someone to introduce us to the necessary strategies that we are not aware of. This unknown realm may be well outside the protection of your comfort zone. Most times what we want, is outside of the boundaries we set for ourselves. We need someone to be there to help stretch us but also to help navigate the way. The right coach has the map with the directions that will take you to the success you are after. Be sure to choose wisely.

Coaches come in all different uniforms. Every coach has strengths in different areas. Everything is not for everybody. What you need today, you may not need tomorrow. What you need in one season you may not need in another so be prepared to be flexible when your needs change. Even if you have been in business for a long time, be prepared to know when the shift occurs to change players on the team to take your business to the next level.

It is also important that while you are thinking about selecting a coach, find one to help launch you but to also help you to narrow down the focus for your business. You cannot be all things to all people. It has been said that if you are marketing to everyone, you are marketing to no one. That means that you have to determine if what you are doing is so broad that it cannot speak specifically to your target audience. Just like the football coach hones the athlete skills to play effectively, you must allow your business coach to help you refine your approach and be conscious of the changing tides whether you have been in business for a while and especially when you first get started.

The primary role of the coach is to teach and to train you to go beyond your current limits. When you invest in a business coach, be prepared to be a student. Just because you have been in business before or in business for a long time, doesn't mean that you know it all! Times change. Trends change. People change. In order to navigate the business landscape, you need an extra pair of eyes and ears to help you sense the world of business around you. If you don't take advantage of these elements, you will be left behind.

It has been found that coaching is most effective when the player starts early at the game because the coach helps the athlete to learn the rules of the game and understand the requirements that are necessary for winning. It is safe to say that you cannot play the game effectively if you don't know the rules. Furthermore, you cannot expect to win if you don't play by the rules. It is critical to continuously play by the rules if you want to sustain your success.

In addition, the coach is responsible to make decisions about how the team plays the game. This means that the players have to give up control and submit to the coaches direction based upon trust. There is a similar relationship that the business owner must have with the business coach. You must be willing to receive instruction on how your strategy should play out. Your coach may come up with a new game plan based upon your current position. You have to be willing to trust that your coach is able to get you to the end zone and respond accordingly. The coach may give you a play, but in the end the decision to act on it is ultimately yours.

Trust is critical. If you do not trust your coach, it will be difficult to follow through with the instructions for the plays that are called by the coach. You will always be second guessing and wondering which will ultimately interfere with your progress. The best combination for success is a trusted experienced coach and a receiving willing player. This combination is the real formula for victory.

▎ LESSON 3 - SECURE YOUR SUCCESS

The most difficult part of getting an NFL contract is not necessarily all of the preparation that went before signing on the dotted line. One can say that the most difficult part of getting an NFL contract is preparing for what the player will do after he gets signed.

Every single area of the athlete's life, in addition to the lives of his loved ones, will be forever changed, in some cases for the better. But if the player is unprepared, this change turns out for the worse. Take a look at these startling statistics for NFL Players in the short period after they retire:

» Almost 80% of NFL players are either broke bankrupt 3 years after retirement

» They experience difficulties in relationships with domestic violence as a major issue

» They suffer from long term physical health concerns

» They receive high pressure from career and family life

» They have too few trustworthy supporters

I am sure that you will agree that this is considered a terrible tragedy for those who have been exposed to such tremendous opportunity. But the fact of the matter is that you will only go as far as you know. These statistics show that although you may be talented in one area does not mean that you are guaranteed to have aptitude in others. We could argue that a player should be trained in all of these area and supported with soft skills before they are allowed to sign up for the NFL. But the choice is ultimately up to the player to be fully educated in the lifestyle that he is signing up for. Too often, the player forgoes the education and leaves the future of his fortune up to chance.

The fact of the matter is that we need to understand what we sign up for when we decided to start a business. We need to see our business endeavors holistically and not make the mistake in making it the end rather than the means. If you are not careful, your business could consume you. You need someone who has the capacity to speak wisdom into all areas of your life. We can also make a case for getting a coach that has the capacity help you with more than one area of your life, not just your business. This may be more than one person. More importantly, you need to invest in a coach that would be willing to invest their wisdom into you but you must be willing to listen to what they have to say. The fact of the matter is you can pay someone to do a job but you can't pay people to care and when someone genuinely does, be grateful and allow them.

The truth is that we do not know everything and if you cannot find a coach who cares enough about you to tell you the truth, get a new coach! Don't be afraid to get a more than one! There are some business experts that know nothing about relationships. There are some relationship coaches that are not well versed in healthy lifestyles. There are some financial planners who are clueless when it comes to what it means to live a fulfilling lifestyle because all they do is work. But this does not have to be you! Set your sights high and choose a coach who is well rounded based upon where you want to go. It's an investment that is guaranteed to pay off in the end.

Here are a few recommendations for securing your future and well-rounded overall success:

Invest in financial planning advice - Athletes may understand the game but they don't always understand finances. Athletes see prominent people spending money, and they believe that their spending pattern should be the same. However, athletes fail to take into account that those prominent members have spent a lifetime learning about financial responsibility and budget strategies.

Likewise, you may be an expert in a particular area of business but doesn't mean that you have what it takes to master the area of budgets, taxes and long term finances. Don't be afraid to get help for what you don't know. It will pay off in the long run and you can spend your time maximizing profits instead of trying to figure it all out. The financial coach can help you make better choices because it is their area of expertise. Be willing to let an experienced trusted financial coach help you figure out the best strategy for what to do with the additional income you will earn from your business and produce a plan that will secure your future endeavors. It is also helpful to learn some things on your own so that you can equip yourself with financial education to understand how to protect your assets from the wrong people.

Set up a structure that will keep you in the game as long as possible but remember that there is life after business so plan for that as well. Develop a long term plan for your business. Get clear about your intentions and then make it clear to yourself and to your coach precisely what you plan to do. Define with clarity what you want to achieve. For example, know what it will look like when you've reached your goal and share that vision with your coach. It will be unique as you are so you have to be able to share your vision with absolute clarity so that you both are clear about expectations. When you fully understand that you will not be able to always do business in the same manner over an extended period of time, you come to realize that you should consider your retirement in stages. A good coach will help you to see past the moment and help you set up a long term financial plan for retirement. The coach will help you consider things that you may not be aware of. As with all coaches, the final choice is yours based upon your desires and preferences.

▌ THE HIGH PRICE OF SUCCESS

A 2009 report from Sports Illustrated found that "78% of former NFL players have gone bankrupt or are under financial stress because of joblessness or divorce" after they'd been retired only two years. Many of the biggest stars in professional sports come from very humble beginnings. Once these athletes earn a lot of money, their family and friends rely on them for financial support. The athletes often feel an obligation to help out their loved ones, and don't watch how much money they are actually giving away.

Successful entrepreneurs experience similar issues especially when they accumulate wealth early but do not have the financial fortitude to sustain themselves over the long haul. Many businesses have filed for bankruptcy due to financial stress because they are inept financially and did not have the foresight to employ the services of a financial coach who could show them the value of forecasting.

A person with a successful business is similar to a professional athlete as it relates to the rarity of achievement. Data from the Small Business Administration (SBA) states that only 66 percent of small businesses will survive their first two years. This means about one third of total businesses will actually fail in these first two crucial years, the major cause being a lack of experience. It is this lack of experience in finances that leads to the financial failure that is also experienced by the professional athlete.

A great football career as a pro athlete can lead to fame and fortune. Unfortunately for some, the riches don't last because they lack proper financial education. Having a successful and prominent career in the NFL does not make you immune from having money problems. Despite all the money that NFL players make during their careers, many have gone on to declare bankruptcy. But this is an important lesson for successful business owners to strategize and get the tools they need to secure their financial future.

The following are reasons are why American footballers suffer failure during and after a successful career that business owners can learn from:

1. They get used to a certain lifestyle. Extravagant spending is ingrained in NFL culture "Players don't see their bills or keep track of their payments. They're in the dark about taxes. They lose touch with their own money."

   Once they retire and the millions stop flowing into their bank accounts, many players find it impossible to dramatically shift gears and adapt to life on a limited fixed income. It's all the more difficult because they're still relatively young and aren't anywhere near ready to embrace the sensible, low-key, downsized lifestyle of the typical 70-year-old retiree. Likewise it would behoove business owners to be cautious with spending. Although a loan may make you feel like you have a lot of money, the fact of the matter is: it's someone else's!...so handle it wisely.

2. They ignore sound investing advice. Get a coach or advisor that you can trust and then listen to what they say.

3. Low financial literacy makes many athletes susceptible to getting scammed or suffering losses in high-risk investments. Pick a coach that has a clear understanding of how investments work and will tell you what constitutes realistic returns and reasonable fees. Don't delegate too much and oversee too little.

4. They get bad advice and make bad decisions. Do your homework before selecting a coach. No one has a perfect history but it is important to understand what you are getting into. Pick the coach that has the best track record of what you are looking for.

5. Too Much Too Fast: Some athletes don't get their big paydays until later on in their careers, but others are given big paychecks as soon as they enter the league. First-round draft picks are virtually guaranteed to be millionaires upon signing their rookie contracts. For almost all of the athletes, it's much more money than they've ever seen. Fresh out of college, a lot of the athletes are not fully prepared to have that much money, and spend it irresponsibly. But that's similar to what it's like when you hit a level of success in business. Don't be fooled into thinking financial permanency when in fact you just got a lucky break. You always need to prepare for when things suddenly change.

NFL athletes have great expectations because their peers are living large and sometimes this is a real motivation for business owners too!

And why not? Isn't this what you work so hard for? Like the flamboyant touchdown celebrations of the athlete the suddenly successful business owner feels that there has to be something to show for their windfall. The public persona of the athlete corresponds to the business talent which makes them attractive to others. They acquire a new set of "friends" that often show up to sap resources, so be careful. It is important to build into your entrepreneurial career someone that you can be financially accountable to in order to secure your future.

It has been said that the lifestyle of a professional athlete is a gift and a curse. It's a gift because of the notoriety and big money that it brings and it can be a curse because of the personal problems that come along with it. In spite of the momentary financial success, it is lack of proper planning has left numerous athletes plagued with social problems.

If you don't believe that an athletic career can be a curse look at some of the results of the lives of players due to the lack of proper life coaching. Many players:

» ...engage in unfaithful immorality indiscretion causing divorce and broken family

» ...are involved in and disproportionate accounts of domestic violence

» ...get caught up hanging with a bad crowd because they have a lot of free time on their hands

» ...end up broke and jobless because they didn't plan an exit strategy

» ...partied hard and fail drug tests, and drug related arrests

» ...have problems with the IRS committing tax fraud and file for bankruptcy and had to auction off most of his possessions to pay the IRS, lawyers, and the government.

» ...have failed business collapsed investments

Some of the stories of pro athletes losing their fortunes, chronicled in the ESPN documentary "Broke" and elsewhere, are astonishing. There are many lessons that can be learned from professional athletes to help your business thrive!

» Plan for success by getting coaching early on

» Be willing to invest in yourself! The more you invest the greater the return you can expect

» The pathway to success requires premeditated action

» Surround yourself with the tools you need to succeed

» Ask better questions to get the right answers

» Give yourself permission to start with a new canvas and be prepared to be creative and create new systems and learn new skills.

» A coach will help you take the risk and be prepared to go beyond anywhere you have been before.

» A good coach could easily become your hero.

Just like the football athlete needs a coach to get to stardom, so do you! All of the above facts and statistics prove why you should not attempt to succeed in business on your own. And with such an abundance of great coaches out there why would you even try?

Dr. LaVerne Adams
The Transforming Center
6410 Haverford Avenue
Philadelphia, PA 19151
DrLaVerneAdams@gmail.com
1 (844) 828-7267

Dr. LaVerne Adams is a Transformational Leadership Consultant, Affiliate Member, Institute of Coaching, McLean Hospital, Harvard Medical School Affiliate, Personality Assessment Administrator, and holds a Doctor of Ministry from Palmer Theological Seminary. She has been recognized by major media for her 25 years of experience in consulting, ministry, and advising high-profile leaders, and has helped to transform the lives of countless people to achieve their personal development goals, peak performance, and fulfillment in life.

She is the CEO and founder of Total Life Consultancy, LLC, the only firm that serves high profile professionals and their families with the exclusive CUPID Life M.A.P. to help them effortlessly perform at higher levels while finding significance. Her Total Life Transformation system encompasses personal development tools that are designed to produce meaning and satisfaction in every area of life in life in a way that ultimately increases the bottom line. She has authored 20 books on personal, social, and global transformation. For more information please go to http://www.TotalLifeTransformation.Net.

ABOUT THE BUSINESS CONSULTANT INSTITUTE

We are thrilled that you have read this entire book and have made it to the end. The consultants in this book have demonstrated from their chapters a wide range of skills, industry knowledge, and size of their clients. They range from work with huge corporate clients to support full business transformations to those who have narrowly defined niche expertise to help specific, small businesses. Some have been consulting for years as employees in larger consulting firms before starting out on their own, and some have leveraged their decades of experience in their careers to recently take the plunge with their own consulting firm.

These contributing authors as a collective group represent the broader demographics of our clients at The Business Consultant Institute. The consultants we attract to our live events truly are a diverse group of business leaders, some who have been leading their own consulting companies for ten years or more, and others who have not yet started consulting but who recognize that, because business consulting is a lucrative industry, now is the time to consider developing their consulting skill set and seek their first client.

Further, those consultants in our higher-level programs, such as our mastermind or those who work with us 1-on-1, are excitedly pouring their energy into accelerating their business growth. Many are enjoying substantial additional revenue to the tune of doubling and tripling their business. Sound good to you, too?

Because you've read this far into this book, we know you have an interest in business consulting – either because you've been at it a while and are now ready to give you revenue a shot in the arm or because you know consulting is smart for you to pursue. Become part of our family. Find out more about The Business Consultant Institute and tap into the resources we have for you at http://www.BusinessConsultantInstitute.com so that you can significantly improve your results, just like our other clients.

If you're ready to see a quick jump in your business' profits, then apply for our Profit Session: http://www.businessconsultantinstitute.com/apply.

And, if you have specific questions, you can reach out directly to us: info@BusinessConsultantInstitute.com or call +1 (855) BCI-0005.

We look forward to hearing from you!

Terri Levine and Pete Winiarski,

Co-founders of The Business Consultant Institute

ABOUT THE FOUNDERS

▌TERRI LEVINE

Terri Levine is the bestselling author of almost a dozen books and the Chief Heartrepreneur™ at http://www.heartrepreneur.com, and is known as the business-mentoring expert with heart. Her latest book, *Turbocharge How to Transform Your Business As A Heartrepreneur™* has become an overnight success. (https:// goo.gl/pdkFyV)

Terri was named one of the top ten coaching gurus in the world by www.coachinggurus.net and the top female coach in the world. She has received recognition from every major coaching organization and association, has been assisting businesses worldwide with creating the right inner mindset and outer actions for business growth. Terri has been mentoring business leaders and team members for over three decades and helped over five thousand business owners to go from ordinary to extraordinary while having the life of their dreams, doing the work they love, loving the work they do, and being financially secure too!

As a keynote speaker, Terri has inspired hundreds of thousands of people through her high-content, memorable, and motivation- al speeches. She has been featured in the media on platforms such as ABC, NBC, MSN-BC, CNBC, *Fortune, Forbes, Shape, Self, The New York Times*, the BBC, and in more than fifteen hundred publications. Her radio show, *The Terri Levine Show: Business Advice You Can Take to the Bank*, is downloaded by thousands of people from her iHeart Radio channel each month. http://www.iheart.com/show/209-The-Terri-Levine-Show/

Terri holds a PhD in clinical psychology, is a Master Certified Guerrilla Marketing Trainer and Coach, and is accredited by the American Association of Business Psychology. She is a Licensed Hidden Marketing Assets Consultant, she is managing director for Polka Dots Powerhouse, and a founding member of the Evolutionary Business Council where she also serves as a call leader, and the Philadelphia Ambassador for the organization. She is a mentor for StrongBrook Mentoring Network, and sits on the board of four nonprofit organizations.

She operates http://www.heartrepreneur.com, mentoring business owners to turbocharge their business to create more revenues and profits while learning to be Heartrepreneurs.

Terri is the co-founder of http://www.businessconsultantinstitute.com and https://www.businessconsultantevent.com, training business consultants to create super profitable consulting businesses.

Terri is also on the advisory board of several companies and dedicates time fundraising for the nonprofit foundation she founded, The Terri Levine Foundation for Children with RSD. (http://www.TerriLevinefoundationforchildrenwithRSD.org)

▌PETE WINIARSKI

Peter (Pete) D. Winiarski is highly sought after business consultant, speaker, media guest, and best-selling author. Pete is known as a business transformation expert and a goal achievement expert.

Having thirty years of experience in leadership roles, Pete leads his consulting company, Win Enterprises, LLC, to help business leaders transform their results with a team of resources who are experts in business transformation, process improvement using "Lean" principles, organization culture, leadership, and goal achievement.

His website, https://www.completebusinesstransformation.com, is an abundant resource for business leaders to help guide their business improvement for long-term and sustainable results.

Pete is the creator of the Win Holistic Transformation Model™, a complete approach for companies to experience lasting transformational change. He is also the co-creator of the Conscious Leadership Model™, and teaches leaders how to maximize their effectiveness as leaders of others by first leading themselves.

Pete is the author of the #1 International Best Selling book, *Act Now! A Daily Action Log for Achieving Your Goals in 90 Days,* and is in process of publishing six other books on business transformation and consulting.

Pete has appeared as a business expert and a goal-achievement expert in multiple media outlets, including ABC, CBS, FOX, NBC, and Industry Week.

Pete has been trained and mentored by Jack Canfield, and is one of just a few people around the world to achieve "Certified Senior Trainer" status to deliver Jack's work.

Pete is the co-founder of the Business Consultant Institute, at http://www.businessconsultantinstitute.com and http://www.businessconsultantevent.com, which trains business consultants to create super profitable consulting businesses.

In his spare time, Pete coaches and plays baseball, enjoys live music, and supports whatever activities his wife and two sons are pursuing.